Lost and Found in Russia

Susan Richards is the author of *Epics of Everyday Life*, which won the P.E.N. Time-Life Award for Non-Fiction and the Yorkshire Post Best First Work Award in 1990. She edits openDemocracy Russia, part of openDemocracy, the website about global affairs which she co-founded. After her doctorate on Alexander Solzhenitsyn from St Antony's College, Oxford University, she initiated the programme of talks, conferences and debates at London's Institute of Contemporary Arts and worked as a film producer. With her husband, the television producer Roger Graef, she started Bookaid, a charity which sent a million English language books to public libraries throughout the Soviet Union.

'A work of great thoughtfulness and enterprise, it sheds a uniquely intimate light behind the façade of the new Russia.'

Colin Thubron

'Susan Richards has long been one of the very best writers on Russia. Her new book is a remarkable blend of travel and reflection, as she introduces us to the vivid gallery of people she meets in the provinces. The result is a brilliant, poignant evocation of a society in transition.'

Robert Service

'A uniquely personal chronicle, and a testament to friendship. Susan Richards's political fact-finding is set ablaze by her intimacy with the discomforts and dangers of life in these remote regions, where the magic of the natural world challenges urban degradation, and where physical deprivation coexists with a richness of belief-systems as strange as the mountains of the moon.'

Victoria Glendinning

Praise for *Epics of Everyday Life: Encounters in a Changing Russia*

'One of the most intriguing books ever written about the Soviet Union.'

Fitzroy MacLean, *Evening Standard*

'The work of a gifted writer, one who describes better than any foreign author I know the bizarre, surreal, Gogolian nature of life in the Soviet Union "new" or "old".'

Sally Laird, *Observer*

'Susan Richards writes ... about the passions, hopes and hard realities of life for the ordinary Russian citizens whom she befriended. Her book is about despair and ultimately about the triumph of the human spirit in a disintegrating empire.'

Sue MacGregor, *Mail on Sunday*

'In Richards's sensitive hands *Everyday Life* ... seem to achieve epic scale ... This vivid and compelling book with its rich confusion of anger, heartbreak, irreverence, scepticism and finally ... love answers to something in the country itself.'

Christopher Hope, *New Statesman*

'A very fine, refreshing and often moving account of a people we have been conditioned to regard as enemies and who are not.'

John Pilger

Lost and Found in Russia

Encounters in the Deep Heartland

Susan Richards

I.B. TAURIS

LONDON · NEW YORK

947,
to3
6
hc

Published in 2009 by I.B.Tauris & Co. Ltd
6 Salem Road, London W2 4BU
175 Fifth Avenue, New York NY 10010
www.ibtauris.com

ISBN: 978 1 84885 023 1

A full CIP record for this book is available from the British Library

Typeset in Sabon by Ellipsis Books Limited, Glasgow
Printed and bound in Great Britain by CPI Antony Rowe, Chippenham

FSC
Mixed Sources
Product group from well-managed
forests and other controlled sources
Cert no. SGS-COC-2953
www.fsc.org
© 1996 Forest Stewardship Council

CONTENTS

ACKNOWLEDGEMENTS

If ever there was a book which depended on the generosity of friends, it is this. I am infinitely grateful to the Russians whose lives I have chronicled in this book. Anna, Tatiana, Misha, Natasha, Igor and Vera (these are not their real names) befriended me after the fall of communism, when visitors from the West were objects of deep suspicion in that part of the countryside. They have had the courage not to withdraw their confidence in my good faith over the years, even now that the relationship between our governments has hardened into a familiar antagonism.

Sixteen years is a long time. Behind this book stands a tribe of supporters, people who backed me even when they no longer understood what I was doing, or why I was persisting. My husband Roger Graef has been my unfailing champion, chief critic and my life support, backed up always by Chloe and Max Graef. Without the three of them, I would not have made it. Equally important was my 'family' in Moscow, Elena Vasilieva, her daughter Ira Vasilieva and son-in-law Alexander (Sasha) Radov. Adventurous, and unfailingly cheerful, Ira and Sasha were my ideal travelling companions.

That same spirit infuses those most experienced travellers, Vladimir Nikolaevich Alekseev and Professor Elena Ivanovna Dergacheva-Skop, to whom I am boundlessly grateful for taking me to meet the Old Believers of Burny.

The key that unlocked my visit to Nina Stepanovna was Sergei Filatov's research on the rebirth of paganism among the non-Slav Volga minorities, published in *An Atlas of Religious Life in Russia Today*, edited by Michael Bourdeaux and Sergei Filatov (Keston Institute, 2005). What I found there would have been even more mysterious without the help of Joanna Hubbs's book *Mother Russia: The Feminine Myth in Russian Culture* (Bloomington, 1988).

Back in England, I am grateful to Mark Lefanu for having offered me a grant from the Society of Authors at a time when publishers were giving me a wide berth. It has been wonderful to be championed by David Godwin and Sophie Hoult, my agents.

As for my publisher Iradj Bagherzade, editor Liz Friend-Smith and copy-editor Elizabeth Stone, they gave me the combination of encouragement and criticism every writer needs.

Whenever I looked like giving up, Colin Thubron steeled me not to. Help came from many quarters, including Gillon Aitken, Sarah Anderson, Linda Blandford, Hilda Deas, Toby Eady, Celina Fox, Lennie Goodings, Deborah Honore, Rohan McCullough, Konstanz Merkel, Stuart Proffitt and Sarah Stacey, and above all from Anthony Smith.

AUTHOR'S NOTE

I have changed the names of one regional business and some regional newspapers to protect the privacy of my characters.

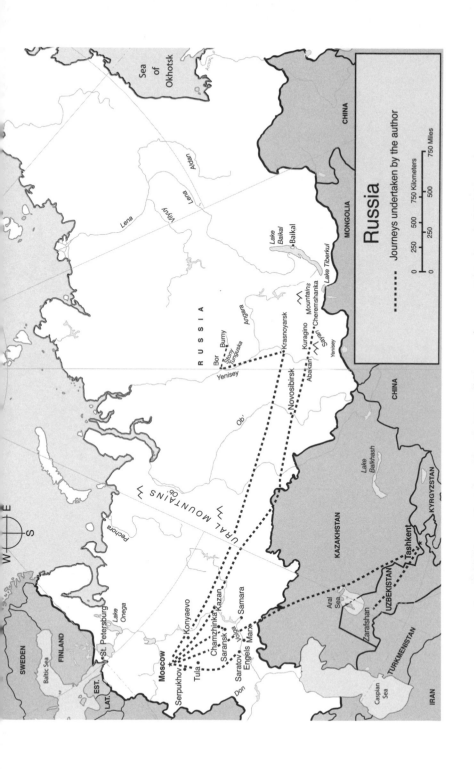

TIMELINE

1990

8 February   Mikhail Gorbachev and US Secretary of State James Baker agree that if Germany reunites, NATO will not be expanded.

1991

12 June   Boris Yeltsin is elected as first President of Russian Federation.

7 July $.5 billion food credit for Union of Soviet Socialist Republics (USSR) approved by the US.

19–21 August   Hardline Soviet leaders launch a coup to save USSR. Mass demonstrations face down the coup.

24 August   Gorbachev resigns as General Secretary of Communist Party of Soviet Union (CPSU).

29 August   Russian parliament dissolves CPSU.

6 November   Yeltsin bans the CPSU on territory of Russian Federation.

21 December   USSR dissolved. Russian Federation and former republics become sovereign states.

1992

29 January   Yegor Gaidar's 'shock therapy' economic reforms launched; most prices liberalised and spiral up.

January   Throughout the year the conflict between Yeltsin and parliament (Congress of People's Deputies) intensifies.

21 March   Tatarstan declares independence from Russia. Fragmentation threatens Russia.

1 October   Chubais launches massive privatisation programme, giving every citizen a 10,000-rouble privatisation voucher.

November   Constitutional Court partially lifts ban on the Communist Party.

9 December   Congress forces resignation of Prime Minister Gaidar.

1993

3 January   Yeltsin and Bush sign START 2, envisaging reduction of nuclear weapons.

28 March   Yeltsin declares state of emergency. Congress threatens to impeach him.

25 April   Yeltsin narrowly wins national referendum on his reforms.

9 July   G7 countries announce $28.4 billion aid for former USSR.

21 September   Yeltsin disbands parliament, introduces presidential rule, brings Gaidar back to run economy.

26 September	10,000 demonstrate on behalf of legislators.
3–4 October	Political impasse turns to armed conflict. Nationalist and communist deputies barricade themselves in parliament, with their militias. Yeltsin sends tanks to shell parliament; 187 killed. Opposition leaders jailed.
25 December	Elections to new parliament (State Duma). Referendum on new constitution with strong presidential role narrowly approved.

1994

16 January	Gaidar quits government over end to reform programme.
Spring	In Kremlin, Yeltsin's bodyguard Alexander Korzhakov comes to dominance.
1 December	First Chechen war begins. Russian troops enter Chechnya.

1995

8 February	Strike of 500,000 miners. Yeltsin starts to lose grip.
2 June	Paris Club reschedules Russia's $9.5 billion debt.
14–23 June	Basayev's Chechen terrorists kill hundreds of civilians. Peace negotiations agree withdrawal of Russia's army from Chechnya.
August	NATO launches air strikes in Yugoslavia.

1996

Spring	Anatoly Chubais offers oligarchs control of key state assets in return for media support and financing of Yeltsin's re-election.
June–July	Terrorist acts in Moscow metro and in North Caucasus. Yeltsin steals election from Communist Party.
30–31 August	General Lebed, Yeltsin's national security chief, signs peace treaty with Chechen leader. His popularity threatens Yeltsin.
15 October	Lebed fired.
1 December	Russian troops withdraw from Chechnya.

1997

27 May	NATO–Russia Founding Act binds NATO not to deploy nuclear weapons or substantial numbers of foreign troops on territory of its new members.
Summer–autumn	War breaks out between Chubais and the oligarchs, and between the oligarchs themselves, when Chubais tries to curtail their 'sweetheart deals'.
Autumn	Search for Yeltsin's successor.

1998

| 16 May | Russia becomes member of G8. |

17 July	Remains of Tsar Nicholas II and family buried in St Petersburg on 80th anniversary of their murder.
Summer	Financial crisis in Russia: government devalues rouble, defaults on its domestic debts and declares moratorium on payment to foreign creditors following collapse of Asian market and commodity prices. International Monetary Fund and World Bank give Russia credits.
16 December	First Iraq War starts. Kremlin disapproves.

1999

Spring	Climax of struggle for succession to Yeltsin.
17 March	Vladimir Putin appointed secretary of Security Council.
18 March	Russia condemns NATO air strikes against Yugoslavia, in response to repression of ethnic Albanians in Kosovo.
19 March	First enlargement of NATO since Cold War, with Czech Republic, Poland and Hungary acceding.
7 August	Chechen terrorists invade neighbouring Dagestan.
26 August	Russian troops march into Chechnya. Second Chechen war begins.
9–16 September	Apartment blocks in four Russian cities bombed. Death toll *c.* 300.
14–31 December	Yeltsin appoints Putin as his successor and resigns.

2000

January–February	Putin revives relations with West, hints at interest in joining NATO.
26 March	Putin is elected President.
May	Putin curtails powers of regional governors and brings Chechnya under direct presidential rule.
12 August	Nuclear submarine *Kursk* sinks, losing all hands.
13 June	Oligarch Vladimir Gusinsky's arrest signals drive to break oligarch power.
November	Independent media curbed.

2001

Spring	End of independent TV channel NTV and Gusinsky's media empire.
12 April	Putin endorses new 'party of power', United Russia.
28 June	Duma passes law banning use of mind-control weapons on Russian territory.
24 September	Following terrorist attacks on New York, Putin supports Bush's war on terror.
13 December	US withdraws from Anti-Ballistic Missile Treaty and fails to back Russia's bid to join World Trade Organisation.

2002

January	Last independent television channel closed.

28 May	Formation of NATO–Russia Council. Putin meets with all NATO leaders.
23 October	Chechen terrorists seize Moscow theatre. 129 hostages die in battle to free them.

2003

19 March	Start of Second Iraq War.
31 March	EU–Russia summit agrees on areas of cooperation: economy; freedom, security and human rights; external security; science, education, research and culture.
5 October	Akhmad Kadyrov elected as Chechnya's leader. Putin starts policy of 'Chechenisation'.
22–23 November	Georgia's Rose Revolution sees President Shevardnadze resign in favour of Mikhail Saakashvili.

2004

13 March	Kyrgyzstan's Tulip Revolution.
14 March	Putin re-elected with huge majority for second term.
29 March	NATO admits Bulgaria, Estonia, Latvia, Lithuania, Romania, Slovakia and Slovenia.
9 May	President Akhmad Kadyrov assassinated. His son Ramzan succeeds him.
Summer	US–Russian relations deteriorate. Georgian–Russian relations deteriorate.
1 September	Chechen terrorists occupy Beslan school. More than 340 die in attempt to free them.
26 September	Election of regional governors scrapped.

2005

January	Demonstrations throughout Russia over proposal to monetise social benefits.
Spring	Kremlin builds Nashi and other loyalist youth movements.
31 May	Oligarch Mikhail Khodorkovsky, owner of Russia's largest oil company, Yukos sentenced to nine years for fraud and tax evasion. Assets of Yukos redistributed among Putin's cadres.
November– December	Ukraine's Orange Revolution.
29 December	Gazprom raises gas price to Ukraine.

2006

1 January	Brief interruption of Russia's gas supply to Ukraine and Europe, due to Ukraine's non-payment, sends shock waves through Europe.
12 January	Duma limits activities of NGOs.
22 February	Vladislav Surkov coins term 'sovereign democracy' to describe what distinguishes Putin's regime from liberal democracy.

15–17 July	Putin hosts G8 Summit in St Petersburg.
13 September	Arrest of Russian intelligence officers in Tbilisi triggers blockade of Georgia and deportation of its citizens from Russia.
7 October	Anna Politkovskaya, fearless critic of Putin, murdered.
23 November	Ex-FSB officer Alexander Litvinenko granted asylum in Britain and dies of polonium poisoning.

2007

30 April	Russia–Estonia crisis after Estonia seeks to move Soviet war memorial.
4 June	Putin warns Washington that it might retaliate if NATO proceeds with missile defence system in Europe.
8 June	G8 summit in Germany.
20–24 July	Moscow–London tit-for-tat expulsions of diplomats following Litvinenko poisoning.
8 August	Russian strategic bombers resume long-haul missions to areas patrolled by NATO and US.
December	Putin ends uncertainty by indicating that he will respect constitution and step down at end of his second presidential term.

2008

7 May	Dmitry Medvedev becomes President of Russian Federation.
8 May	Putin becomes Prime Minister.
7 August	Georgia's President Saakashvili tries to regain control of South Ossetia. After six days of fighting, Russian troops invade Georgia and destroy all military installations.
September	Global financial markets crash, ending Russia's eight-year economic boom.

For Roger

PREFACE

This book grew out of my visits to a small, apparently unremarkable town. It begins when Russians were in shock, after the fall of communism. It ends when the country, flush with petrodollars and resurgent pride, is succumbing to global recession. It is the story of a nation going through a nervous breakdown, pulling through, but paying the price. It is about a people lost and found, about their search for meaning.

The vast stage of provincial Russia where the book is set barely connects to the world of Moscow and Petersburg. Its strangeness offers an explanation as to why we in the West are often baffled by Russia.

The friends I made in that small provincial town are the backbone of this book. For better and worse, their lives mirror Russia's fortunes in its transition from chaos to order. I have tried to capture their experience. But I have come to accept that it is in the nature of the relationship between our cultures that they will think I have failed.

Anna, the tomboy, was born on the same date as me. On the surface we do not appear to have much in common, though in some obscure way we recognised that our lives are connected. Once, my friendship may have offered her support, but now things have changed so much that it runs the risk of damaging her. When we met, she was ready to sacrifice her life to build a free and democratic Russia. Today, she has found refuge in Russia's resurgent Church.

Curly-haired, irrepressible Natasha was endowed at birth with privilege and talent. Following her rainbow had led her to that obscure country town. To the locals, she and her dashing husband Igor seemed every bit as exotic as I did, as a foreigner. Our otherness made us objects of suspicion.

The pale beauty Tatiana, with her innate wisdom, was the peacemaker in the volatile group. Back then, her husband Misha was one of millions of ants struggling to make the chaos work for them, fetching and carrying, dodging the heel of the law. Now, he is Mikhail Ivanovich, an important manufacturer. He and Tatiana may take their holidays in Provence, but when I look into Tatiana's grey eyes I am afraid for her.

Hope brought us together. The year was 1992, and the euphoria of the Gorbachev period had evaporated. The story behind our hopefulness goes back two centuries, to when Catherine the Great became empress of Russia. A German princess, she dreamed of building an island of European values on the wild eastern frontier of her empire. Her people posted advertisements in Germany, promising fertile land, housing and livestock to anyone who was prepared to settle there. Thousands responded. For a year they travelled east, then sailed down the Volga River. When they arrived they found nothing to match the promises. They were left in the wild steppe, a prey to vengeful Tartar horsemen.

Russian history seems to move in circles. Fast forward two centuries, to 1988 and the final days of communism. Again a Russian government was promising the descendants of those original German settlers that they could settle the same piece of land – since when the Nazis invaded the Soviet Union the entire community was deported, lest they collaborate. After the war, for decades they lived in exile in remote parts of Siberia and Central Asia, accused of a crime they did not commit. Finally, almost fifty years later, Gorbachev's government agreed to give them back their original homeland, by way of making amends. What is more, the German government was offering the homeland money, in the hope that this might deter Russia's Germans from moving back to Germany, as was their right.

This was what attracted Natasha and Igor to move there from the Caucasus, Catherine the Great's original dream of building an island of European values on the steppe, with German investment. It drew me there, too. We were all desperate for reasons to be hopeful. Even if the rest of Russia was paralysed, I longed to find one small piece of countryside where people would be busy building the microcosm of a Russia worth living in.

But instead of a buzz of activity, I found a place embalmed in sullen silence. What had happened? No one would tell me. In fact, hardly anyone would talk to me at all; and yet it was that wall of silence that drew me back there over several years. It seemed to me that if I could understand, really understand, what was going on in the fog of confusion hanging over one small place, the larger picture of Russia in that confused time might become more comprehensible.

From there, I slipped through a crack in the wardrobe, into another Russia.

On the borders of early maps you sometimes find blank places where the mapmaker's information peters out. Sometimes these are decked out with pictures of dragons and fabulous monsters, the creatures of travellers' tales. That was where I was travelling during Russia's lost years, way off the map of my known world. In the course of my journeys, President Boris Yeltsin sank deeper into a stupor, the oligarchs squabbled over Russia's wealth, miners went unpaid and teachers fainted from hunger in front of their pupils.

The agony of transition was throwing up strange manifestations that defied my plodding, Western rationality. While I could not share these collective visions of shining beings and visitors from distant planets, nor could I dismiss them – too many people were seeing them, and their roots in the culture ran too deep. It took me a long time to accept that perhaps I had just ventured into a place where reality was different.

In these places off the map of my world I met another face of Russia, too, one where time had almost stopped, under the carapace of communism. There, choreographers, KGB colonels and other urban refugees were happily building their New Jerusalem in Siberia, as sectarians have done for centuries.

But it was deep in the forest that I found myself face to face with the heart of whatever it is that makes the Russian people different. I found it hundreds of miles from the nearest road or railway, in a community vigorously pursuing the dream of a Russia which had never opened up to the West.

Older still was the tradition of paganism which, having survived ten centuries of persecution, had bubbled to the surface in parts of the countryside in that in-between time. There, I met the witch of Russia's fairy tales, who was busy healing victims of the upheaval.

The hardest parts of this journey began when I tried to write about my experiences. That brought me up against the limits of my own language. How wise Wittgenstein was when he concluded that there were some things about which we should stay silent. But having once embarked on this book, I did not have that luxury.

I have never managed to reconcile the reality of my world with that of this other Russia. But now, I would not want to.

From the start of my journey, there were hints of stranger things to come.

1992–1993

Communist rule had only just ended when I set out on my travels. For the next few years, the overriding goal of President Yeltsin's government would be the dismantling of the massive planned economy. Yeltsin had banned the Communist Party and implemented a programme of 'shock therapy': price controls were relaxed, the currency was floated and a mass programme of privatisation had begun.

Prices shot up twenty-six-fold in a single year. Russia's colonies taking their independence had already served to dismember the old economy. Economic activity had halved and inflation was taking off. Since the Central Bank kept printing money and offering cheap credits to industry, it quickly rose to 2,000 per cent, leaving the rouble worthless. By mid-1993 over 40 per cent of Russians were living in poverty – as opposed to 1.5 per cent in the late Soviet period.

Almost at once, the old party elite and the factory bosses started privatising the institutions they managed. Within three to four years, 60–70 per cent of state enterprises were privatised. The bosses siphoned off money and raw materials from state enterprises into co-ops, private banks and out of Russia, into offshore companies. This was not illegal, for there was no procedure in place for transferring assets into private hands. Between 1991 and 2000 it is reckoned that $1 billion was secreted out of Russia every month.

The public were issued with vouchers worth 10,000 roubles (around $20) with which to buy a stake in this giant sell-off of state assets. But there was no framework of laws or financial institutions to regulate financial activity; so companies appeared out of nowhere, promising fairy-tale dividends to those who invested their vouchers, then disappeared with the money.

Could radically different intervention by the West have changed things? Certainly, the architect of the reforms, Prime Minister Yegor Gaidar, and their implementer, Anatoly

Chubais, were heavily reliant on Western advice. This came from two quarters. There were the free marketeers (the International Monetary Fund, Jeffrey Sachs and his Harvard clan) who believed that economic man behaved the same in any circumstances: as soon as the centrally planned economy was dismantled, a free market would spring up in the space, like willow herb in a bombsite. Others argued that nothing in Russia's culture and history had prepared its people for the marketplace. It was not just that Russia was emerging from seventy years of communism, they protested, but there was no pre-revolutionary tradition to graft on to either. For under tsarism the culture of private ownership and the independent business sector were both weak. Besides, they pointed out, Russia had no institutional infrastructure to handle these changes – no legal framework, stable banking system, checks and balances. Reforms had to be introduced gradually, as in Poland, and they had to be backed by massive long-term aid and assistance from the West.

However, free market fundamentalism was at its height. Besides, Yeltsin's economic team was driven by the need to prevent the return of communism. Any strategy of gradual reform would be subverted by the old Soviet bosses, who were still in charge. Yeltsin's colleagues saw themselves as kamikaze pilots, whose mission it was to break the tradition of Russian autocracy and introduce Russia to the marketplace and democracy. They were indeed attacking the vested interests of everyone with power, from the old Party bosses and officials to the army and security services. By December 1992 opposition to the reforms was already so fierce that Gaidar had to resign as Prime Minister.

Three features of this period would throw long shadows over the future. The failure to establish the institutions of an open society would discredit the notion of liberal democracy before anyone in Russia had experienced it. The presence of Western advisers laid the seeds of bitter resentment. Finally, a collective fear of anarchy rooted in living memory generated such intense anxiety that order and stability became precious above all else.

On the political front, Yeltsin had missed the opportunity to call fresh elections after the Communist Party's coup attempt in August 1991, when he was viewed as a national hero. So he was saddled with a parliament dominated by former Party officials and powerful Soviet-era factory managers. A coalition of communists and nationalists had united to oppose all reforms aimed at introducing market reforms and a liberal democracy. With every month, rumours of another communist coup grew stronger. When the courts lifted Yeltsin's ban on the Communist Party, it made a strong comeback under its effective new leader, Gennady Zyuganov. By the autumn of 1993 Russia appeared to be on the brink of civil war. Yeltsin and his parliament had reached an impasse. The president decided on drastic action to save his reform programme. In September he banned parliament and called fresh elections. That speech triggered a bloody showdown. Armed crowds marched on Moscow's Ostankino television centre. While the 'democrats' manned the barricades, nationalist and communist deputies holed up in the parliament building with their private militias. Yeltsin ordered the army to intervene. Reluctantly, it obeyed. Tanks surrounded the White House and opened fire. They bombarded the deputies and their gunmen into submission, at the cost of 187 lives.

Yeltsin then implemented his plans to win a mandate for a new legislature, as well as a constitution giving him broader powers. In the elections for the new, weaker parliament (now called the Duma) voters endorsed Yeltsin's new constitution, while punishing the more democratic candidates.

When the White House bombardment was over, a mood of suppurating resentment set in:. 'Freedom' had brought nothing but poverty, corruption, confiscatory privatisation and criminality.

1992

THERE BE MONSTERS

———❖———

I had an appointment in Samara. The sun was high and there was no shade on the dock. I was getting anxious. I had been offered a lift to the Russian–German homeland in a boat, two days' sail down the Volga. My friend's instructions, written in her neat Cyrillic hand, were clear: '12.00 a.m. sharp. 2 August. Samara riverfront – N. Gastello'. If I was late, she warned, the boat would not wait for me. It was now 12.30. I scanned the empty river for a glimpse of Zhenya's boat. He had promised to take me to the area of the Russian German homeland, two days' sail south down the Volga.

It was high season, and the railings, kiosks, flowerbeds and crowd control notices suggested the place should be teeming with people and boats. But the mooring was empty, apart from a triple-decked Soviet cruiser whose white hull loomed over the orderly promenade. There was not a soul to be seen.

No one was taking holidays that year. The Soviet Union had been dissolved seven months ago. With inflation at 20 per cent and rising, a mood of apocalyptic gloom had set in over Russia. The country had lost its colonies and the Communist Party, which ran everything in the empire, was banned. During that last terrible gasp of communism shops were empty and food was rationed. Yet the minute prices were freed, the shops filled with food. Few people could afford to buy.

Travelling anywhere that summer was hard. I had arrived from Siberia the night before, after spending weeks tracking down exiled Russian Germans. With prices rising day by day, transport was in chaos. Twice my journey had ground to a halt. In one town the buses had been 'privatised' by their drivers in lieu of wages. Then my flight was grounded for lack of fuel. It only took off because a bull-necked man with a phalanx of bodyguards had a word with the pilot, and the fuel was found. I was lucky to have got here at all. But getting to the region where I was heading would be even more of a challenge, a fact I did not yet appreciate in the general confusion.

It was one of many things I failed to grasp. When a society starts falling apart, the surface of things remains deceptively tranquil. Overprotected as I was by my Russian friends, I had not yet realised how rapidly the mood of the country was going from sweet to sour. In the euphoria of the late 1980s I had travelled freely across Russia, passed from hand to hand by welcoming new friends. Now Russia was unravelling, and it was no time for foreign travellers. I was trying to get to Marx, a small town near the city of Saratov. That was suspicious in itself, as I would soon find. But I was looking for something particular – for reasons to be hopeful.

As I stood on the empty promenade, I was not actually sure whom I was waiting for. I had never met Zhenya, just caught a glimpse of him in one of the films he had financed. He was one of a new breed in Russia, a businessman. Elena had talked a lot about him. She was the woman who adopted me as family when I wrote my first book about Russia.

One day Zhenya had walked into Moscow's Cinema Centre where she worked, declaring that it was his mission to save Russian cinema. In one of the films he went on to fund, the director had given him a walk-on part. Elena had showed me the film. She stopped the video to point him out: 'Look – that's him! That funny little figure.' He was in the back of the shot, barely visible. Now, months later, all I could remember was that he had a straggling beard that reminded me of one of Chagall's Jewish fiddlers.

When I told her my plan, Elena made it clear she thought I was mad to be travelling anywhere that year. But she knew I had set my heart on going to Saratov. All I needed was a few contacts there. This time no one had been able to help. Only later, when I learned that it had been a closed town, did I realise why the usual network of friendship did not extend there.

Then, one day she came home from work bursting with news. 'Your trip to the Volga – it's sorted!' she announced. Zhenya had dropped in to Elena's office and told her he was sailing down to Saratov. She asked if I could go too. He not only agreed, he even offered to introduce me to people there. This was one invitation I was not going to miss.

But one month later, on Samara's empty dock, it seemed as if he had stood me up. I was hunting around on the promenade

looking for someone who could help when a woman appeared
on the deck of the huge cruise liner. Why not ask her? As I
walked up the gangplank the ship's name caught my eye: *N.
Gastello*. I froze. So this was it, the boat. There in front of me
all the time.

This was not all right, not at all. It could only mean that Zhenya
was a mafia boss, and a big one. I had been expecting something
so different, a little gin palace, perhaps, but not this. It was vast,
the sort of ship that used to ply up and down the Volga, entertaining Soviet holidaymakers to the strains of martial music.

A man in a white uniform and cap had now appeared as well,
and was saluting me. 'You must be Susan,' the woman shouted,
'I'm Olga – the cruise manager, and this is our captain Boris
Nikolaevich. We've been waiting for you!' I pulled myself together,
shook hands and followed Olga to my cabin. Plump and motherly, she was hardly my idea of a mafia moll. Maybe the *N. Gastello*
was just a business venture? But no. That year no one could afford
holidays.

The cabin was luxurious, with starched white sheets. Out of
the porthole I watched the crew casting off. There was no going
back now. When lunch was announced, I realised how hungry I
was. On my travels I had been camping on floors, eating out
of tins.

In the dining rooms, which were supported by gilded Corinthian
columns, Olga ushered me to a seat of honour at the captain's
table. Opposite sat a young man with tattoos, a scarred vulpine
face and stubs for teeth. A dandy with a brutalised face and plucked
eyebrows sat beside me. That decided it: those faces belonged to
the criminal underworld. Smiling waitresses were heaping our
plates with delectable food, but I had lost my appetite.

The problem was that, along with the invitation, Elena had
given me something: 'Zhenya said you were to take this.' Wrapped
in newspaper, the brick-sized package contained stacks of roubles
fresh from the bank. They were worth $100, a fortune in Russia
that year. I refused the package, but Elena could be very obsti-
nate: 'I'm not taking it back! If you want to go, you've got to
take it! Anyway, it's nothing to him.' In the end I gave in, resolving
that when I did meet Zhenya I would return his money, and we
would have a laugh about it. I had been carrying it round my
waist for weeks. Now I was gripped by anxiety: in Russia, accepting

hospitality incurs serious obligations. A Hogarthian image flashed into my mind of Zhenya and his thuggish cronies in my London house, feet on the table.

The powdered dandy interrupted my thoughts.

'How do you know Benya then?'

'What?'

'Benya – your host!' he repeated, looking surprised. Yes, he did say Benya.

'Are you all right?' asked the powdered youth.

Well, no. In Russia the name Benya is not like Tom, Dick or Harry. It is what the writer Isaac Babel called the Jewish gang-land prince in his stories of pre-revolutionary Odessa. As Scrooge is to English misers, Benya is to Russian gangsters. Benya, the great extortioner, waltzes through them in multi-coloured clothes, splashing money around, a rogue with panache. So Elena's friend was a literary gangster. How very Russian.

A man with yellow eyes sat down opposite and smiled, or rather leered at me. His face was long and he had a straggling beard. I smiled back politely. Then I remembered the bearded figure in the film Elena showed me. I looked again. This must be Zhenya, or rather Benya. It had to be.

How to describe what happened next between that man and me? It felt as if I was standing on the edge of a cliff, being pulled towards the edge, though Benya did no more than fix me with a pair of terrible, yellow eyes. I was spellbound, falling. The prospect was terrifying, but I was powerless to resist the pull of those eyes. It was irresistibly sweet. I came to and started to struggle. How long we battled it out I have no idea. I did pull back from the edge, but the effort left me shaken and horrified.

I got up and hurried back to my cabin. Behind I heard footsteps and a man's voice saying 'Syusan, Syusan.' There was a glimpse of those yellow eyes as I slammed the door. I sat on the bunk, thoroughly frightened, and furious with myself. What was this? I was an experienced traveller. I loved nothing better than travelling on my own. What was I frightened of? So what if the man was a mafia boss? I was in no danger on this boat. But I was not just frightened. There was something here that I could not name, something worse than that.

I had a lot to learn. The man was just a minor monster, but I came from a world which was properly mapped, where travellers

ran across real dangers, not from monsters. I did not yet understand that I had left that world behind.

I must have dozed off after that. When I woke, the light through
the porthole had softened. It was late afternoon, and the cabin
walls were thrumming to the syncopated beat of live jazz. I lay
there, watching reflections of the water playing on the ceiling,
mortified by my overreaction, packing my fears away, yet reluctant to venture out of the cabin for fear of seeing Benya again.

Finally, the beat of the music lured me out, down a spiral staircase. On the landing below, a wiry sun-tanned American couple
stood admiring the theatre designs on the walls. 'Great music, isn't
it? We do Dixieland, but we're nothing compared with this lot,'
said the man. A trumpeter, he had been invited to St Petersburg
for a jazz festival. When they arrived, they found the event had
fallen victim to the chaos. Hearing of their plight, Benya offered
them a place on his cruise. 'Did you hear last night's concert?
Night after night there are these amazing musicians playing! Last
night was the greatest – this singer, she's a sort of Russian Edith
Piaf. I've never heard anything like her . . .'

'So what do you make of this Benya?' the trumpeter went on.

'He's quite a character,' the trumpeter's wife chipped in. 'Every
now and then he turns up in this white Mercedes, chauffeur-
driven—'

'With one hub cap missing,' added the trumpeter.

'Is he on board now?' I asked.

'Well, he was last night. You can tell when he's coming. His
girlfriend gets all dressed up. Then it's party time! He's quite a
guy – climbs on to the car and dances on the hood, wearing these
wild clothes – yellow shirt, red trousers and green socks.'

'D'you suppose he's mafia?' the trumpeter's wife asked, as we
walked down towards to the music. I let the question go. Whoever
our host was, the costume made it all too clear that he was model-
ling himself on Babel's king of thieves.

The main deck was packed with people, listening to the music.
Pale, plump and dowdy, they looked reassuringly ordinary. A
trombonist stepped forward and began a solo. He had the face
and body of a clown. He played with an intensity that made even
the babies in their sunhats stop and stare. Sleepy middle-aged
men emerged from their cabins and their plump wives dropped
their knitting.

We were held in the skein of the music. The man's playing was as effortless as breathing. It touched something in his listeners, transmuting the pain of living in the rubble of the great socialist experiment that had been inflicted on them, their fathers and grandfathers. He played to them of the happiness which no one could take away, the happiness of this moment in the sunshine, floating down the Volga. My own anxiety ebbed away, absurd.

When the trombonist finished his solo I turned to leave and saw Benya threading through the crowd towards me, yellow eyes fixed on me, leering. He was wearing only the briefest of red trunks and a gold chain round his neck. I lost my head and dashed up the stairs, making for the cruise manager's cabin. As I pounded on the door I heard Benya's footsteps on the stairs. After an interminable wait the door opened: 'Susan! What a lovely surprise!' Olga was standing in a large, light cabin lined in panelled, pale wood. I slipped inside and closed the door. The cabin was dotted with bouquets of dying red roses. Olga had company, two women friends.

'Is everything all right?' Olga asked. 'You look, well – flustered.'

'I'm fine.'

'Come on now, don't be so English. You look as if you've seen a ghost,' said a woman with a boyish face.

'It's nothing, really . . .' I could hardly say I was running away from our host.

'Has someone been bothering you?'

'No, no . . .'

'I'll deal with him,' said the boyish one.

'No, no, please.'

'Oh, I bet it's Boris,' Olga said. 'He was ogling her at lunch. He's incorrigible.'

'You mean the one with the straggly beard? So that's not Benya?'

The three women burst out laughing. They laughed extravagantly, holding on to one another. 'Benya! She thought he was Benya!'

'He's not on the boat at all,' Olga explained kindly.

'Well, what did I say about Boris?' the boyish one said triumphantly.

'She'd better stay with us,' murmured the third woman. 'It's funny – Westerners can't usually tell these things.'

*   *   *

Boris was Benya's *extrasensor*, his healer and spiritual advisor, they explained. The boyish woman assured me fiercely that he 'wouldn't bother me again'. He did not. For the next two days she insisted on collecting me from my cabin and chaperoning me back again. I had no idea why I needed this protection. But I was grateful to her. 'You were quite right about that fellow,' she confided. 'He's bad news – seriously spooky. We were only just talking about him, before you came in. Can't think what Benya's doing keeping him around.'

As I knew from my earlier travels, the transition from communism had brought to the surface all sorts of spiritual quackery. People were always talking about 'energy fields', 'bio-rhythms', dowsing and long-distance healing. A hypnotist called Kashpirovsky became a popular idol because of his mass-healing séances on television.

If this were a novel, the fleeting appearance of Benya's *extrasensor* would serve as a warning of monsters ahead. But this is not fiction. Life's little joke is that we are equipped for experiences only when they are over. The warning was one I would understand later on – too late to turn back.

BENYA'S ARK

After that I had a good time on the boat. Elsewhere in Russia my friends were living on bread, milk and potatoes. Here every meal was a feast. Solemnly, we ate our way through cutlets, meat pies, trifles, soups, pastries, pancakes with sour cream and smoked fish, salads drenched in mayonnaise. As Benya's guests we ate without ceremony, packing our bodies like suitcases before a long journey, preparing for a return to life in the wreckage of Russia's empire.

The star among my friends was the 'Russian Edith Piaf', whose concert had astounded the Dixieland trumpeter. With her long, dark hair and soulful eyes Elena Kamburova looked like one of those characters who gaze out from early Christian Coptic grave portraits, their eyes trained on eternity. The dying red roses in Olga's suite were tributes from her concert the night before.

Later on, back in Moscow, I would watch the reticence fall off like a cloak as she walked onstage. She seemed to live fully only in those moments of performance. For the time being, I watched her sing on the screen of a faulty video recording taken the night before. Though the image was distorted, the velvet-dark sound was undamaged. She was indeed the apotheosis of Russia's great tradition of singer-poets.

As we sat out on deck, Kamburova was sewing a present for Benya. It was a bearded cloth doll with multi-coloured clothes and pockets for his pens and pencils. 'How else can I thank him?' she murmured. 'Anything that money can buy he can get himself.' They were devoted to Benya. It was all very puzzling. The cream of Russia's creative intelligentsia, they were unlikely to accept hospitality from a mafia boss. But how to ask about Benya without making my misgivings rudely obvious? Was he a Party boss who had walked off with the funds? When all business dealings were illegal, the Party controlled the biggest scams. The richest oligarchs to emerge from the confusion of those years would come from that background.

Finally, angling for information, I asked Olga about the thugs who were lunching at the captain's table. She burst out laughing: 'Of course! You must've thought you'd landed in some mafia stronghold! Well, rest assured – Benya's not like that.' Not long ago, those two young hoods had attacked him when he was carrying a huge sum of money, she explained. 'Being Benya, he invited them to join him! We tried to dissuade him, but he reckoned that since he wouldn't be able to shake them off, he'd try to convert them – that's Benya all over. So far, it's worked. He certainly needs protection. Times are changing, it's becoming dangerous – at least they keep the others off.'

Benya grew up in a mountain resort in southern Russia. Theatre was his great love. The dean of a Leningrad arts college, on holiday in a resort, spotted him in some production and encouraged him to apply for a theatre course at his college. All would have been well if Benya had not decided to redecorate his student room in Leningrad. Halfway through the job, he dragged a refuse bin in from the courtyard for the rubbish. The police turned up and started poking around in the bin. They found a dead body, and pinned a murder charge on Benya. When the charge would not stick, they saved face by charging him with 'appropriating state property'. Of course, the refuse bin belonged to the state, as did the brushes and paint. In those days everyone lived like that, stealing odds and ends from a state that owned everything.

Benya was given a minimum sentence of three years. The conviction ended his chance of a career in theatre, or in any other profession. After his release, he took casual jobs as a maintenance man here, a nightwatchman or caretaker there. But theatre remained his passion. Night after night he would be there with carnations for his favourite actor or singer.

When Gorbachev came to power, Benya started trading. He was quick-witted, and, having no stake in the old regime, he could move fast. He started importing Japanese video recorders, which allowed early glimpses of life in the abundant West. Then he moved on to personal computers, each of which could be sold for the lifetime salary of an average professional. He made his first fortune well before the fall of communism. He was a talented deal maker, the legacy perhaps of generations of Odessa Jewish traders. When the first chink of freedom allowed, he opened a little theatre. He seems to have had little use for money personally. He kept on the move in his white Mercedes, brokering deals, trading goods wherever they were in short supply. When he had made enough, he started bankrolling films, which was how he met Elena. Later, when I asked her why she had not told me that he called himself Benya she explained that she would not invoke Babel's mafia lord because 'it's unworthy of him'.

Zhenya-Benya was a grand jester, riding a carnival moment of chaos. He was a wanderer in the service of a higher truth, only his truth was not religious. Dressed in his multi-coloured clothes, sleeping in his white Mercedes, he belonged to that tradition of social outcasts touched by grace, Russia's holy fools. He believed that Russia could be redeemed, but only by its artists.

His fantastical career reached its high point that summer of 1992 when he hired the N. Gastello, filled his ark with his favourite artists and indulged them with every luxury. But by that time the mafias were starting to carve up the territory between them. It was becoming dangerous for a loner.

As the N. Gastello steamed into Saratov I prepared to leave, but Olga told me Benya was expected. He was throwing a feast. Everyone was dressed up. Benya's girlfriend, in her flowing dress, presided over the table of honour. But the chair beside her remained empty all evening. Over dinner, the thug with tattoos entertained me with filthy underworld anecdotes, which he said were 'English'. When he smiled his scar seemed less terrible. 'The name's Yuris – if you're ever in trouble in Petersburg, call me up . . .' Beside him sat the extrasensor, my nemesis Boris, looking very ordinary in a badly cut jacket and white socks. Since Olga had taken me under her wing, he made himself scarce.

After dinner Boris whirled Olga round the deck. Relaxed now, I danced with the jazz pianist who had played on deck that afternoon: 'I hate this country,' he confided, flicking his pony-tail. 'Life's hell here. But when I got the chance to stay in America I found I was condemned to Russia.'

We leaned on the rail, peering over the river into the darkness. It was so broad that we could not see the east bank. Somewhere out there lay Marx, the town where I was going to chronicle the making of the new Russia. Thanks to its history, I told the pianist, thanks to foreign investment, this place would be transformed long before change came to the rest of rural Russia.

He sighed. 'I wish you luck. But remember that foreigners come here and see change because they want to. In fact there's only one riddle, and that's insoluble – why is Russia the way it is?' 'I'm fed up with this Russian fatalism,' I replied. 'Things are going to change now – and I'm going to watch the preview.'

VISIONS AND FAKES

Next morning the boat was going to head back to St Petersburg. Late that night in Olga's candlelit suite my friends tried to dissuade me from leaving. 'Don't be a fool,' said my boyish protector, 'no one'll have time for you – they'll be too busy grubbing round for the next meal. Stay here. We'll have fun, and you'll get to meet Benya.' It was tempting. I had been counting on Benya to introduce me to people in Saratov. All evening we had still been half expecting him. But his chair remained empty.

My protector had put her finger on another problem. The glasnost years, when everyone wanted to know a Westerner, were over. Now it was the fault of the West that people's magical expectations had failed to come true.

Staying in Saratov was going to be difficult for other reasons, too. When the boat docked, Kamburova's concert agent in the city had come to pay his respects to the singer. He enquired if I had a visa for Saratov.

'I don't need one now!' I responded airily. Under the old regime, each city required separate entry visas for foreigners.

'In Saratov you do,' he replied grimly.

'Russia's full of rules which no one obeys,' I responded. But I noted the triangle of anxiety between his eyes.

'In Saratov, rules are rules.'

'Come off it, Sergei,' remonstrated Kamburova's pianist.

'You don't understand – nothing's changed here! I'll help you with a visa, but you'll have to go back and apply from Moscow.'

He told me that Saratov had been a city closed to foreigners until only a few weeks before. Until then, they were allowed only to travel past the city by train in the dead of night.

What to do? From the boat, I could see Saratov stretching uphill from the Volga as far as the eye could see, towards the 'yellow mountain' of its Tatar name. It looked dauntingly large. No hotel was going to let me stay without a visa. I could be handed over to the police simply for being here. The only hope was to stay with someone. My one contact was away. 'Maybe he'll be back tomorrow,' a woman's voice said when I rang. Or maybe not.

Saratov sounded grim, but I was reluctant to return to the Russia I knew with Marx only a bus ride away. I slept fitfully in my luxurious cabin and woke out of a strange dream. After travelling through a desert I arrived in a place which looked like a north German city, with cobbled streets and Gothic churches, except that everything was carved from solid stone. Giant Coca Cola bottles and finned 1950s Cadillacs were carved into the buildings, but it was unclear what their function was. The city was humming with unfathomable life, but I could only make myself understood by writing in trochees, dactyls and spondees, the language of scansion.

After breakfast, the captain of the N. *Gastello* blew the hooter. The sun glittered on the deserted waterway as I hugged my friends goodbye and walked down the gangplank. Perhaps my punk contact would turn up. A woman was standing on the promenade. Tiny, with a full skirt and wicker basket, I recognised her from the evening before, when the boat had docked. She had joined us as we enacted the ritual the singer Kamburova had adopted whenever she arrived in a city, feeding the stray dogs. When the price of food doubled and tripled, people started turning their dogs out. Pedigrees and mongrels, they sat on the pavements like unemployed men, hoping for their luck to change.

The tiny woman and I waved to the N. *Gastello* as she sailed north. Then, flashing a dazzling smile which showed her worn teeth she asked, 'Are you Susan? I'm Vera. Elena told me that you needed help. Would you like to stay with me?' I put down my bag and hugged her. As Vera and I started up the hill, through crumbling streets of neoclassical buildings, she talked of Kamburova: 'Her songs have been my lifeline. So I'm thrilled at the chance of doing something for you!'

Before the Bolshevik Revolution, Saratov used to be called 'the Athens of the Volga'. Then, it was a rich merchant town, trading in timber and hard wheat. In the Second World War, it was spared destruction, thanks to the battle of Stalingrad to the south. Since then time had been wrecking what the tanks spared. Now scaffolding held in place the bulging walls and extravagant wrought-iron balconies above the plastic shop signs. Vera lived in a small flat off a leafy street near the city centre. Outside her front door an enormous black mongrel sat waiting. 'Jack's a stray – he followed me home one day.' Her flat was cluttered with books and paintings. 'My son's away, so you can sleep in his bed. Excuse the mess.' Her son's walls were hung with Led Zeppelin posters. 'I hate housework. If I spent my time looking after the flat, I'd have time for nothing else,' she said as she cleared a path through the dust to the bed with a mop.

We sat drinking tea on her rusting balcony overlooking an inner courtyard full of plane trees. Vera played me Kamburova's songs on an old gramophone. The rich, dark voice floated over the courtyard, transmuting the drabness and the tragedy of everyday life. 'Pessimistic', the Soviet authorities had dubbed her music. She had operated in that fertile margin beyond Soviet approval, but this side of prohibition. 'When I had nothing else, I had Elena's songs,' Vera murmured.

Vera herself was born into the Soviet elite. She trained as a physicist, and held a prestigious, well-paid job in an armaments factory. 'But it wasn't feeding me,' as she put it. So she gave it up, became a librarian and retired into her own world, avoiding newspapers and television, protecting herself from Soviet reality behind barricades of music and the poems of Tsvetaeva.

A light breeze rustled the leaves of the plane tree. In the courtyard below a babushka in a flowered housecoat fell asleep in the sun with a brindled cat on her lap. 'Isn't it wonderful?' murmured Vera, her heart-shaped face glowing. 'It's taken me a long time to learn to live in the moment. Now I see how lucky I am.'

I failed to see the luck. Saratov had been closed to foreigners because its industry was largely military. Her husband had been an engineer in an armament factory. He was unemployed, thanks to Reagan's deal with Gorbachev. One of her sons was a student, and her own salary as a librarian was barely enough to keep the three of them in porridge, potatoes and windfall apples.

Despite her plight, Vera's radiant cheerfulness marked her out. Before the fall of communism the population of this closed city was well paid, its shops well stocked and its housing, schools and colleges among the best in the empire. Then the arms factories closed. Now people walked with eyes lowered, faces averted from one another. In

shops, I was served reluctantly. When I asked the way, people pretended
not to hear. To them, I was an outrider for the victorious armies of
capitalism. In Vera's company it was different. Few could resist smiling
at this diminutive woman whose radiant, heart-shaped face told one
story, while her darned clothes and worn teeth told another. One
morning, we passed a blind man groping his way to avoid the open
manholes and gaping holes where the asphalt had collapsed into the
sewers. Vera slipped her arm through his and we walked him home
across the city centre.

Marx was tantalisingly close now, but first I needed contacts there.
I was in a hurry as my Russian visa was running out. But each time
I mentioned that homeland for Russia's Germans, people clammed
up. The project had clearly met with vigorous local opposition. Why?
No one would tell me. I even met a radical who talked about how
he tried to quell that opposition by applying something he called the
algebra of harmony. He was happy to talk about the equation.
$\frac{H}{S = Hmax - H}$ But I got no satisfactory answer when I asked him why
people were so opposed to a project from which they stood to gain
so much.

When I returned to Vera's flat, perplexed and bruised, she would
smile her dizzy smile and pull me into her cocoon. She too thought
I was mad to be pinning my hopes on Russia's economic regenera-
tion: 'This is only the beginning. The chaos will get worse, far worse.
But we have to be cleansed. It will be terrible, but there's no alternative. Until then, nothing'll thrive here.'

The apocalyptic tenor of such remarks made me wary of asking
about the source of her inner radiance. However, over supper in her
cramped kitchen one evening, she answered my unspoken question:
'Have you heard of Vissarion?' My heart sank. Vissarion was the
leader of a cult. 'He came in the nick of time – I was losing hope.'
Russia was a fairground of beliefs. The Moscow metro was plastered
with bright advertisements for the Bhagavadgita; smiling American
missionaries were plying their trade in the streets like hookers; in the
bookshops, the long forbidden works of Gurdjieff and Madame
Blavatsky were walking off the shelves; the Moonies and Scientology
were thriving. Among the home-grown cults, there were six prophets
in Moscow that summer who claimed to be the Second Coming.
Vissarion was one of them.

Vera's face glowed as she talked about him: he revealed himself
on Red Square on New Year's Eve, just as the Soviet regime was

passing into history. 'It was crammed with people celebrating. He was wearing nothing but a red robe and an old fur coat. He preached to the crowd.' She showed me photographs of his paintings. They were crude. There was a video, too: with his saccharine smile and red robe he might have been playing Jesus in a provincial theatre production. 'Brothers and Sisters!' he pronounced, in a sing-song voice. 'The time has come when you must choose between the paths of Good and Evil.' The end of the world was nigh; only those who followed Vissarion were going to survive . . .

After that, we skirted round the subject of Vissarion. Vera was not deceived by my polite interest and I distrusted the source of her radiant spirituality. The appeal was obvious. The Orthodox Church could not respond to people's needs, as it was emerging from what some believed was the worst period of sustained persecution any Christian church had suffered since the late Roman Empire.

Next day, I understood Vera's desperation better. When I arrived back at the flat bringing a bottle of Napoleon brandy, the colour drained from her face. 'It's my husband – he's . . .' Her voice dropped: 'alcoholic'. She hid the bottle on top of a cupboard. I had hardly met the man. Handsome, with a ravaged face, he left early and arrived home after we had gone to bed.

I might have guessed. Russian men were managing the Soviet collapse much less well than women. In the early 1990s, a million more men would die than if the old regime had continued. With the arms factory closed, Vera's husband had nothing left to do but drink. No wonder she had grown desperate, living with him in a single room. She had planned to leave him when her sons grew up, but the collapse of the economy had dashed those hopes.

As for the Napoleon brandy, it was fake. The twenty-nine-year-old marketing it would soon emerge as Russia's richest oligarch. Mikhail Khodorkovsky, favourite child of the old Party, was already running his own bank. Within a few years he would control Russia's oil. Soon after, he would be behind bars. At least his brandy did not poison or blind, like many of the fakes.

I had still not reached Marx when I ran out of time. Something had obviously gone wrong with the project to rebuild that homeland for Russia's Germans with foreign money. But what? I was clearly unwelcome in Saratov. I was in the city illegally, and my Russian visa was about to run out. But even as I packed to leave I was determined to come back and find out what lay behind that wall of silence.

1993

OPENING THE CAGES

―――⟶➤●◄――――

I reached the Volga town of Marx only that winter. What drew me was a sense that I had to be in Russia at that moment. Russian history had been shaped by long periods of stability interrupted by sudden discontinuities like this. I had a hunch that the character of its people was forged at such times. Ordinary Russians were in a fog of anxiety, and the fog was nowhere thicker than in that Volga region.

How could the local population be opposed to a plan from which they stood to gain so much? Ethnic tension, which had erupted right across Russia's southern border, had been a crucial factor in the unravelling of the Soviet empire. But these Russian Germans were white and indistinguishable from Russians. Most did not even speak German. On my last day in Saratov I had met a young woman who had a flat in Marx. She had invited me to stay there, 'in the unlikely event that you ever come back'. Anna was a local journalist and she had championed the cause of a homeland for Russia's Germans. We met briefly, in the offices of the city's only liberal newspaper, where she worked. A tall, gangling young woman, she moved awkwardly, as if her clothes were lined with prickles. Her lively, boyish face was framed by a tonsure of dark hair. She appraised me guardedly from a pair of large brown eyes whose whites were tinged with blue. They sparkled with intelligence. Over meatballs in the paper's canteen – which poisoned me for a week – she said something intriguing: 'I should warn you – do you remember what happened when Gerald Durrell freed the animals in his zoo? He opened their cages and they wouldn't leave – just sat there and howled. They refused to go back to the jungle and start hunting for food again. Well, that's us – that's what we're like in Marx.' I laughed. But she was not smiling.

My fellow passengers on the battered bus from Saratov sat in silence, bulky in their overcoats, buttressed in with bulging bags. The windows were iced over with crystalline patterns. Melting a hole with my gloved hand, I peered out. There was nothing to see but the snowy steppe stretching away to meet the snowy sky.

I thought about Benya, mysterious host of my cruise. I finally got to meet him in Moscow, over supper at Elena's. He could not have been less like the flamboyant outlaw of Babel's Odessa. He looked like an out-of-work clown with his long face, straggling beard and sad eyes. Rather than multi-coloured clothes, he wore an old hand-knitted jersey. He was accompanied by a bodyguard, an athletic young Kirghiz whose smart pale blue suit did not conceal the bulge of a gun.

I felt there was something very wrong, but Elena was reassuring: Benya was famous for getting into scrapes and out of them. His luck was down, but he would soon bob up and start splashing money round again, she said. Yet soon after that supper he went missing. In his empty offices, the telephone rang and rang. At first his friends assumed he had gone to ground, as he did whenever he had promised more money to his artist friends than he could deliver. Now he had just surfaced after months of silence. He had turned up in a police station somewhere in Siberia, wearing no coat or trousers. It was minus 30 outside and he was penniless. Exactly what had happened he would not say, but he appeared to have been acting as middle man in a negotiation that went wrong between the Kirghiz and Chechen mafias. The Chechens defaulted, and the Kirghiz held Benya responsible. They kidnapped him and stripped him of everything he owned. The Kirghiz whom he introduced as his bodyguard that evening was in fact his jailor.

The bus was late by the time it rattled to a halt by some rusting factory buildings on the outskirts of Marx. Anna was standing by a telegraph pole, shoulders hunched against the cold. As I stepped down, the sun came out from behind a cloud, throwing Anna's shadow and that of the telegraph poles on to the snow like exclamation marks. 'We must hurry – the light's going to fail,' she said brusquely, striding off down a street of dilapidated wooden houses.

I followed, hampered by a heavy bag. Anna crashed down on the frozen snow. Then I went flying. Still she kept on hurrying. Finally she stopped in a snowy wasteland. 'This is the old German cemetery. In summer it's littered with bones.' Clearing the snow away, she showed me toppled headstones and tombstones engraved with Gothic inscriptions in German. 'They ripped the place apart in '41. And they're still doing it today.' 'Is the memory still so strong – after half a century?' Striding off again, she muttered: 'Memory? You'll find no memory here!'

As I hurried to keep up, slipping and falling, I remembered a sad little story by Daniel Kharms about a carpenter who left home one day to buy glue. He fell over, banged his head and popped into the chemist for a plaster. On the way home, he fell down again and went back for another plaster. Again and again he fell down, and each time he went back to the shop for another plaster. Finally the chemist suggested he buy the box. 'No!' said the carpenter optimistically. 'I won't fall down again!' But by the time he reached home he was so covered in plasters that his family did not recognise him and turned him out on the street . . .

Kharms was one of the 'repressed' writers whose work was finally enjoying cult status in Russia. A comic, a performance artist before the phrase was coined, he used to make his stage appearances out of a cupboard. When he was arrested in 1930 he was charged with 'distracting the people from building socialism with . . . absurdist views'.

It was dark and bitterly cold by the time Anna stopped again. A full moon, yellow as double cream, shone on a white, empty space where a statue of Lenin stood pointing at the remains of a neoclassical Lutheran church. 'This is where they held the anti-German demonstrations.' 'I don't really understand why they were demonstrating,' I began, but Anna shot me a dark look and strode off again.

Anna's Spartan little flat at the top of a high-rise block was barely heated. There was no hot water and the bathroom fittings, sink and lavatory cistern were laid out on the floor. Still, it was a relief to have arrived. Now we could talk. 'So why were people here so against the German homeland?' I began. 'Surely they stood to gain so much from it?' She frowned: 'Hmm, that's what you'd think,' she began, then tailed off into silence. She offered me strong tea. She offered me a pancake; but she left my question unanswered.

I asked Anna how she came to be living in Marx, since she worked in Saratov. She threw such a poisonous glance at me that I recoiled. 'It's a long and boring story,' she said with finality. After that she tucked up her legs on a high stool and sat in silence, like a pinioned owl. I was baffled. Last time we met she was a different person – relaxed, amused. Today the tension was coming off her in waves. She seemed afraid, and I felt myself catching that fear, without knowing what there was to be afraid of.

I ventured another question or two. But she answered monosyllabically, and with such daunting finality that I relapsed into silence as well. On the kitchen wall hung a photograph of the moon-faced Yegor Gaidar, architect of the economic reforms. All round him Anna had stuck pictures of happy dogs cut out from coloured magazines. The walls at least told me that she supported Yeltsin's economic reforms.

It was only just after 5 p.m. An interminable winter evening stretched before us. Had there been anywhere to go I would have left. Had there been anything to eat, I would have eaten it. Anna's little pancake had whetted my appetite. 'This is how hunger begins,' the first line of a ditty by Daniel Kharms came back to me.

> The morning you wake, feeling lively,
> Then the weakness begins,
> Then the boredom begins;
> Then comes the loss
> Of the power of quick reason,
> Then comes the calmness
> And then the horror begins.

I just wanted supper. Kharms died of starvation.

This evening was my initiation into the world of silences. Silence can have many different qualities, as I would find. All I knew about this one was that I could barely control the impulse to get up and leave. Later, I would learn the reasons behind it, though never from Anna herself. She was young, and had not known the harshest years of Soviet censorship, but already her words and opinions had cost her dear. Although we would become friends, she was never going to forget that, as a foreigner and a writer, I was potentially dangerous.

By the time Anna finally laid out a mattress for me on the floor I was charged with her tension. I lay there hurt and baffled. Why had she invited me, if she thought I was some kind of spy? What had been going on that was so terrible she could not talk about it? Now and then a chilling scream penetrated the walls.

'What's that?'

'Oh, that's my neighbours' idea of fun.'

I was lost in the fog. Nothing had prepared me for the low-level collective hysteria that had Marx, and indeed Russia, in its grip. Factories were folding. Ordinary people, beggared by inflation and rising prices, were unpaid for months on end. Meanwhile, the old Soviet bosses were stripping state assets, appropriating raw materials, salting money away for themselves. Here in Marx those bosses were egging people on to take out their grievances on people like me, cartoon capitalists who were supposedly prowling round, eyeing Russia's wealth. That would come later. But at the time, the nation's wealth was worth less than a large Western corporation.

Twice in the course of the night, Anna sat bolt upright. 'What's up?' I whispered. It was as if she were waiting for that dawn knock on the door. But that was absurd – this was not the 1930s.

'Nothing. Go to sleep.'

I had intended to stay in Marx for a few days, but I changed my mind: I was going to catch the bus back to Saratov next morning.

When I woke Anna was lying in bed in her overcoat, hat and gloves: I had been sleeping with her only extra blanket. If I thought that my change of plan would please her, I was wrong: 'You can't. I've fixed up all these appointments for you.' So with bad grace I trailed behind her along the icy streets to my first appointment. 'Boris Pilnyak went to school there,' she volunteered. Looking up at the nondescript school block, I went flying across the icy ground. Pilnyak was a popular, stylish writer, a star of the 1920s literary scene. 'Was he a Volga German?'

'Of course,' she replied.

The meetings were a waste of time. The mayor looked as if he was having a nervous breakdown. The museum curator tried to sell me his museum's archives. A schoolteacher with a pudding-bowl haircut and beard that spouted like a jet of water from his chin fired platitudes at me like missiles. Anna maintained her Trappist stance, refusing to divulge anything. Later I learned that the mayor was a frustrated reformer, while the schoolteacher was the local demagogue who had roused crowds against the German homeland by invoking memories of the Nazi invasion.

'What's wrong with everyone?' I grumbled.

'Now do you understand? No one here's going to talk to you!'
'But why?' She refused to elaborate, but I detected a glimmer
of sympathy.
During one of these pointless meetings Anna ran off to draw
her monthly salary. 'I must spend it, or it'll be worthless,' she
muttered, patting a shopping bag bulging with notes. 'But what
on? I used to buy books, but they've disappeared now.' During
my next meeting, she spent it all on a red and white summer dress.
When she held it against herself in the snowy street I caught a
glimpse of the dashing young woman Anna might have been had
she not lived in that place, at that time.
As we trudged down the street someone hit me on the head
from behind. The weapon was only a long sausage, but I had had
enough. Bruised, hungry and perplexed, I let out a volley of hopelessly outdated Russian curses. Two young men scuttled away,
looking aghast. For a moment Anna stood petrified. Then she
laughed. She laughed so much that she almost fell over again. 'They
thought you were German!' she gasped. I did not see the joke.

FALSE PREGNANCY

That night, Anna returned to Saratov and I stayed on. Some friends of hers had offered me a bed. She walked me to their ramshackle wooden house, then strode off to catch the bus. Snow-bound clouds hung over the town. The icy street was empty and the town was wrapped in silence. Between the houses, high fences sealed off the yards from the street. Presently, the door opened to reveal a small, curly-haired woman. 'Come in, you must be freezing. Where's Anna? Ah, yes, she and my husband aren't speaking at the moment,' she laughed and rolled her eyes.

Natasha spoke in English, fluently. At that juncture, it was extraordinary to meet anyone in the provinces who spoke a foreign language well. As I peeled off my outer garments I complimented her. 'Thanks, but here it just marks you out as a suspicious character.'

In her bare kitchen a three-legged marmalade cat was licking itself on an upturned log of wood. 'You must be hungry if you've been staying with Anna,' she went on. Natasha had a lively, snub-nosed face and high Slavic cheekbones, though she was deathly pale. As I ate, she told me how she and her husband had ended up in Marx. 'We were living in the Caucasus. When Gorbachev announced the plan for a German homeland, we thought it was all going to happen here.' She sighed and lit a fresh cigarette from the stub of the last. 'We were just married. In love. Full of dreams. I saw this ad in the paper. *Delightful private house on the banks of the Volga.* I bought it sight unseen. "It doesn't matter if it isn't exactly what we want," we said to ourselves. "Once the Germans get things going we'll be able to do anything – restore it, build another."

'Everyone warned us. My father pleaded with me. My cousin Borya, who's a KGB general, travelled across Russia to get me to change my mind: "Don't be a fool, it's not going to happen!" he said. He must've known something we didn't. But we wouldn't listen. You see, it was the new beginning we'd been longing for.'

Natasha sighed and poured us tea: 'To think – I gave up my little house in the Caucasus for this barrack! It had this garden full of flowers..When we arrived I asked the driver why he'd stopped. "This is it," he said. "You're joking!" I said.

'Now we can't get out. Who'd buy a house in Marx now? We can't even get work. Igor's a brilliant engineer, and he knows all about computers, but he's been out of work for months. I'm a journalist, I've got a degree in mathematics and I speak English, but I can't even get a job teaching!'

'How do you manage?'

'I've got a few private pupils. Mostly, we just sell things. We had all these pictures, crystal, furniture . . .' Now the room was bare, except for beds, a table, some chairs and books.

While Natasha was talking, a man appeared in the doorway and stood looking at me disapprovingly. He was strikingly handsome, with olive skin and a trim moustache that curved down each side of his mouth as far as his chin. His black eyes, underscored with dark rings, were sad. 'Ah, Igor.'

'So why can't you get a job?' I asked him.

'Because I don't belong,' he replied. 'It's a town of serfs! There are no educated people here – we've only got each other,' he replied, fixing Natasha with his soulful eyes.

'I used to be sorry for them,' he went on. 'Then I realised you can't do that – you've got to judge them. I'll give you an example,' he said, walking to the sink and turning the tap. 'Take this tap – quite simple, you might think. It turns on. It turns off. Well, our neighbours don't have running water.' I murmured something sympathetic. 'What was that? Did I hear you say "poor things"?' Igor rolled his eyes. 'They could have had it long ago – free of charge. But guess what?' He was in a lather now. 'No, you couldn't guess, you come from the West. Those "poor things" of yours would rather live like that. Yes! The idea of change, any kind of change, terrifies them. They revel in their backwardness – in the Caucasus, where I come from, a man will at least pretend to be brave. In Siberia – Natasha's from Siberia – they've got a different kind of courage. But not in Marx! I tell you – you've come to the real Russia here!'

Natasha was watching with amusement. 'I can't tell you how lonely it is. And ugly! You'll damage your eyes! Listen – when they needed bricklayers to build the new Catholic church they had to go to Saratov – no one here could remember how to lay bricks straight!'

On it rolled, Igor's litany of contempt and self-pity, acted out with extravagantly theatrical gestures. He pulled out a bottle. 'In the Caucasus we wouldn't call this drink. But you can't be too careful nowadays. It's the only stuff you can trust. The rest's all doctored.' The bottle, 96 per cent proof, came, improbably, from France. The couple proceeded to teach me how to drink raw alcohol, using fruit juice as a chaser.

A few glasses later, Igor pulled his log closer to the table and looked me in the face. 'Come on, you can tell us,' he said, cajoling. 'Why have you come?' I explained, not for the first time.

'Don't give me that malarkey.' He was hectoring now. 'Who sent you?'

'What do you mean? No one!'

'Who did you say you were working for?'

'I don't work for anyone.'

Natasha sat back, relishing the spectacle of her husband baiting me. He pressed on.

'Who paid you to come?'

'It's not quite like that. You see I'm a . . .'

'Come off it,' he interrupted, sarcasm boiling over. 'There you are – sitting in your nice London house with your charming children and your loving husband. And you expect us to believe that one fine day you decide to come and see how people live in the town of Marx! I don't believe you.'

'That's not my fault.'

'Ah, I get it!' Igor interrupted. 'You're here for a bit of rough! You'll go home and dine out on horror stories of your brave trip to the heart of barbaric Russia.'

'I came because I want to understand.'

'Understand? The woman wants to understand!' Igor bellowed, rolling his dusky eyes. 'When has the West ever wanted to understand Russia?'

'I can't answer for the West.'

'You don't seem able to answer for yourself either.'

'And you don't seem able to listen.'

It was almost dawn and I was fed up with being bullied. I lost my temper. 'Look, I may be a fool for trying to write a book about Russia right now. I'm clearly a fool to have come here. But what about you? I can leave – you're stuck. Anyway, who'd send a spy to a dump like this?' There was a long silence. Then Igor fell about laughing and Natasha threw her arms round my neck and started kissing me: 'Honey, honey, look to me – I am waiting for you so long,' she slurred, her impeccable English smashed by drink. 'You're a wunafull, wunafull . . .' Horrified, I disentangled myself and locked myself in the front room, where Natasha had set up a camp bed.

I lay awake, stung by Igor's accusation that I was either a spy or a sensation tourist. How different it was when I set out on my travels in the last years of Soviet power, researching *Epics of Everyday Life*. Then, I wanted to find out how ordinary people were handling the revelation that they had been lied to all their lives. Often, I was the first Westerner they had met. It was people's resilience that struck me then. Where was that resilience now?

I woke early next morning to the sound of a howling cat. I had slept badly, mocked by my naivety at thinking that any island of prosperity could rise up here, out of this drowned land. During the night I remembered something else too. A Moscow journalist friend had come to Marx ten years ago to research an article about irrigation. He had not been welcome either. 'In the evening I was eating in a restaurant when something hit me on the head,' he told me. 'I took no notice. Wham! It happened again. I looked round. No one there. Wham! And again. Three men at the far table were throwing their bones at me.

"Is that what you usually do with your bones?" I asked them.
"Who are you?"
"What business is that of yours?"
"Who are you?"
Jostling, threatening, they followed him out of the restaurant. He used the only weapon he had – the names of the local Party bosses he was going to see. 'Hey, brother, why didn't you say so before? We'll see you back to the hotel, make sure you're all right.' Watch it, my friend concluded: they don't like strangers in the town of Marx. I had laughed at my friend's story, thinking how different it would be now. Yes, it was: it was worse.

The howling cat was sounding desperate. I unlocked the door

to find her scrawny and heavily pregnant, clearly about to give birth. After failing to rouse Natasha and Igor, I wrapped myself in a blanket and watched over her as she went into labour. On the wall hung a photograph of Natasha wearing a striped jacket and a cap made of newspaper on which was written the word MARXLAG. A strand of barbed wire ran across the picture.

By the time Natasha and Igor woke up the feline drama was over. The cat's convulsions had produced blood and afterbirth, but no kittens. Like the Volga German homeland, it was a false pregnancy.

STILL BIRTH
PHANTOM pregnancy
ABORTED FAILED p.

THE RED CARDINAL

Anna did warn me that no one in Marx would ever talk to me about the political tornado which had hit the town. She was right. But back in Moscow I started researching. The story I pieced together captured in miniature the tragedy of Russia in the twentieth century.

When Soviet communism set out to liberate man from the tyranny of nature, the countryside around Marx was accorded a highly significant role. The land, which was fertile, though inclined to drought, was earmarked to become the market garden for the whole empire. Once the Volga was dammed and the land irrigated, the town's hinterland would become a 'zone of guaranteed harvest'. When agronomists objected that the soil was not suitable for irrigation they were labelled bourgeois saboteurs and dispatched to the camps.

The task of 'novelising' the First Five Year Plan for the region was given to Boris Pilnyak, who went to that lycée in Marx. Pilnyak was deeply opposed to the harnassing of literature to political ends. In 1929 he had himself been denounced as a bourgeois saboteur in a hysterical press campaign. This project was his chance to redeem himself. Stalin also had a score to settle with Pilnyak, as the writer had published a story in 1926 that more or less openly accused him of having engineered the death of one of his rivals, Mikhail Frunze. The Great Joker assigned him Nikolai Yezhov, head of the secret police, as his literary mentor. *The Volga Flows into the Caspian Sea*, published two years later, tells the story of the heroic workers who foil a scheme by capitalist saboteurs to blow up the dam they are building. But this creaking tract won Pilnyak only a few more years. He was arrested in 1937, accused with gallows humour of wanting to kill his literary advisor, Yezhov.

The plan to create that 'zone of guaranteed harvest' also ran into trouble. The new dams prevented the river's low east bank from flooding the steppe in spring, moistening the soil for the growing season. So by the late 1950s, the region was suffering from drought. Cattle were dying, and at one point the population even had to be evacuated.

Manpower and resources were drafted in to solve the problem. Teams worked night and day, in non-stop shifts, to build the Saratov canal. For a while it looked as if these efforts had worked. Grain harvests rose by three or four times on the irrigated land, and the result was held up as a model for Soviet agriculture. Yet they were in such a hurry that they did not line the canals and ditches with cement. So they leaked. The water table started rising, bringing salt to the surface and souring the earth, just as the agronomist had warned.

The Party bosses ignored the problem. The more they irrigated, the more subsidy they could wring out of the state. Gradually, to keep the subsidies rolling in, the whole project moved from fact into fiction: directors of state farms were pressured to sign papers stating that work was complete which had barely begun. Those who agreed were promoted, those who refused found their careers blocked. Of all the Soviet money-making scams, irrigation was the most lucrative, since subsidies were not paid on the basis of harvest yields but on the amount of water poured on to the fields.

Yes, really, the more water they poured on the fields, the more subsidy they were paid. By the end of Soviet power, this approach left almost half the region's finest farming land salinated and unfit for agriculture. No wonder those in power did not want a German homeland. New money from Germany would have meant new people, asking awkward questions.

The man who ran this operation for twenty years was Ivan Petrovich Kuznetsov. Marx was his power base. He commanded a workforce of some 30,000, and won a medal as a Hero of the Soviet Union. A boss in the old Stalinist mode, he worked from early morning until late into the night, employing staff in two shifts – two secretaries, two chauffeurs, and the rest. Day and night people waited outside his office: the bosses of housing trusts, factories, state farms, Party secretaries and colonels whose battalions were assigned to construction. It was Kuznetsov who decided which roads and housing blocks would be built, and who was assigned housing.

They called him the Red Cardinal, King of the Shadow Economy, and his connections reached right up to the Politburo. Detailed information about him was hard to find: even at the height of glasnost those who knew kept their mouths shut. But gossip suggested the scale on which he worked: in 1988 the Gorky car factory received an order from Saratov for 150 cars to renew the town's pool of taxis. Only seventy arrived. A similar fate befell a planeload of humanitarian aid from Germany.

When President Yeltsin visited Saratov after the fall of communism, he announced publicly that it was time to depose Kuznetsov. The irrigation boss responded in venerable Soviet tradition, by retiring to hospital with a 'heart condition', and demoting himself to deputy head of irrigation.

The Red Cardinal was no longer the boss. But was his power broken?

A-LITTLE-BIT-ME

Back in London, a battered envelope dropped through my door one spring morning. It was from Anna and it had taken two months to arrive. It was remarkable that it had done so at all. Salaries of Russian postal workers were well below subsistence level; letters in and out of the country were being routinely dumped, or opened in the hope of finding money.

It arrived just after President Yeltsin had surprised everyone by winning support for his reform programme in a referendum. He staged it in order to leapfrog parliamentary opposition to his reforms. Some 58 per cent of the voters backed Yeltsin personally, while 53 per cent backed his economic programme.

A sheaf of poems fell out of the envelope: 'I don't know what waits for us tomorrow,' she wrote in eloquent, fractured English. 'It might be dictatorship, a coup, chaos or civil war. I have not lost my hope, of course, but impartial analysis of our Russian atmosphere shows we must be ready for all. So I want to ask you a favour. If something will happen with me, all my poems will perish with me together. I would not want that to happen. My poems are my trace, my sign on this Earth.

'I often recollect words of my friend, a psychologist. When she saw the photo of you and me she said that we have something in common in our eyes. And you remember, we were born on the same day.

'I think that you are . . . ' She broke into Russian, 'a-little-bit-me. A-little-bit-me lives far away, in safety in England, in a fairy-tale world of elves and gnomes. And that makes me feel good, at peace.'

After reading this enchanting letter I sat there, stunned. Was this the same person who had frozen me out throughout that interminable evening? I was ashamed of myself. Anna must have been in deep trouble. How easily I had dismissed the possibility, misread the situation, behaved like a cartoon Westerner, unable to imagine that in provincial Russia today people could still be listening for that knock on the door.

From other people in Marx, I had learned more about her after we parted. When things got ugly for the town's small Russian German minority, Anna was one of the few Russians who publicly rushed to their defence. As a result, she lost her job on the local paper, and was turned out of her flat. The townspeople turned against her too: Marx was full of stupid rumours to the effect that she had a Russian German lover, that she gave birth to an illegitimate child.

I had to know if she was all right. There was no way I could ring her, as she had no phone. I tried reaching Natasha and Igor. After the usual delays, the Russian operator said in that familiar, Soviet categorical tone: 'There's no such place as Marx'. How good it would be to be able to write the place off as a chimera, a nasty, neurasthenic state of mind, but it was real.

'I've been there!'

'There is no such town as Marx,' repeated the robotic voice. 'But I can put you through to Engels instead.'

So there it was, the partnership between Marx and Engels, still indissoluble, reincarnated in bricks and mortar. Later, I learned why Marx was not on the phone. The town's telephone system was still being switched manually. The operators had been offered automation, but fearing for their jobs, they refused.

I scanned Anna's poems for clues as to the source of her trouble. I found none. But I recognised the voice of a real poet. One of them perfectly captured the desolation I felt when I arrived in that provincial town:

It was a battered bus that brought me
to the country, as if to prepare me for what I would find.
It smelt thickly of burned out stars
and the dampness of the starry waste.

Lumps of dark red brick
lay around like meteorites.
The red-eyed cur, abandoned since spring
(its owner was Rita-the-Slain),

Loomed everywhere, as if it had
innumerable bodies which, though wasted,
were still sinister. It was no astronaut, but man
that dared to live among the groves

of clay-defying elms, which grow by the shaggy river
and reach towards the hills.
Brave is the man who lives
so ill-defended from himself at such a time!

Resolute he strides into the nothingness
carrying his irreparable hump, the earth,
having pronounced an irrevocable 'yes'
to the crimson-grey, unpeoplable Universe.

THE OTHER SIDE OF DESPAIR

'I think that you are a-little-bit-me.' With these words Anna reeled me back to Marx like a fish on a line. As I travelled down there on the train, I imagined what the town was going to look like in summer. It might have charms I could not have guessed at.

But no, Marx turned out to be even uglier without its cosmetic blanket of snow. The rows of decrepit residential blocks, the concrete high rises and rusting sheds lacked any pastoral charms. There were no redeeming features in the abandoned building sites, broken benches and rutted, puddled streets where the infrequent traffic showered muddy water over passers-by, but where, if you turned on a tap, there was no clean water to be had for whole days on end.

Anna's boyish face was brown and her tonsured hair gleamed. But when I moved to embrace her she shied away. When she heard how anxious her letter had made me she looked horrified. 'Forget it – it was just a little winter gloom.'

There was more to it than that, though. Because of her brave stand on the Volga German issue, Natasha explained, Anna was invited to Moscow for a trial period working on *Izvestia*, Russia's oldest liberal newspaper. It was the first move towards offering her a job. When no offer was forthcoming, she fell into a depression: her chance of escaping the provinces was over. 'You can't blame them,' Natasha commented. 'She's a good journalist, but she can't play the game – they'll have written her off as hopelessly provincial.'

When I went to stay with Anna the first things that caught my eye in her cramped hallway were two photographs on her wall. One was of me, looking almost as wary as Anna. The other was of Elena Kamburova, the singer who had befriended me on Benya's cruise. Since my last visit, she had given a concert in Saratov, and

Anna and Igor (who had taken the picture for the paper) had both fallen under her spell. During the evening of interminable silences that followed, I clung to these gossamer connections.

The following morning we went for a walk along the backwaters of the Volga. Anna strode ahead, pursued by demons. Only once we had settled on a spit of wooded land surrounded by inlets did she start to relax. 'Did you know that the man who introduced us is the KGB officer on our paper?' she said with a hint of a smile: 'When I saw him again he asked whether I thought you were an agent.' I realised that whatever suspicions she might once have had were over now.

There was a sudden flash of yellow-green wings overhead. 'That's an oriole – there's a nest up there.' Anna knew her birds; she had read biology at university, she told me. The trunks of the willow trees were standing in water and the air was filled with the fluff of seeding poplar trees. Two pink-grey ring doves were flying to and fro across the water, as if harnessed together, cooing their murmuring song. A water rat swam across the inlet, breaking the surface with its nose.

'I'm sorry I was so unfriendly when you were here last,' she said after a long silence. 'I used to be so pro-Western. Then I started meeting people from the West.' She pulled a face. 'Mostly journalists from Germany. They treated us as if we were animals in a zoo, rare specimens of malformation! You're different. At least you're interested in us as people.' Then, after a long pause, 'You know what it's like to live on the other side of despair.'

Her words caught me off guard. She was right, of course. But how did she know? After all, she had succeeded in choking off every substantive attempt I had made at conversation. Despair had brought me here to Marx. When Gorbachev opened the Soviet empire in the late 1980s I had become enthralled as she had by the dream of Russia's Westernisers, who wanted to see Russia become a European state, with the institutions of liberal democracy – civil society, free speech, democracy and the rule of law. The Slavophiles, on the other hand, insisted that the Western path of development was not right for Russia; the country's backwardness protected qualities in her which allowed her a different and spiritually superior way forward. I had been fascinated, as I imagined she had been, by the idea of this piece of countryside having an ongoing, supportive connection with Europe, through the Russian German connection. We both dreamed, as Catherine the Great had once done, that this rural region would become a haven of prosperity and civilised values.

After this promising flash of intimacy, our friendship developed with painful slowness. I sensed that she was holding herself together with difficulty. She responded badly to questioning and rarely volunteered information about herself. She was like a wild bird, poised to fly off if I got too close. So when we spent time together I took to sitting very still, hoping she might just come to trust me. Often, her large dark eyes were wary, defiant. Only now and then, when she let her guard slip, would her face light up with amusement or curiosity.

It was Natasha who told me why Anna would not talk to me in the winter. An article she wrote had had a devastating effect in the town of Marx, and she was not going to risk that happening again. It was a bizarre story, but it made it amply clear why that Russian German homeland could never have got off the ground in any circumstances.

In October 1991, shortly after the Communist Party's attempted coup, a government spokesman announced that the Russian German homeland would be established by the end of the year. By that time, local opposition had died down. It was even dawning on people that the development might improve their lives.

Their elected representatives disagreed. They announced a State of Emergency in the region and called a grand meeting in Marx. In speech after hysterical speech, the deputies declared that unless the decision were reversed they would close all borders and roads to the province and destroy the bridges over the Volga. The town's prosecutor, backed by the police chief and the head of the local KGB, warned them that such actions would contravene the criminal statute book. But they were shouted down with cries of 'Monster!', 'Eunuch!' 'Coward!'

Anna covered the event for a Saratov paper. Her article merely reported the facts, but that was enough: unlike Marx's paper, *The Banner* (formerly '*of Communism*') it said nothing about the 'thousands of demonstrators' because there were none. Indeed, the episode would soon have been forgotten had a Moscow journalist who was visiting his mother-in-law not read Anna's article. Vastly amused, he rewrote the story under his own by-line.

It appeared on the front page of one of the most sensational national newspapers, *Moskovsky Komsomolets*: 'From now on the deputies of Marx's town council are as free as birds,' the article began. 'No one's going to take any notice of them. The regional prosecutor, the chief of the KGB, the head of the police and the judges have all declared in black and white: "We disassociate ourselves from the actions and proceedings of the present council. We've got enough trouble with hooligans already . . ."'

The people of Marx opened their favourite paper to find that the whole country was laughing at their elected representatives. Instead of joining in, they closed ranks: for all their faults, the deputies were *theirs*. Solidarity in times of crisis was an ancient reflex. It was born of Russia's geography and climate, the experience of scratching a living out of this tricky soil, watered by patchy rainfall in a land situated too far north for easy living. The survival of the group was a safer option than individual initiative in these obdurate circumstances.

Marx's chiefs of the KGB and police were forced to resign and the judges to apologise. Only the town prosecutor refused to back down and survived in office. He retreated behind his desk, armed with heart pills and the complete works of Chekhov, and took to lobbing missiles at fools who wasted his time.

That buried the last hope of a homeland for Russia's Germans. It was not Anna's fault; but, nevertheless, her words were instrumental.

I was reminded of a story by Nikolai Leskov, supreme chronicler of provincial life in nineteenth-century Russia. The peasants on a well-managed estate had gone on the rampage, smashing machinery and burning buildings down; so the baffled owner hired someone to find out why. The estate's English manager could cast no light on what had triggered the revolt. All he had done was build new factories and introduce modern farming techniques, he said. And of course he had never beaten them.

The investigator met a wall of silence when he talked to the peasants. No, the Englishman had not beaten them or worked them too hard, they agreed. There was nothing wrong with the new factories either. But in the end, one peasant cracked. He said the Englishman had meted out this terrible punishment to a lazy peasant: rather than beating him, he sat him on a fancy armchair, tied him there by a thread – 'Just like a sparrow!' – and forced him to watch his fellow peasants work. That was what set the peasants off.

Russians will endure almost any hardship, these two stories reminded me. What they cannot endure is the suspicion that they are being laughed at, humiliated. No wonder I had run into a wall of silence when I first arrived here. My questions had picked the scab off a very fresh wound.

TIED BACK TO BACK

Natasha and Igor greeted me like an old friend, and insisted that I stay with them. It was a relief to have my own room in their house on Engels Street, since the air of Marx was still thick with mistrust. Walking through it was like heading into a strong wind.

The couple were in a state of shock. When they arrived in the town the only local newspaper was the ponderous *Banner of Communism* – which was to sack Anna for supporting the Germans, and kicked her out of her flat. The couple had persuaded the town's tractor factory to let them start a paper of their own. They called it *The Messenger* and they wrote and produced it entirely themselves. They wanted to liberate the townspeople with their words, to bring them that sense of freedom and opportunity which fired Russia's urban population during the glasnost period. And it did become a popular little publication. Every issue sold out. But for reasons they could not explain, the factory had just sacked them and appointed another editor.

The success of an enterprise binds people together, while failure divides them. Since my last visit, Natasha had been corresponding with an old admirer, who had moved to Canada and become a successful businessman. Recently, he had asked if she would join him there. 'I'm not in love with the man, of course, but he's nice enough, and he's had a soft spot for me for years.'

'Does Igor know?'

'No – for goodness' sake don't breathe a word! It may all come to nothing. But whatever happens, when that letter arrived, I came back to life.' She had indeed. In the winter she was deathly pale and remote, like a faded photograph. Now her snub-nosed, high-cheekboned face radiated energy, and the eyes under that mane of brown curls sparkled.

The house, which belonged to her, was on the market. 'That

means nothing though – everyone in Marx is trying to get out. But who'd buy a house here now?' She had told Igor she wanted a divorce. 'We had this terrible fight. He attacked me with a kitchen knife. It was scary – but funny too. Yes, really! After that I realised I'd got to get out fast. I just want to start my life all over again!' When the house was sold, she would return to Siberia. Her father would help her get started: 'I won't need much. I've done with possessions. Antiques, pictures, china – I've had it all. Even the junk we've now got weighs me down. I just want to be free! The years I've spent in Marx have taken their toll on me, I know that. But I was given a lot. I've still got enough of what it takes to begin again. I can't wait to travel and see the world!'

In the meantime, Natasha was spending most of her time out of the house. She left in the morning and did not return until supper time, though she had no work but the odd English lesson. Where she went she did not say. 'Igor's become impossible. I can't bear to be with him. He won't take a job, and he's quarrelled with all our friends.' But in the evening, the three of us would sit long over supper, my company seeming to act as some sort of buffer between them.

As for Igor, he paced up and down the house like a caged animal, rolling his dark eyes, releasing his frustration in scathing diatribes against the backward dolts of Marx. With his dark southern features and distinctive moustache trimmed round his mouth he might indeed have been a zoo animal, so exotic did he look in that small town. Natasha accused him of being lazy and spoiled, and the accusation stung. Yes, he did turn down a job editing a newsletter for the mayor: 'But not because I'm lazy – I just won't work for fools! I'd be only too happy to work, if there were anything decent on offer. What I won't do is to put up with the old Soviet way of working – and I don't see a new one emerging. Look around you. You'll see nothing but people who've been broken by the system – I was too. When I came out of the army I worked at this place where they were developing something like the photocopier. After a while, I started coughing blood. I asked for ventilation. They did nothing. I asked nicely. I explained, I pleaded. Useless. In the end I just stopped working. They finally sacked me for negligence!' He sighed: 'In the life of everyone in this country you'll find some such story.'

In fact, Igor was not lazy. He was just in despair. He really did love nothing better than work. His ex-wife, who had set up a dressmaking business in Moscow, had commissioned him (in exchange for a ton of sweets, a currency more reliable than roubles) to devise a machine for making shoulder pads. He was putting the finishing touches to his invention. Whenever he came back from working on it he would be in a sweet mood.

Leafing through back issues of *The Messenger*, I understand why Natasha and Igor lost the editorship. To start with it was lively and intelligent, a breath of fresh air after the thudding provincialism of *The Banner (of Communism)*. But gradually, Natasha and Igor's despair at the town's Luddite opposition to change spilled on to the pages.

The articles were unsigned, but there was no mistaking their voices. Igor was the thunderer: 'Don't be fools! If you haven't got the strength to meet the challenge of this new age yourself, don't make it worse for others than it already is. Don't betray those who saved Russia from the communist nightmare! Have a little patience, help each other with a word, a crust, a smile. And particularly the children – they will never forgive your treachery, your greed, your ignorance . . .'

Natasha's style was more literary: '"When will he come, Russia's liberator?" we complain. We can't make up our minds to take that step ourselves. Hello, it's me! I'm a free person in a free Russia! I'm not a worker, I'm an individual, and I hate lies and slavery!' she wrote on the occasion of Russia's newly established Day of Independence. 'I believe that sometime this day really will become a national holiday. But before that can happen, each one of us must "squeeze the slave out of ourselves, drop by drop" as Chekhov advised us.'

As I sat there, reading their articles, I heard music. A funeral was passing in the street below. A saxophonist and two trumpeters led the way, playing wildly out of tune. Four men carried the bandaged body in an open coffin. A crowd followed, then a procession of cars and buses. The man looked quite young. He had lived a few doors down, said Igor. He fell ill after spraying his carrots. 'It'll pass. Just drink lots of milk!' the doctor said. Next day he was dead.

Death was lurking in any can or bottle on sale now. Half the products were fakes, but which half? Mostly, the labels were convincing enough. The day before, I went out to buy a feast for Natasha and Igor: a fresh fish, a good Spanish wine, cheese and a bottle of French mayonnaise. The 'wine' turned out to be raw alcohol, apple juice, water with a touch of something petro-chemical. The 'mayonnaise' was furniture polish with added vinegar.

'*Obmanul cheloveke*' ('I had one over on him'), the very phrase expressed satisfaction at having deceived someone. People who lost their jobs were making money by mixing these poisonous potions for their neighbours. Gone were the controls of a developed society. If you bought rotten goods, there was no redress. Nor, for the carrot-sprayer's widow, would there be compensation. Here, it was 'fate'. It was not Germans, or even Kuznetsov, people feared now. It was each other.

Igor and Natasha's rows would flare up out of nowhere. One day, Natasha and I were picking strawberries in a patch of ground behind their house. The plants were a relic of the couple's early days in Marx, when they thought the town was going to be their permanent home. 'But it's no good – this place, it gets to you,' Natasha commented, surveying the muddle of weeds and long grass.

Natasha and I were talking about a friend of theirs called Misha when Igor joined us. He was an ex-engineer turned trader whom I had just met. He would not survive as a businessman, Natasha was saying; he was too innocent. 'It's good to meet someone who's so confident in the future,' I was saying. 'He's so open.'

'Misha's not open,' Igor interrupted. 'I'm the one who's open. If people don't like it they're just stupid.' Misha had tried bringing Igor into his business, but Igor had quarrelled with everyone.

'They're not stupid,' retorted Natasha. 'You just can't get on with them.'

'I can't lie, even if everyone else does. You excuse everyone else's lies, but not my Truth.' They were off.

'People lie for lots of reasons: not to cause pain; because they don't want to disappoint someone.'

'Look, I'm no fool. If a girl says some bloke likes her I'm not going to contradict her. But lies are different. You've got to understand,' he went on, turning to me, 'how lies permeated every corner of our working lives. It became so much part of us that we have no idea how to live without lying at every step. That's why I won't work with these fools! I'll give you an example: Ivan's got thirty hectares of land and the state says he can produce x on it. In order to produce that he'll have to work not just the thirty, but another fifteen he's kept hidden from the state. If that's how he's worked all his life, how d'you expect him to start living without lies? The clever man, who's praised and rewarded – oh you're so wonderful, here's a medal – is the one who'd got his hands on those extra hectares. Then I come along with what I've produced on my thirty hectares, and I'm sacked for living like an honest man! So here we are, heads fogged with lies and people don't like it when I tell the truth!'

'See what I mean?' Natasha said to me, before turning to Igor: 'Have you finished?'

'What do you expect me to do, smile and say "You're right"? Every day the wall between me and the rest of the world gets thicker. I can smile and lie and say they're right when they're not, and the wall gets a teeny bit thinner. I can lick arse and it'll get even thinner. Or I can break my bones and it'll disappear entirely. What should I do? You tell me!'

'You're insufferable,' Natasha sobbed, running into the house. Igor stood shrugging his shoulders, as if to say 'What's with the woman now?'

Later, he told me a story he came across when editing *The Messenger*. During one of the waves of mass arrests in the 1930s, a young Volga German couple from Marx who were very much in love were locked for a month in a basement on some phantom charge. They were tied together, back to back. 'And guess what became of their great love? When they were freed they ran off in opposite directions and never clapped eyes on one another again.' He paused. 'That's what Marx is doing to Natasha and me.'

TURNING RUSSIA ROUND

It was early evening in Marx. The breeze off the fields smelt sweet and the sky over the steppes was vast. Under the poplars of Lenin Alley groups of young men in nylon tracksuits, trousers hitched tight to display their manhood, were flirting with the mini-skirted, bubblegum-popping girls. It was a welcome sight: their youth carried its own sort of promise.

Natasha and I were invited to supper with Misha and his wife Tatiana. We walked past broken benches, hacked-down trees, abandoned building sites and row on row of jerry-built, battered residential blocks. The crippled, gifted art teacher I had just met walked this way to work every day: 'I read all the way there and back without lifting my eyes from the book,' he confided. 'It's the only way I can survive the ugliness.' Marx was affecting me like that too.

In one of the battered blocks, we found Tatiana scrubbing crayfish in a red and white spotted kitchen. There were crayfish everywhere: in a bucket on the floor, crawling along the sideboard; boiling on the stove, steaming in a pink pile on the table. Tatiana was young, with large grey eyes, full lips and wavy, ash-blonde hair. 'I hope you like crayfish,' she said shyly, standing on one leg, wrapped in an apron, unconscious of her beauty. 'There's nothing much else to eat. Some boys were selling them by the roadside and Misha bought a sackful.'

She and Misha had come to Marx to serve out their obligatory provincial stint after graduating as engineers from Moscow's elite Baumann Institute. Marx's secret electronics factory used to employ 500 engineers to work on the electronics for Saratov's arms factories. It was deemed a prestigious placement. So hush-hush was its operation that even its workers did not know the factory's real name. They turned out toy cars too, to give the factory an alibi.

Now the bright young engineers like Misha and Tatiana had left, and toys were all the factory was making. Those who remained earned a token amount, when they were paid at all. Tatiana was happy that Misha was earning enough for her to be able to stay at home and look after their daughter, Polina.

Presently, Misha walked in wearing football clothes. Star of the factory's football team, he was putting on weight now. He was fair, like his wife, with blue eyes and a gentle face which lit up when he smiled. Natasha had described him to me as 'the only honest businessman in Marx'. When I told him he laughed. 'Honest? Not me! Well, it depends what you mean. I don't stick to the law – no one could. But in the sense of being decent, I try.'

What Natasha meant by saying that Misha and his partners were honest was that they had not set up their business by stealing from the state. Those who could did so by paying some factory manager to 'borrow' his employees' wages for a month or two. The workers went unpaid, but another business was born. Misha kick-started his business by driving to south Russia, where Tatiana's mother worked in a sugar factory, filling the car with sugar, and selling it in Saratov. Now they traded in soft drinks and chewing gum. Though the family lived modestly enough, unlike most people they could eat fresh food every day, and treat their friends.

Misha was shy with me. But as the liqueur bottle grew emptier, he relaxed: 'I know you think we're just traders in cheap goods, but you wait! I'm going to knock out my rivals. I'm going to be a power in this province. We may have started by lying and stealing from the government – there was no other way to start. But we'll soon be beyond that. Even now things are sorting themselves out. And there'll be no stopping the people who come through these years. We're going to be fabulously rich.'

Misha's words were addressed to me, but his eyes stayed on his graceful wife as she moved round the kitchen. 'Only then will we get round to tackling the chaos you see all around you. Mark my words, the West'll have to watch out! Who'd be a businessman in the West? They're going mad with boredom – you've got a *system*. Where's the fun? Here you build your own world every day. It's a game of skill, and there are no rules, just ways of getting through. We may have lived under a regime where the more water you poured on to your fields, the more subsidy you received, but that's over. Now we count every kopeck. For me every other trader in town's a competitor – I'll do the lot in! It's tough, but fun! We're going to turn Russia round!'

Later, when I went to stay with them, I would watch Misha leap into his little Zhiguli each morning as if throwing himself into the saddle, and drive off in a cloud of dust to his own Wild West. He talked little about the risks he was running, even to Tatiana. But she overheard the whispered late-night phone calls. She saw how he was ruining his health, how he twitched and muttered in his sleep, and woke stare-eyed with fear. 'I don't know how much longer I can stand it,' he muttered one morning at breakfast. 'My nerves are shot. The games we have to play, day in, day out, to stay out of the clutches of the police; hiding in ditches, paying them off. Everyone talks about the mafia, but the government are the racketeers. You can come to an arrangement with the mafia, if you know how to talk to them.'

Misha was born in Ukraine, into a peasant family. His parents survived the great famines that killed some five to eight million Ukrainians – no one even knew how many. His father, badly wounded in the war, lay concussed for six months. Only because his officers valued him was he, an ordinary soldier, given the precious American drugs that saved him. After that he was sent to the camps on some trumped-up charge. Through all this he remained a man of great sweetness, Tatiana said. Misha had inherited that quality. How indeed was he going to survive in the jungle of Russian business?

Tatiana had an inner poise that set her apart from the anxious strivings of her husband and friends. Her pale beauty was typical of her father's people, the Mordvins, a Finno-Ugric minority who had lived on the River Volga since long before the Slavs settled the steppes. For a beautiful young woman, she was curiously lacking in vanity. At school, she was said to have been so ugly that the other children kept their distance, calling her 'Sergievna', 'Sergei's daughter'. Through hard work she won a place at Moscow's prestigious Baumann Institute for engineering. Once there she grew her hair, changed her image and fell in love with another scholarship kid from the sticks, Misha.

Staying with her, I began to appreciate how looking after a small family could occupy all her time. In theory, Marx had running water, gas and electricity. But in practice, one or other and sometimes all three were turned off for periods every day. Keys were another problem: there was nowhere in town to get one cut, so Tatiana was the only one in the family who had one. The family appeared to live with all 'mod cons', but there was nothing modern or convenient about their lives. Their washing machine had not worked for five years, the man who came to mend it having walked off with a broken part and never returned. The town had a launderette, but it was a long way away and it tore clothes to shreds. So, like everyone else, Tatiana washed the family's clothes by hand. As for the telephone, since Misha was earning reasonable money, they jumped the five-year queue to get one installed. But you could use it only for local calls. For all others, you had to walk half an hour to the main post office. There, you booked and paid for the call, returned home and waited until the manually operated switchboard chose to put you through.

When I first came to Marx I was surprised to find educated people sleeping on broken sofas, keeping their baths full of water, using cupboards without handles, and eating cold spaghetti. Now, watching Tatiana struggling with the pointless trials of everyday life, I appreciated how hard it was to bring up a family without taking to the bottle, or sinking into a depression. Sanity required that you did only the minimum required to keep life going.

Just before I arrived, the balconies fell off an entire block of flats while the owners were asleep in their beds. As the town fell ever further into disrepair, the future too was retreating.

CONNOISSEUR OF SILENCES

All this time, the person I was most anxious to get to know was the awkward, brave, poetical Anna. But like a bird, she would dart in for a crumb of friendship before hopping out of reach again. Years later, I was astonished when Natasha told me she had been deliberately leaving her diary out on the table for me to read. I wish I had known. For she was still stone-walling me with her silences. What I write here about her came out only much later, when she started to relax.

Anna grew up in a remote Volga village where cleverness was regarded with suspicion. An only child, her parents worked on a collective farm. It was her maternal grandmother who largely brought her up. The old woman was educated at a Leningrad school for blue-blooded girls, before war swept her out to the steppes. Anna's childhood was marked by the tug-of-war between her grandmother's middle-class expectations and those of her rural father. But Anna remained obdurately herself.

She always hated being cuddled and never joined the village girls who flocked together, giggling and sharing secrets. I imagine her crouching awkwardly over a book or watching a trail of ants cross the porch of their wooden house. In July, the month of the falling stars, I see her creeping out of the house in the evening to lie on the rough grass of the steppe, and breathe the smell of wormwood. When the night sky lit up with summer lightning, I picture her rushing outside to wait for the cloudbursts that followed.

She came to trust animals more than people. Anna's mother had a gift with animals, and the household was full of them. When someone ran over a dog, or found a bird with a broken wing, they left it with her mother. A man brought an owl which had been shot and wounded. The bird refused to leave when it was healed and lived with the hens. It never attacked the chicks, or took more than its fair share of food. There was a crow that could not fly, too. On summer evenings, it would sit by Anna's mother in front of the house and defend her against anyone who came too close.

Only rarely did the wider world intrude on village life, as it did on the day of the oranges. It was midwinter, and the snow was deep on the steppes when Anna's grandmother sent her out to the shop. Usually, the same meagre array of goods sat there year in year out. But that day the shop was glowing: there were oranges everywhere. Anna had never seen one before. A freight train from Central Asia had overturned, carrying fruit for the Party elite. The villagers went home with bulging bags, then queued again. All winter, the snow remained littered with orange peel. Not until she went to university was Anna able to start exploring the mysteries suggested by the sudden appearance of those oranges.

Before the fall of Soviet power I used to argue about the past with a Moscow friend called Grisha. He insisted that in Russia you could not afford to look back, because you would not survive what you found. I argued that only by facing the past could you move forward. In Marx, Anna watched me struggling to get people to talk about the past. She even introduced me to people. But it was only later that she admitted how hard she had battled to do the same herself.

Misfortune had rained down on this part of the Volga during the Soviet period. It was bitterly fought over in the Civil War, being a rich grain-producing region. When the Bolsheviks secured it, the Volga Germans' reputation as farmers proved their downfall. Though mostly smallholders, to the Bolsheviks they were 'kulaks', class enemies. The grain quotas imposed were three times higher than elsewhere. Sometimes, they were higher than the harvests themselves. By 1920 the requisitioning parties were taking people's last food, and next year's seed corn as well. The poor killed their livestock. They ate grass and the thatch off their roofs.

As famine loomed, the German peasants exploded in rage. They buried their grain and staged armed revolts. They were not alone: much of the Russian countryside was in rebellion, but on the Volga it was worse. It was a brave Bolshevik who ventured unarmed into the countryside from Marxstadt (as Marx was then called).

They risked being ripped apart. In the town square farmers were selling mechanical reapers for a loaf of bread.

By 1921 96.9 per cent of the region's population was starving. Hunger broke the peasants' rebellion. In the early twenties, when other parts of the countryside were enjoying a respite, here on the Middle Volga a quarter of the population died in famines. Cannibalism was commonplace.

Until glasnost, it was a punishable offence to talk about these matters, and people were still afraid to talk. I became a connoisseur of silences. There was the habit of fear, and the hope that if they stayed silent, the horror would die with them. But the toxic past had a way of seeping through, burdening the children with a distress that, being ignorant of the past, they had no way of combating.

Mostly, I retrieved clues and omissions, fragments of narrative. But there was too little matter, too much dammed-up feeling. The most devastating stories were the hardest to verify. For instance, I kept hearing how, after the Wehrmacht invaded in June 1941, the secret police tried to lure the Volga Germans into collaboration, in order to justify their impending deportation. Aeroplanes with fascist markings flew over the fields where the Volga Germans were harvesting. They dropped paratroopers, wearing fascist uniforms and armed with Valter pistols. The women, old men and children rounded them up with their pitchforks and scythes and marched them into the nearest Party headquarters. They found that these 'spies' did not even speak German. Some were Poles; others broke into fluent Russian when cornered. One pulled off his shirt to reveal his NKVD uniform underneath.

Saratov's leading historian of the Volga Germans told me that this was a Volga German myth, born of a pathological need to prove their innocence. He had found no evidence of it in the archives. But the clues I picked up suggested it did happen. General Anders, some of whose Poles were involved, mentions it in his memoirs. Someone I knew had heard a retired Russian colonel from the Ministry of the Interior testify publicly that the 'spies' were all shot, to destroy all evidence of this failed attempt to provoke the Volga Germans into betraying their country. In Siberia I met an old German who told me that a Soviet German Party apparatchik confessed on his deathbed that he was there when the harvesters brought in one such 'spy': the German Party workers were sworn to secrecy, and, terrible to record, they remained faithful to their promise, despite being deported for a crime they did not commit.

All this reminded me of a Russian saying: the real fools are not those who think they can predict the future, but those who believe they can predict the past. In the end, maybe my Moscow friend Grisha was right when he said that in Russia you could not afford to look back. Here, the past was toxic. It could be taken only in small doses.

Glasnost was well under way before Anna learned that her village was German before the war. There was only one Russian family in the village then, and they were still there. She got to know the grandfather. He never talked about what he had seen, but he confided it to paper. He wrote compulsively; when his eyesight failed, the family took his pen away. He went on writing in pencil. When the lead wore down, he kept writing. Anna strained to read the words from the indentations he left on the paper: he recalled the summer day when armed men arrived and rounded up his neighbours. When they were gone, he described galloping for his life on horseback, pursued by a stampede of maddened cows: udders bursting, they were desperate to find someone to relieve them of their milk.

Anna's family was haunted by the past, too. One night when she was little and her parents were away she woke up to find her grandfather sitting with an axe in his hands, muttering about not being able to go into his room because 'they' were waiting for him. After that, her parents hid all the axes and knives in the attic, leaving only one blunt knife in the kitchen. As he grew older, her grandfather's 'enemies' loomed larger. He would shout in his sleep, tormented by the fear that 'they' were coming for him.

Anna tried to find out what had traumatised her grandfather. Although he had escaped the famines, prison and labour camp, he was a Pole during years when that was cause for deportation. He disguised his name, pretending to be Belorussian.

When his family were evacuated from Leningrad, he volunteered to stay behind. He endured the Wehrmacht's 872-day blockade; that winter of 1941 when, with the temperature at minus forty and rations down to two slices of bread a day, gangs were killing for ration cards, trading in rats and human flesh. He was one of the wraiths with lumpy green faces who came through, when some 800,000 died of starvation.

Anna concluded that his trauma went back further, to 1938, when one in ten of the adult population was behind wire, and the secret police had their monthly quotas of arrests to fulfil. One night, armed men took Anna's grandfather away. The family thought they would never see him again. But next morning he walked through the door, a free man. That was unheard of. When a Jew who admired Anna's grandmother was arrested she blamed her husband, and tried to turn Anna against him. But she loved her grandpa.

'After his death I went into his room, and I could feel his terror,' she told me. 'The walls of his room were steeped in it.' So perhaps was the next generation. One of Anna's cousins spent years in an asylum, while tension surrounded Anna like a high-voltage fence. At night she barely slept, as if afraid that if she relaxed she might lose control.

Someone described Anna to me as a *pravednik*, or truth-bearer. It was a phrase that the writer Nikolai Leskov used to describe some of his heroes. He took the concept from the story of Sodom and Gomorrah, where God is challenged to spare the cities for the sake of a handful of innocents. The *pravedniki* in Leskov's stories were ordinary men and women distinguished by their readiness to sacrifice themselves for others. By this definition, Anna was a *pravednik*. But with the collapse of the Russian German homeland, she had lost her cause.

I had been looking for someone to blame for the failure of that plan to revive the homeland for Russia's Germans on the Volga. Anna's conclusion was that there was no point in blame, that only the bone's prayer and the wind over the steppe would heal what had been done.

THE DEVIL'S TUNE

When Natasha's KGB cousin advised her not to move to Marx, because the German homeland was not going to happen, he knew what he was talking about. The KGB ran a brilliant campaign of destabilisation against the re-establishment of that homeland, and it seems to have worked. What follows is an account of what I think happened, though thanks to the wall of silence, piecing together any coherent account was hard. If I am right, the story is fascinating for what it reveals about the way Russia's secret service goes about its work against its own people.

The operation was probably hatched in 1989, when Gorbachev's liberal policies were running into trouble. The problem was that the Russian Germans had been promised a homeland, and their cause was legitimate. But with violent ethnic clashes breaking out over the Soviet Union's southern flank, the prospect of creating a new ethnic enclave in the middle of Russia, particularly one connected to a European power, was alarming.

The man who ran the KGB's Russian German desk was Alexander Kichikhin. In Russian his name sounds like a sneeze, so let's call him Sneezer. His task was to discredit the Russian German leadership so severely that the collapse of the project could be blamed on them. This was not easy, since under glasnost many of the KGB's traditional tools of manipulation had lost their effectiveness.

First, Sneezer set out to win their trust. He claimed to have been duped into believing that the Soviet Germans really were fourth columnists for the Nazis in the Second World War; now that he knew the truth, he had become the Volga homeland's chief advocate. To demonstrate this, he wrote a series of articles in the national press which 'proved' how Marx's irrigation boss orchestrated opposition to the homeland. The move worked: many Russian Germans began to trust him.

Next, Sneezer set about ensuring that they would elect a malleable leader. His choice fell on an ambitious young Russian German scientist. The man was sounded out: was he interested in becoming leader of this new German homeland? Hearing of this, his fellow Germans fell into Sneezer's trap. They assumed they were about to be granted their homeland, and duly voted the scientist in. From then on Sneezer's task was easy, for the scientist was excitable and politically very inexperienced.

By this time Sneezer had worked himself into such a position of trust with his victims that they appointed him as a delegate at the Russian Germans' conference. There, he made a speech claiming that twenty-two out of thirty-four of their old leaders were KGB collaborators. This unleashed a storm of mistrust and paranoia, and destroyed the reputation of the one Russian German leader with any political experience.

Finally, presumably in order to prove conclusively that he was 'their man', he camped out in Red Square, in the summer of 1990, to protest on behalf of Russia's German minority. He wrote to the President, the Prosecutor-General and 200 Soviet deputies. Ridiculous though this all was, Sneezer got away with it. He proved adept at exploiting the weaknesses of the Russian Germans, their demoralised state, their simplicity and inflamed sense of historical injustice. For he knew how law-abiding they were, how much they longed to be accepted by Soviet power. He understood the psychology of their despair.

To this day, some Russian Germans still defend Sneezer's efforts on their behalf as well-intentioned. But this is what I believe happened to that plan to give Russia's Germans back a homeland. It was a dark tale, so dark that I was struggling to keep my hopes alive. To undo that authoritarian conditioning was going to take far longer than I had imagined. But the process had begun, slow as it was – I could that see in Marx. Starting with the most basic unit of society, the individual, people were just beginning to imagine how they might live differently; how they might slough off the old obedience, learn about personal choice, risk and responsibility.

AN ABYSS OF STARS

I had grown fond of my friends in Marx. But as the town returned to sleepy normality and the story I was following dried up, I was thinking of giving up. Then something intervened which changed the course of my travels.

I had seen only one faintly encouraging project in Marx. It was a settlement being built way out on the steppes to house a community of refugees from Uzbekistan. The refugees were Russian Germans, and the project was being financed by German money. The men were helping with the building, working at furious speed, all day and into the night under arc lights. In my desperation, I was wondering whether perhaps I should be following the fortunes of this new settlement instead. So later that summer I decided to visit the Uzbek town from which the Russian Germans were fleeing.

I asked Ira (daughter of my Russian mother, Elena) to come with me. With inflation rising all the time, she could not afford a holiday. But with my dollars, I was rich enough for two that year. Together we looked for Zarafshan on the map. It lay north-west of Tashkent, below the Aral Sea, a long way from anywhere. We presumed it was an agricultural settlement, for large numbers of ethnic Germans were deported to Central Asia after the Nazi invasion, and farming was their major occupation.

The one hitch was that Ira had to be back at work in nine days. This was time enough for the trip, but not for me to get a visa to enter Uzbekistan. Ira, who was an experienced traveller, proposed that I borrow a Russian passport. It was she who taught me how to travel cheaply in the glasnost years by posing as a Soviet citizen. 'But it's an independent country now!' I demurred. She just laughed: 'How many times do I have to tell you? This is Russia – trust me, nothing'll have changed.' I wavered, but not for long: if I wanted to travel with her my options were limited. Looking back, I realise how typical Ira's reaction was: few Russians really understood at that juncture that their empire had gone for good.

When the plane touched down in Tashkent, it seemed Ira was right. The bored officials barely glanced at my passport. I began to relax: the rest of the journey involved only a domestic flight from a smaller airport. Next morning when we turned up for this flight I had almost forgotten the risk I was running. The air smelt of blossom and woodsmoke and Ira and I were in a holiday mood.

We agreed that Ira would do the talking, lest my accent give me away. But I need not have worried. The plump Uzbek woman on passport control spoke Russian much more heavily accented than mine. She let us through. We passed through the second control with similar ease. Only when a girl in the baggage section called me back did I become alarmed. They asked to examine my locked bag. My heart thumped: she would see that everything in it was foreign. She and her colleague examined the contents minutely. Then they let me go. We were through.

A few minutes later passport control called me back. My heart was pounding so loud by this time that I thought everyone in the drab departure hall could hear it. The woman apologised, but explained that they had just been fined for letting a foreigner through. Could they take another look at my passport? 'It doesn't look very like you,' she said dubiously. This was an understatement. The woman who had lent me her passport had a broad Slav face. Mine was thin. She had peroxide hair. Mine was brown. 'Of course it's me,' I said breezily.

'You've lost a lot of weight.'

'Thanks.'

'What's your name?'

'Tamara Vladimirovna.' My mind blanked out on my surname, but Ira leapt in: 'Su-kho-no-gaya,' we chanted indignantly.

'OK, OK, no need to . . .'

In silence we stalked away and sat in a far corner of the hall, not daring to look at one another. There was nothing normal about these precautions, and on a domestic flight too. What kind of agricultural settlement place were we going to?

Our fellow passengers were Russians, not Uzbeks, and their pale faces and briefcases suggested they were not farmers. 'They'll probably be waiting for us with machine guns,' Ira whispered as we boarded the plane. 'Learn your passport details.' As the plane's shadow followed us over unbroken desert I muttered the details of my fake identity to myself. By the time the plane touched down I knew who I was – but not where we were.

The heat made the air buckle as we stepped out of the plane. The low hills all around looked like crumpled brown paper. There were armed guards, but they did not appear to be looking for anyone in particular. Relaxing slightly, we boarded the bus heading into town. It drove along suspiciously good roads, between well-built five-storey blocks, letting passengers off as it went. Whatever this place was, it was large and rich. There was no trace of an old Uzbek town, or of agriculture. Apart from the desert scrub, there was hardly a plant in sight. A sign by the road read:

'THROUGH THE WILL OF THE PARTY AND WITH THE PEOPLE'S HANDS THE TOWN OF ZARAFSHAN SHALL BE BUILT HERE.'

Finally, Ira and I were the only passengers left. Where did we want to go, the driver asked? 'Oh, just drop us in the centre of town,' said Ira casually. He turned and peered at her suspiciously. 'Centre? What centre?' Hastily, I produced the address I had been given. It was that of the mayor, Oscar Wentland. Muttering, the driver let us off by a cluster of five-storey blocks identical to the others.

It was midday and there was no one around. We looked for a telephone. Spotting a wraith-like woman resting her shopping bags on a bench, I approached her. 'If you're after a phone there aren't any'.

'Could you—'

'Must go, must go . . .' she said, scuttling away.

We sat down and looked around us. Not a door slammed, not a window opened in the neat white housing blocks. The desert sun beat down on our heads. We sat in silence.

'I'm sorry, Ira.'

'Don't worry – let's go to Bukhara instead.' That ancient city, key staging post on the great Silk Road, was due south of us, a long bus ride away. A bird shat on Ira's head: 'That means good luck,' she said brightly.

No one answered Oscar Wentland's doorbell. We decided to

find somewhere to leave our bags before exploring the town. On the floor above an old woman with a deeply fissured peasant face came to the door. When I explained why we had come her eyes filled with tears. 'My family's German! Come on in.'

'Come quickly!' she bawled down the phone. 'The relations from England have arrived!' She came back carrying a photograph album: 'Oscar Wentland! Fancy him having family in England! My mother was a German baroness, you know. No, really,' she went on, catching our scepticism. 'Grandpa was a professor at Vilnius University. Look at this!' It was a photograph of a swan-necked beauty in a high-necked Edwardian dress. 'That's her. She was always composing something. So was Father – his first wife was Rachmaninov's niece.' I tried not to laugh.

'And that's Father,' the old woman went on. 'He was high up in the Comintern.' Soviet intelligence had created the Communist International in the 1920s to harness the wishfulness of Western intellectuals to Soviet ends. It succeeded beyond its wildest imaginings. Bright young Hollywood directors, the intellectual cream of the Left Bank, of Berlin and Cambridge – they all proved susceptible. But for all their success, in the late thirties, the Comintern spymasters were charged with being Western spies themselves. Could the handsome dreamer in the yellowing photograph really be the father of this garrulous peasant? Only when she took her guitar and started singing did I believe her. For the light, ironic German romances she sang in a cracked, melodious voice were not Soviet. They belonged to that sophisticated, Central European culture that had been broken underfoot by marching armies.

A ring on the doorbell interrupted our recital. A tall, angry woman in scarlet strutted in on very high heels. Oscar Wentland's wife, Ludmila, cut the old woman and marched us downstairs to her flat. Closing the front door, she stood with her back against it. She had bright pink spots on her cheeks: 'You might have warned us.' Phone lines to Zarafshan were down, I explained, but Ludmila went on. 'If only Oscar were here.' He was away on a business trip. She sounded desperate.

I reassured her. 'Don't worry. Just give us a few telephone numbers and we'll . . .' 'You don't have a clue,' Ludmila interrupted. 'You can't even step outside the door – they're looking for you.'

'Who?'

'Who d'you think? The FSB.'

I sat down rather suddenly.

'Don't you know anything about this place?' she asked, incredulous.

'Well . . .' Ludmila's face passed from incredulity to fury. Then she laughed until the tears fell.

Zarafshan was a closed town, she explained. It was built around a vast complex of gold and uranium mines. Under the old regime foreigners had not been allowed here. 'In theory the security was strict, but in practice it was all right. Now it's awful! It's a punishable offence not to announce the arrival of a foreigner to the FSB within twenty-four hours. You'd have been fine if it hadn't been for that old bag – she's the town gossip. The news was round the factory in minutes. You can't stay here – they know where you are!'

'We'll leave – we'll go to Bukhara.'

'Not a chance,' Ludmila answered, serious again. 'You can't get out of here. There are no buses, and the next flight is tomorrow. Sit down. I must make some calls.' She walked out, closing the door on the phone's long extension cord.

We huddled on the sofa, considering our options. Ludmila could hand us over to the FSB, or she could hide us, but she was the mayor's wife; she had to go on living here. When 'they' caught up with us how was I going to explain my frivolous decision to borrow a Russian passport?

Ludmila returned looking calmer. 'Let's get you out of here. Hurry!' We sprinted to her small car and headed out of town, towards those crumpled brown hills. As town gave way to scrub, and scrub to a leafy suburb of small dachas, she relaxed slightly. 'It'll probably be all right. Oscar'll sort something out. He's arriving tomorrow morning from America. I'll just have to keep you out of the way till then.'

She drew up at a bungalow set in a grove of fruit trees. We spent the afternoon at the dacha, picking up fallen apricots, which Ludmila split and laid in the sun. We worked in silence. I was mortified. The whole escapade was so unnecessary. Ludmila was taking a big risk. A gold mine! Now the airport security made sense. A car drew up and I retreated under the trees. But it was only a friend of Ludmila's. Sasha ran the airport. His fair-haired good looks were marred by a squint so severe that to look directly at us he turned his face to one side. 'How did you hear about us?'

he asked. 'Germans – what Germans?' Then he too laughed. 'You really don't have a clue, do you?'

'You're in deep trouble,' he went on, squinting, grinning from ear to ear. 'You couldn't have picked a worse person to talk to than that hag. The news'll be all round town. They'll catch up with you – it's only a matter of time. I'd get out if I were you.' Get out! I had to walk away or I would have said something rash. He knew very well that there was no way out until tomorrow.

I went on collecting apricots, leaving Sasha talking to Ira. As I passed with an armful of fruit he was telling a story. 'This tall, shining figure was walking towards him. "Stop!" he shouted – the figure went on coming. He shouted for his mates. One fired a round of bullets – the figure went up in a shower of sparks.' Was he pulling Ira's leg? But the slight smile on his face looked more like embarrassment. 'They found the guy who'd fired the shot lying on the ground with one hand round a telephone receiver. It'd been ripped out of the wall. There were signs of a fight all around. The guy was unconscious, paralysed from the waist down. When he came to he was scared witless. Kept saying "they" were coming for him. "We came to help you with your ecological disaster," they said, "and you met us with gunfire. We'll be back. Meanwhile, we're borrowing your legs. You'll be paralysed for ninety-three days." And they did come for him again. It was in the ward – in full view of lots of people. He was carried to the door by invisible hands. He clung on to the doorpost – people rushed up and dragged him back to bed.'

'So what happened?' Ira asked.

'After three months he recovered the use of his legs.'

When Sasha left I asked Ira what that was all about.

'Something that happened recently on night watch at the mine.'

'He was pulling your leg—'

'Things like that are happening all the time, he said.' When I asked Ludmila to explain she groaned. 'I've not seen a thing myself. Ask Vasily Vasilevich. He's Oscar's best friend. I'll be taking you over there when he's finished work.'

Vasily Vasilevich was the engineer in charge of supplying the water that kept the 50,000 people in this desert town alive. The light was failing when Ludmila drove us over, and the windows of his bungalow were dark. 'He'll be here any minute.' I got out of the car. A dry wind was blowing off the desert. The sound of rustling leaves was magnified by the emptiness. The headlights fell on chunks of stone stacked along one side of the house. I was looking at them when a voice from the darkness said: 'Let me give you some light.' The bare bulb revealed a thin, tanned man in his fifties in faded brown shorts and a half-buttoned shirt. With his bright blue eyes and enchanting smile, he looked like some desert Ariel.

'People think the desert's dead, but that's because they don't know how to read it – the Syr Dar'ya used to run near here on its way to the Aral Sea. Now every drop of water we use comes from 200 kilometres away. Look at this – it's jaspar. That's white opal. Here's a fossilised tree. It wasn't always desert here, you know.'

We sat on the verandah drinking fermented camel's milk. The wind rustled the leaves of his orange grove. I looked into the darkness and thought of the FSB, out there looking for us. Vasya was talking about the region's early history, showing us photographs of rock drawings, images of animals, men and strange discs, said to be about 4,000 years old. The pool of light on the verandah seemed to hold us in a spell of safety.

When I confessed how heedlessly I had flown in on a borrowed passport Vasya laughed. As a boy growing up in Siberia, he had stowed away on a plane for Moscow. 'There was just room round the oxygen containers. It was summer, but there was ice forming on every surface. We'd have frozen to death if the plane hadn't stopped at Tomsk. We arrived in Moscow none the worse for wear and had a marvellous few days exploring the city.'

Ira mentioned Sasha's story of the shining man. 'What's that all about?' Vasya walked over to his collection of stones and handed us fragments of grey-green stone, light, like pumice. 'I've had it tested by a lab. It's sand that's been heated to an extra-ordinarily high temperature. Do you see the slight curve?' he said. 'They're part of a saucer-shaped crater, about twenty metres across.'

'Do you mean a UFO crater?' Ira asked.

'Yes. We see things like that all the time.' Despite the smile, he was serious. 'The earth here gives off an energy they need. Vortex energy, they call it. They come to recharge themselves. But they also come to help.'

It began a few years ago, he explained. People started bringing stories to Ludmila's husband, who was First Secretary of the

Communist Party. They were seeing UFOs, shining beings, all sorts of odd things. They wanted Oscar to 'do something'. He handed the problem over to Vasya.

'And what did you do?'

'Oh, this and that! But Oscar's their chosen man, not me.' Overnight, Vasya, a loyal Party member, had been drawn into a world teeming with invisible creatures. There was a hierarchy that ranged all the way from shining beings down to hairy runts, poltergeists and little devils: 'There are rough types too. They're the small ones, who haven't made it. They throw things around, beat people up and do all sorts of spiteful things.'

He was talking lightly, a slight smile playing on his face. Was he teasing us, I wondered? As if in response he went into the house and returned carrying a photograph: 'Take a look – I'd just put a new film in my camera. When I developed it I found this image on one of the first frames I'd taken when I was winding on the film.' The photograph was black, except for one corner, which was brightly lit, with a leering face. The snout was long, like a pig's, and there was the blurred outline of something like a paw over its mouth. 'What on earth is it?' I asked. 'It's a *domovoi*,' he replied.

At that point, I gave up trying to make sense of anything. We were back in the world of monsters. *Domovois* were creatures from Russian folklore. After the alarms of the day, it was comforting sitting there, held in the ring of light cast by the bare bulb, listening to the fairy tales of this unlikely Scheherazade. The wind off the desert was blowing up, tossing the branches of Vasya's orange trees. The darkness was alive with fantastical possibilities, ones which kept at bay the real threat that Zarafshan's secret police were closing in on us.

Above us the stars hung so low that they seemed almost within reach. A young man dropped by to return Vasya's night binoculars, which he had borrowed to watch for UFOs. I picked them up. Through them, the heavens came alive: there were gashes of greenish yellow light; luminous patches as faint as sighs; stars whose light throbbed and swelled. A sky like that made anything seem possible.

We stayed late, reluctant to move beyond the circle of safety that Vasya had drawn around us with his stories. As he walked us to the car, Ira asked how his own views had been changed by these experiences. 'For twenty years I was a good Communist. And I've always been a pragmatist – I'm an engineer after all,' he replied. 'But now I know there's a higher force controlling and guiding us. The beings are clear about that. "You must live in such a way that your good deeds outweigh your bad," they tell us. They're leading us, prompting us – sometimes very harshly. But always in the direction of good.'

We said goodbye reluctantly. 'I'm sure I'll see you again,' he said. 'Oscar'll sort you out. Drop by any time.' We drove back in silence. The headlights lit up five-storey blocks on either side of the road, blocks where those people lived who had brought their Party bosses these weird stories.

I spent the night clinging to the side of Ludmila's narrow sofa, Ira's feet in my face, dreaming I was falling into an abyss of stars.

PIECE OF GREEN PUMICE

Next morning, Ludmila's husband, Oscar Wentland, arrived by the early plane. The Party type, stocky, fair-haired and Germanic, he breathed authority. He sat us down and laid out the situation: if the FSB found us, he would be unable to protect us. But he could help us get out of town; the next flight was leaving in an hour. Meekly, we agreed.

He looked at his watch. 'We still have time. Do you have any questions?' When I told him what prompted my visit he gave a hollow laugh: 'They're broken people, parasites. They don't even speak German. They're only going for the free housing.' I bit my tongue. I did not like the way he was talking, but time was short. When Ira asked him about the shining beings Oscar's response was brisk: 'I might have guessed it – Vasya's been telling you stories. Flying saucers, little green men . . . You must take what he says with a pinch of salt. I'm different. I've never seen anything paranormal myself.' So that was that. The cock had crowed and the creatures of the night had vanished.

Sasha led us to the plane by a back route and ran with us across the scorching tarmac under the pounding desert sun. The plane's propellers were turning as he bundled a man and a woman off to make room for us. 'Mind you keep your dark glasses on,' he said by way of a farewell. 'I dread to think what they'll do if they catch you with false papers and no visa.' As we flew back over the Kyzylkum desert, Ira and I sat mute, shaken.

My luck ran out on the last leg of our journey. What did it was the fact that the passport had run out four weeks earlier. Tashkent airport's wiry Uzbek security chief led me behind a green curtain. 'Come on, you're not really Sukhonogaya, are you?' Blushing, I admitted it. The man looked incredulous; he was used to dealing with real criminals. Brushing aside my amateur attempt to bribe him, he took my passport and disappeared through the green curtain.

He reappeared and summoned Ira. She returned looking subdued, and gave me my passport: 'Hurry. The plane's waiting. I'll come on the morning flight.'

'What's going on?' I asked. Ira lowered her voice: 'He offered me a deal. You can go if I spend the night with him.'

'And you agreed!'

'I'll manage. He's not a bad man. Don't worry.' She was looking at her shoes. The Uzbek was grinning from ear to ear: 'Go on then. Don't worry – I'll take good care of her!' There was a long silence. I thought about the prison cell which was probably waiting for me. I was very tempted. But I couldn't leave without Ira. 'No. Thank you, but I'm not going. If Ira's staying, so am I.' We stood awkwardly, frozen in indecision, a ridiculous trio. Then the pilot poked his head through the curtain: 'Well, are they coming or not?' The police chief growled. 'Ah, what the hell. Off you go, both of you. But you owe me one . . .'

Back in Moscow, the rubbish was still piled high in the stinking streets and the cups in the sink were still unwashed. They were reassuringly real. From the baroness's daughter and the gold town in the desert to the UFOs and hairy devils, our adventure was receding hour by hour, becoming no more than a tall story. There were so many questions I wished I had asked. What did Vasya mean when he said that Oscar was 'their' chosen man, for instance?

Ira's mother was away. I slept a lot, cleaned every surface and met up with Ira in the evenings. 'Thank heaven you were there,' I said as we stood on the balcony, watching the children playing on the swings. 'If I'd been on my own, I'd be going crazy now, wondering whether I'd imagined it all.' We found ourselves avoiding meeting up with other people: what could we say? We could turn our trip into a funny story, but that would have been too easy. We liked Vasya, and he was no fool. 'I knew people were going to laugh at me,' he said when we were leaving: 'But I can take that. We've got to tell the truth, for the sake of, well, humanity.'

He gave me a fragment of stone. It came from a UFO crater, he said. He would spot them on his flights over the desert to check the water pipes. The outline would appear suddenly, from one day to the next. Some were radioactive, but this one had healing properties: 'For those with the gift, it has the power to put them in touch with other worlds.' Back in Moscow, we looked at it. Whatever it might have been in the Kyzylkum desert, now it was just a piece of pumice, with a greenish glaze.

SIBERIAN CASSANDRA

On the train down to Saratov I tried to find a way of writing about our Zarafshan trip, but it was no good. Up until now, the language of reason had served my needs perfectly well. But that language was no use when it came to Zarafshan. Unless I could find a way of understanding it, I was not going to be able to write about it, at least not without mocking Vasya. He did not deserve that.

This time, I found the very banality of Marx reassuring. Experimentally, I mentioned the trip to Natasha and Igor. It came out as a funny story and they laughed. I did not mention it again. I was uncomfortable, on this frontier between the mapped and the unmapped territory, between the world of reason and the land of those fabulous monsters.

I took a bus out to Stepnoye, where those families from Zarafshan were living. The houses looked like rows of freshly painted toys, abandoned by some giant child on the red mud of the empty steppe. The incumbents had moved in months ago. But with few exceptions, they had made no effort to organise the community, or even to plant their own gardens. I was incredulous: these people had what every Russian dreamed of – new housing, land, opportunities. But they were sitting in their houses, looking out over the red mud, getting drunk. What were they waiting for?

I spent the day with a biologist. Galya and her nuclear physicist husband (he had worked in Zarafshan's uranium mines) were the only people in the settlement with a higher education. She was rearing chicks, growing vegetables and planning a fish farm. At one point she turned round, put her hands on her hips and hissed: 'Look here. You're amazed that no one's opened a shop, that they haven't planted anything. You don't understand – if these degenerates haven't got something, they'll do without. The notion they could improve their lives wouldn't enter their heads! I'm ashamed for you to see this. But what shames me most is that I'm one of the few people here who's got any idea that there's anything to be ashamed of!' Galya was spring-loaded, so close to breaking point that I feared what would happen if I touched her.

Late that night, I ventured to ask about Zarafshan's paranormal epidemic. Galya groaned. 'If I hear the word UFO again—' But her husband interrupted. 'Yes, weird things were happening all the time. For instance, one night, with some other scientists, I saw a cigar-shaped craft heading for the airport. As a scientist, what struck me was the way it stopped in the sky, then streaked off in another direction. That just didn't make scientific sense. But that's what I saw – we all did.' Perhaps it was collective hysteria, I speculated, relieved to be talking to a scientist. 'No, there was more to it than that,' he said firmly.

Next morning I took the bus back to Marx. Broken people, Oscar called them. I had bridled at the judgement, but he seemed to be right. I could not bear the implications. I got off the bus feeling wretched. The street was flanked by housing blocks which looked as if they had been bombarded with mortar fire. Keeping my eyes lowered, I kept walking for the sake of walking, to avoid returning to Engels Street. How Igor was going to crow! He had tried to dissuade me from going to Stepnoye. 'They'll be broken people, serfs,' he said, eerily echoing Oscar's words. 'You can set them up in new houses, give them land, but they'll be sitting there drinking themselves to death. Gimme, gimme – it's all they know!' Could it really be that he was right? That all over Russia, people who had lived with guaranteed jobs had unlearned the most basic instincts?

A sudden wind swept across the steppe, slapping the town, bending the poplars, sending washing flying. Soon, the wind would stop and the rain would sheet down. When it came, it was like a bucket being tipped over the town. I must have looked Job-like when I walked into the house on Engels Street. For Igor made tea, wrung out my wet clothes, and kept his judgements to himself.

When the sun came out, we walked across the square, past the ruined church and the statue of Lenin, down to the pier where the Volga ferries used to dock before traffic on the river stopped, when the Soviet music ended. During the famines of the 1920s barges full of starving people searching for food, had docked here. Then, in September 1941, thousands and thousands of Volga Germans sat here, surrounded by armed guards, waiting to be deported. All this belonged to a past which had for so long been forbidden territory.

We looked out to the white cliffs on the river's far bank. A nightingale sang in the elms and the fish were rising, leaving ripples on the surface of the water. 'To live surrounded by this beauty, and to squander it so – that's what makes me mad!' sighed Igor. He talked about the happy times he and Natasha had spent here, messing about in a boat in the early days. But when he started complaining again, I snapped. 'It's your fault. You're chasing her away. I think you're just bored. Go ahead. But soon you'll have destroyed your love and you'll be alone. Is that what you want?'

Igor looked shocked. But when Natasha arrived home he was contrite and loving. After supper, I poured out my heart about my trip to Stepnoye. 'So now you see,' Natasha said after a long silence. 'We thought we were different, that when the Party lost power it would be fine. We thought we'd spend our time *being free*! We had no idea how much we'd all become products of the Soviet system,' Igor interrupted. 'We knew what we wanted freedom from. But not what we wanted it for.' Yes, that was what lent the edge to Natasha and Igor's despair. As elite intellectuals, who opposed Communist Party rule, they assumed they were part of the solution.

'You in the West were our dream,' Natasha went on, hitting her stride, the Siberian Cassandra. Her wild curls stood up and her pale face shone. 'And when it collapsed, we blamed you. You weren't to blame. We just had no idea how to be free. We were like those prisoners who refuse to leave because they've nowhere else to go. However hard you try you'll never really understand what it was like to live in a country that was one great concentration camp. I'm not using the word loosely. It's no reflection on your intelligence or empathy. It's just that you were born free.

'When the Soviet Union fell, the country went through a sort of nervous breakdown. We came here looking for a new beginning. We didn't understand that there are no new beginnings in Russia, only long and terrible endings. We didn't realise that nothing could change until people find themselves.'

That night, long after Natasha and Igor were asleep, I sat by the open window with the three-legged cat on my knee, arguing with myself. If Natasha was right, if there was no new beginning in sight, I really ought to pack up now, go home. I had come all this way only to find that the people of Marx had reacted to the future they were offered by closing in on themselves, giving in to ancient fears. Now, on top of that, there was Stepnoye and the sight of those 'broken people' sitting in their brand-new houses. I had ventured into territory where no foreigner should go, learned what I did not want to learn. It was beyond weeping, impenetrably dark.

Hold on, now, hold on. What about your friends in Marx? Don't you care what happens to them? And what about that trip to Zarafshan? Ira and I had caught only a glimpse of what was going on there. But the situation did seem to bear a vague resemblance to the events that had hit Marx. There, too, a coherent community appeared to have responded collectively, possibly also with collective hysteria, with its own local variant of the crisis triggered by the end of the communist empire. The people of Zarafshan had not given in to the same ancient fears, though. An aspect of the Russian psyche had been thrown up from the depths in that desert town that baffled me. But it was intriguing.

How absurd the premise was with which I had set off on my travels. I had come here expecting the Russians to behave in a Western, indeed Marxist way. I had assumed that they would be rebuilding Russia on a Western model, too. How arrogant! Slowly, from the vantage point of Russia's provincial hinterland I was starting to appreciate how differently many Russians responded to events from that Westernised elite in Moscow and St Petersburg.

Of course I had no idea what Russia's future was going to look like. But if I was serious about wanting to understand the underlying forces shaping it, perhaps I should learn more about Zarafshan and the collective visions of those miners and engineers. I had been offered the opportunity of peering into the collective unconscious of this other Russia. How could I resist that?

THE ART OF MIND CONTROL

Back in London that winter, I tried to write up our trip to Zarafshan. Again, I found myself off the map, back in the terrain of fabulous monsters. I even thought of leaving the story out of this book, but that seemed faint-hearted. It was easy to write about those shining beings and hairy devils as a comical traveller's tale. But that brought me no closer to understanding how someone like Vasya, an engineer and senior Communist Party member could have believed what he heard, and been so changed by it.

Digging around, I learned that Soviet scientists had taken the esoteric powers of the mind much more seriously than we in the West, for reasons that went back before the Russian Revolution. The discipline of psychology was new then, and embraced everything from psychoanalysis to psychic research as well as the occult. Hypnosis was being studied by mainstream scientists in the West too, as a physiological or neurological phenomenon. Only after the First World War did Western science settle for a purely materialist explanation of energy.

Once a socialist revolution had taken place in Russia, you might have expected the same to happen there. But the wild expectations bred by the new regime led to a different outcome. The new 'scientific' ideology aspired to do more than redesign human nature; it dreamed of mastering the whole world of natural phenomena.

Some scientists saw the revolution as an opportunity to reclaim the Fourth Dimension from the mystics and occultists. They set out to tap the source of energy behind it in the name of socialism. So while the esoteric powers of the mind became taboo in the West because they defied a materialist paradigm, in the communist empire, ironically, these powers went on being studied.

The leading pre-revolutionary authority on hypnosis was a scientist called Vladimir Bekhterev, who died before he could fall in the purges. He was interested in those realms of human behaviour that bypass conscious processes: religious hysteria, pogroms, demonic possession. A radical himself, he welcomed the Revolution, though that did not stop him from regarding it as an example of hypnotic influence on a mass scale.

Bekhterev was not mystically inclined himself, but he could see no essential difference between physical and spiritual phenomena: to him, they all seemed to derive from the same 'world energy'. After his death most of his ideas were publicly discredited. But he had used hypnosis effectively to treat mental illness, and his pioneering work remained a standard Soviet treatment. Nor was his research on hypnosis and other mysterious powers of the mind entirely abandoned. In secret laboratories his disciples carried on the work quietly, still funded by the state.

The early buzz of Soviet interest in the esoteric powers of the mind had other spin-offs, too. Under Stalin they became a branch of the Soviet entertainment industry. Telepathists and hypnotists regularly gave public performances. Stalin himself was so interested in the subject that he subjected the regime's leading psychic, Wolf Messing, to a series of tests he devised himself. Commandeered in mid-performance, Messing was ordered to steal 100,000 roubles from Moscow's Gosbank. Using his hypnotic powers, Messing was reported to have walked into the bank, under the scrutiny of official witnesses, and proceeded to sign a blank piece of paper in lieu of a cheque; the cashier duly handed the money over. Next, he was required to enter Stalin's heavily guarded country dacha without a pass. Messing hypnotised the guards into believing he was Lavrenti Beria, Stalin's top secret policeman, whom he looked nothing like.

In the 1960s, triggered by Western press reports of America's use of ESP, Soviet laboratories researching the subject opened all over the place. For a few years the subject was discussed in the Soviet press before the embargo fell again.

Some have claimed that Soviet interest in mind control played a part in the regime's approach to controlling people's hearts and minds. The writer Maxim Gorky was certainly well known to be interested in the Fourth Dimension, and he was one of the chief architects of Socialist Realism. I certainly remembered how, when I was researching *Epics of Everyday Life*, the strands of this Soviet preoccupation with the Fourth Dimension were surfacing all over the place. At the time, I laughed to see people rushing to their television sets for mass séances. But when I met Benya's yellow-eyed *extrasensor* on the *N. Gastello*, I did not find it funny. In fact, for all my Western rationality, I was terrified. Now I was starting to understand why. Had the man tried to attack me physically, I would have known how to defend myself. But he attacked my mind, where I felt most intimately myself, and what is more he came very close to hypnotising me. It was a humbling experience to find that, whether or not I believed in it, I was every bit as susceptible to the Fourth Dimension as all those credulous Russians.

1994–1996

The Russian economy was in a state of collapse by now. Most people were earning far too little to survive. Many of those still in work were not being paid for months, while their bosses, or the banks, speculated with their wages. So why were people not starving? Each family was its own mystery, unfathomable from outside. Professionals were abandoning their jobs and turned to trading. Someone's daughter was selling herself to foreign businessmen, someone else was selling their father's wartime medals. Grandparents were growing potatoes for their children's families in the city. Teachers were fainting from hunger in their classrooms. In the last year of communism the average life expectancy for men was sixty-eight. By 1995, that figure had plunged to fifty-eight.

By the end of 1994, the mass privatisation programme was over. But despite this huge shift in ownership, the old Soviet factory managers were still in charge of industry. The attempt to give citizens a stake in the privatisation had failed; and speculators and those in the know were making fortunes. Foreign investors were also realising that chunks of Russia's industry could be bought for a song.

The main goal of Yeltsin's reform team now was to get inflation under control. For until that happened, the economy could not grow. But a battle was raging at the heart of government. While the reformers were trying to kick-start a market economy, the Central Bank was pumping money into the economy in the old Soviet way. The result was hyperinflation. By the end of 1994 consumer prices would be 2,000 per cent higher than in 1990.

By 1995 Chubais had managed to lick inflation, but he got little credit. For a new problem had succeeded this: the government was running out of money. It was borrowing on capital markets. Soon, this would spiral out of control, sowing the seeds of the great financial crash of 1998.

Among the gamblers, a handful had emerged with vast assets. At this level, it was a rough game, involving bribery, blackmail and violence. Each oligarch was running their own intelligence corps and corporate army. By 1996 the relationship between them and the government was entering a dangerous phase. Chubais offered the oligarchs a deal. They could take shares in Russia's oil and mineral wealth in return for lending the government money. He knew that it was risky handing them such power. But he reckoned that they would make better owners than the old Soviet factory managers.

By now, two of these oligarchs were running television channels. Vladimir Gusinsky's NTV was joined at the end of 1994 by Boris Berezovsky's ORT, a partnership with other oligarchs. This channel reached every home. Though not owned by the state, it had sworn loyalty to Yeltsin's government. In the spring of 1995, ORT's executive director was gunned down by his own front door. This murder shook Russia. People assumed that the assassins worked for someone in the state security services who was unhappy to see Berezovsky controlling the channel.

Russia had entered a murky period when the really significant changes that were happening were taking place in secret, a long way from the public eye. This was not helped by the fact that by 1995 Yeltsin's health had broken down and he had retreated from public view. The country was awash with rumours about his drunkenness and the corruption of his inner circle. The election due in 1996 looked bound to return the Communist Party. Yeltsin's cronies were urging him to cancel it.

Back in 1994, they had persuaded him that a brief, triumphant military campaign in Chechnya, to put down the secessionists, would boost his ratings. Instead the government was now bogged down in an unpopular war. Gusinsky's television channel NTV was partly responsible for its unpopularity, as it had been capturing huge audiences with its reportage of bloody scenes.

The outcome of the coming election looked certain. Polls showed that the cheated, impoverished, humiliated, exhausted Russians wanted a strong leader to put things right. Gennady Zyuganov's Communist Party was on the way back.

The election battle was joined in the spring of 1996. Until then the frail President's entourage managed to keep him isolated even from his own key ministers. He was about to succumb to their pressure to dissolve the Duma, postpone the election and break the constitution when Prime Minister Chubais forced a meeting with him. Only then did Yeltsin learn what his entourage had been hiding: that only 3–4 per cent of Russians were going to vote for him. Shocked, he rallied from his sick bed, accepted backing from the oligarchs and set about stealing the election from Zyuganov.

Despite Zyuganov's massive popular support, Yeltsin commanded all three national television channels, thanks to the oligarchs. After waging a very dirty campaign indeed, he went on to win the June election by a narrow margin, collecting 53.82 per cent of the vote to Zyuganov's 40.31 per cent. After that, he returned to his sick bed, while the oligarchs joined the political scene.

Does the end justify the means? Nine years later, from his prison cell, the richest of those oligarchs, Khodorkovsky, would conclude that it does not: that by stealing the election for Yeltsin, the oligarchs had poisoned democracy's chance of taking early root in Russia. 'This was when the journalists stopped constructing public opinion and started serving the master, while independent social institutions became voices for their sponsors,' he wrote.

President Clinton, however, praised Yeltsin's election victory as a milestone in Russia's democratic progress. Russian voters had 'turned their backs on tyranny', he exulted. But Khodorkovsky was right. It would have been better if the Communist Party had been allowed to win that election, by democratic means. The Westernisers had won the battle, but lost the war.

1994

LEGEND OF THE GOLDEN WOMAN

———⟫●⟪———

Moscow was like Babel that summer. Everyone and everything was for sale. The city had cast off its penitential monochrome Soviet style, and with it all restraint. There was a terrible energy on the streets, and colour too: hoardings had appeared, bright dreams of Chrysler cars, Snickers bars and catfood, dreams which felt like foreign conquest to an older generation. When the sun came out, the city stank from the piles of uncollected rubbish. Homeless people milled round the railway stations. The pavements were choked with struggling people, traders, beggars, drinkers, thieves. But the sound of the city was changing: above the ground bass of traffic rose the screech of car alarms, the signature tune of a new propertied class. And now and then the sinuous form of a glamorous young woman threaded through the shabby crowd.

On the streets, the mafias were in control, and shootings between rival gangs were not uncommon. Benya had turned up again, penniless, after a year's disappearance. He was lucky to have escaped with his life. A determined loner, his friends feared for him now that the mafias were organised.

Ira was just back from shooting a documentary film about Zarafshan. Late into the night she poured out stories, consulting her notes, showing me documents and scraps of film. From the start, Zarafshan's was a tragic story. A deported Soviet German geologist called Kinder had discovered the site after the war. Wild with joy, certain that this would clear him of the charge of collective treachery which was still hanging over the Russian Germans, he peppered the Party with reports. They took no notice. When they did take a look, in the 1960s, they got terribly excited too. But they ignored Kinder's role. In despair, he hanged himself. Even that was not easy. For he was a tall man, and the ceilings of

Tashkent's residential blocks were so low that his feet trailed on the ground.

They used convict labour to build the settlement. After two years of working under the desert sun, short of water all the time, the prisoners staged a desperate revolt. They were gunned down by their Caucasian guards, and a fresh batch of prisoners completed the work.

Zarafshan was one of those secret, closed towns run directly from Moscow by the Communist Party headquarters. Its mines were incredibly rich. They produced 60 tons of the purest gold a year, as well as uranium, silver and tin. The housing was good, the shops well-stocked, and the pay high. But when Uzbek nationalism resurfaced under Gorbachev, Zarafshan's elite workers, who were mostly Russian, found themselves stranded: it was rumoured that Uzbek nationalists were planning to cut the water pipe. When the empire fell, they lost the remaining privileges that made their jobs worthwhile. Inflation shrivelled their pay and Zarafshan became a prison.

That was when the visions began. In Ira's footage Zarafshan's ex-Party bosses described how terrified people started coming to Oscar, the mayor, begging him to make 'them' go away. The stories then became a flood: shifts of two hundred miners were all seeing the same silvery shapes, leaping sideways, disappearing, defying the laws of gravity and thermodynamics. Next, some mediums from the city of Tomsk, hundreds of miles away, reported receiving cosmic messages addressed to Oscar. Oscar delegated all this to Vasya, and said nothing to Party headquarters, fearing the men in white coats might come for him.

Then one day, a UFO brought work to a standstill in one whole section of the mine. For hours, in full view of the workforce, it hovered there, training its searchlights over one of the great machines which separated the ore from the rock. The machine was used day and night, but the operators refused to go near it while the silver disc hung there. Once the 'visions' started affecting production, Oscar let Moscow know. To his surprise, they flew in teams to investigate.

The Ministry of Atomic Power and Industry produced a report which tentatively suggested that this remarkable outbreak of the paranormal was connected to the fact that 'people are living in conditions of maximum extremity . . .'. In other words, Zarafshan was an ecological disaster. The mines were not ventilated, and the incidence of lung cancer was high. The cyanide being used to separate the ore from the rock had poisoned the desert for miles around. There was also the problem of water. The nearest river, the Syr Dary'a, was seriously contaminated with pesticides, thanks to the cotton-growing settlements which had been built along it. In addition, extravagant extraction of water during the Soviet period had caused the world's largest inland lake, the Aral Sea, to shrink to half its former size. Pesticides from its dried-out bed were being carried all over the region. Wherever they landed, people sickened.

What struck me about Ira's footage was the way Zarafshan's bosses kept trying to get Ira to understand, really understand, that all this was as real as their conversations with her. Their accounts suggested a widespread acceptance of the idea of aliens at a high level in the Communist Party hierarchy. This time, even the pragmatic Oscar admitted to Ira that 'it happens everywhere – the only difference is that we accepted it'. He said that he had started taking the cosmic messages seriously when 'they' pointed his men towards rich seams of ore the miners would have missed. They also helped avert serious accidents.

Official interest in Zarafshan came to a head two weeks before the Party's attempted coup, in the summer of 1991. A message for Oscar from 300 aliens, refugees from some planetary disaster, was intercepted by the Ministry of Defence's mediums(!). They wanted Oscar's permission to settle near the town. Without telling Oscar, the Party dispatched a helicopter full of troops to Zarafshan, led by one General Nazarov. The mobilisation orders bore Gorbachev's signature, and that of the last Soviet Defence Minister, General Yazov, ringleader of the Communist Party's attempted coup, whose trembling hands would be captured by CNN's cameras as the tanks rolled into Moscow.

General Nazarov and his men landed in Zarafshan, waited all day, arms at the ready, and finally received a message from the aliens, relayed via the Moscow mediums: 'Your intentions are aggressive – we're going to Orion instead.'

This deluge of weird information only compounded the problems I was having writing this story. I was reminded of the legend of the golden woman which European travellers to Russia had been bringing home with them for centuries. The Vikings were the first:

they reported she was made of solid gold. Seven centuries later, when Muscovy threw off Tatar rule and re-established links with Europe, the story resurfaced. Baron Sigismund von Herberstein, dispatched to Russia on diplomatic missions by the Habsburg court, featured her in his *Description of Moscow and Muscovy*, in 1549. The statue consisted of three figures, one inside another, he said, and had a hollow 'singing' interior. A few decades later, when Richard Chancellor came home from Russia after his abortive search for a northern sea route to China, he brought back news that the golden woman was an oracle. Giles Fletcher, dispatched to Russia by Queen Elizabeth in 1588, even sent an expedition off in search of her. He concluded that the 'golden hagge' was just an old wives' tale, inspired by a rock shaped like a woman. But even in the mid-twentieth century there were still said to be Russians here and there in the countryside who maintained that there really was a golden woman hidden somewhere in Russia's forests.

Some of those travellers must have believed, or half-believed, in the golden woman while they were in Russia. But by the time they reached home, she was just a tall story. I had no idea what had gone on in Zarafshan. But I had started to appreciate that quite a lot of Russians really did see reality very differently from me.

THE PATH NOT TAKEN

My friends in Marx were muddling through somehow, concentrating on getting through from day to day. But they, like me, had expected that democracy would take root in Russia after the fall of the Soviet empire. With every year that passed, that was looking less and less likely. Now, they seemed depressed, rudderless. A huge, unresolved question was hanging over their lives: who are we now if we're not communist? What does it mean to be Russian?

Under communism, nationality was meant to fade away, replaced by a new Soviet identity. Now, whatever their other difficulties, Russia's ex-colonies in Central Asia, Caucasus and the Baltic States were enjoying a newly recovered sense of self. But for the Russians it was not so easy. Ethnicity was not enough, for the Russians were not all Slav. Territory could not be the defining factor either, for this vast land straddling Europe and Asia had no clear borders to the west or south.

Before the Revolution, the Orthodox Church had bound Russia's imperial subjects together. But although opinion polls showed people were now fascinated by belief, they were not interested in their Church. As yet only 10 per cent identified with it. This was hardly surprising. Orthodoxy had been savagely persecuted in the Soviet period. All but 8,000 churches had been destroyed or re-used and some 200,000 churchmen lost their lives, the finest among them. As an institution, it had survived only by submitting itself to control by the militantly atheist state. The Church was going to take time to recover its voice and place in society.

All this was very much on my mind when I read an extraordinary story in the paper: some geologists on a field trip in the forests of Siberia had come across a community of Old Believers. They had been cut off from society for so long that they knew nothing about aeroplanes, let alone communism. They were survivors of the great schism in Russia's Church in the eighteenth century, which had split the country in two. In order to escape persecution, they had fled to remote parts of the country. Under the tsars there were still thriving sectarian communities all over Russia, but after the Revolution information about them dried up.

I was amazed that these people, who had turned their backs on the very notion of progress, could have escaped communism, while remaining in Russia. Surely these Russians must be part of the answer to that question: who are we, if we're not communist? I started dreaming of visiting an Old Believer community. But it was only a dream. When I began travelling in Siberia, I found that, though there were sectarian villages all over Siberia, most were falling apart, their young having left for the cities. Even if I could identify one that was still vigorous, I could hardly turn up there on my own. For as an independent woman, a non-believer and a Westerner, I represented everything they abhorred.

It was a rare piece of good fortune that I happened to meet one of the few people in Russia who could help me. Vladimir Nikolaevich Alekseev was on a visit to the British Library as part of a delegation of librarians. He was tall, deep-chested and handsome, with a bushy brown beard and twinkling eyes, and he ran the country's greatest repository of Old Believer books, in Novosibirsk.

Every summer for thirty years, he told me, he and his wife had spent travelling down rivers, into the forests in search of outlying Old Believer communities. The Old Believers' lives revolved around their old texts, he explained. As their communities dwindled, many were no longer being used. They did not relish the prospect of their books falling into the wrong hands and they were happy to let him acquire them for Novosibirsk's library.

In due course I met his wife, Professor Elena Ivanovna Dergacheva-Skop, a formidable personality and distinguished scholar of the Old Believers. They asked me to join them on their next trip. They were going to visit their favourite Old Believer community, where they considered the Old Belief was best preserved. The village was called Burny, which means 'stormy', and it lay deep in the forest, a long way from any road or railway. To get there involved travelling north up the River Yenisei, then east down the Stony Tunguska River in boats. I did not appreciate as I travelled to the Siberian city of Krasnoyarsk for the start of the expedition quite how intrepid the Alekseevs were to organise such an expedition at that juncture. Inflation was still running at 19 per cent a month; the economy was barely functioning and transport was paralysed for lack of fuel and passengers.

Thirteen of us boarded the sturdy river steamer. There were a group of Elena Ivanovna's students and a couple of other Britons: a history lecturer called Alan, and his wife, who taught Russian. I sat on deck, my back to the throbbing engine, looking out over the cold, boiling waters of the Yenisei. We had left behind the rusting industrial hulks of Krasnoyarsk. Soon we would be passing the hidden bunker city which had been carved out of the ground in the paranoid Cold War years. I scanned the banks for signs of it. I had come up from below to get away from Alan, who was irritating me intensely. He knew a lot about Russia on paper. But never before had he been in a place where things did not work. He did not speak the language, either. With every day that passed his plump, rubicund face was looking more aggrieved.

The Yenisei rises in the mountains on Mongolia's north-western border and runs through the landmass before debouching into the Arctic Ocean. It marks a natural boundary between the low swampy plains of western Siberia and the virgin forests of the central Siberian plateau. To the east, the forest stretched away, unbroken in places, for thousands of miles all the way to the Sea of Okhotsk.

The river was so wide here that the banks had shrunk to two green strokes of a pencil on either side. For centuries, these waterways were the main thoroughfares through the landmass. The Cossack commander Ermak brought his little expeditionary force down this network of rivers when he subdued the Mongol khanate of Kuchum and conquered Siberia in 1581. It was a commercial venture, paid for by rich merchants pursuing the fur trade. Later, from the mid-eighteenth century, rivers became the main conduit for transporting convicts and rebels to Siberia. The leaders of Russia's two great early peasant rebellions, Stenka Razin and Emilian Pugachev, sailed up the Yenisei into exile. So did the Decembrists, those dilettante revolutionaries who, having tried to overthrow the tsar in 1825, had caught the democratic virus after driving Napoleon's troops back from Moscow. Stalin travelled up this river into exile too, as did hundreds of thousands of Soviets consigned to the Gulag.

A day and a half later, the steamer dropped us off at the mouth of the Stony Tunguska River. It was ten o'clock at night and raining, but still light, being so far north. As we hauled our rucksacks up the wooden steps from the foreshore Alan lagged behind, attaching trolleys to his large cases. 'This is no place for luggage trolleys!' snapped Elena Ivanovna. 'Leave it to the boys!' 'Oh, shut up. Leave me alone!' growled Alan.

We were laying out our sleeping bags in the barrack-like hostel when Vladimir Nikolaevich summoned us to the largest dormitory. 'I know you're all longing to get to bed,' said Elena Ivanovna, holding us with her blue determined gaze. 'But I have to say this: the chipmunk is a bird, and it flies low. In other words, from now on we're an Expedition, and an Expedition only has one leader. However absurd the order, I'm the boss and you do what I say. There's only one way, and that's mine.'

Day One. Bor consisted of a muddle of wooden barracks at the mouth of the Stony Tunguska River. Balanced on the edge of a vast reach of forest, it must once have been a bustling transit point, servicing the gold and copper mines and expeditions of geologists. Now the only other guests in the hostel were a group of drunken, gap-toothed ex-convicts. The airport at the end of the dust track was a graveyard of rusting planes. Planes passed overhead, but they no longer stopped at Bor. Vulpine hunting dogs sprawled on the track lay undisturbed. The original plan was to travel upriver along the Stony Tunguska River in two large flat-bottomed river boats. But one boat was missing, presumed holed in the shallows upriver. The only other one large enough was expected back tonight. Meanwhile, the Alekseevs asked that we refrain from speaking English outside the hostel: if word got round that there were foreigners in Bor, the price of transport would soar.

Day Two. The boat was back, but there had been so little rain that it could not make the final stretch of our river journey. Now the Alekseevs were trying to get hold of a plane. We made the odd foray to the two wooden huts that served as shops. The students played cards. Alan fretted, and I retreated behind a book.

Of all the rebellions against the Russian state, that of the Old Believers was the one that caught the popular imagination. Ostensibly, the schism was provoked by a series of what to us would seem tiny changes Patriarch Nikon ordered for Church rituals and texts in 1653: the spelling of Jesus's name; the number of Hallelujahs in a service; the number of fingers with which worshippers crossed themselves. His reasons for doing so were pragmatic. Since the fall of Byzantium, Russia was the last great power in Eastern Christendom not overrun by Islam. It aspired to leadership of the Orthodox world, but in order to achieve this it had to bring its own religious practice into line with the rest of Orthodoxy. The priorities of the Old Believers were different: for them, all that mattered was the tradition they knew, and that was inviolable. They fled to the forests and outlying regions. Tens of thousands retreated into their wooden churches and burned themselves to death.

Of course, the reasons for the schism lay deeper, in the issue of Russia's destiny: should it open up to the West, or not? Over the next two centuries it became more overtly political, embracing a fifth of the population. For merchants and those with land, Peter the Great's reforms offered a way forward; but not for the poor. The Old Belief became a movement of resistance to the encroaching power of the modernising, power-hungry state.

In Krasnoyarsk, before we boarded the steamer, another scholar of the Old Believers had been saying to me that most Russians today did not understand them: 'They see them as quaint, with their stern expressions and long beards. They think of them as having valuable icons and books – yes, it's a dangerous time for them, they're being robbed, even scholars steal things from them! What they can't see is that the Old Believers are an essential part of Russia's identity. They're the living continuation of that first rift which opened up in Russia in the seventeenth century. They're vital to our understanding of ourselves. Ever since then it has opened up again and again whenever there's a civil war. As there was during the Revolution. As there is today! Look at the struggle between Yeltsin and the parliament – it's the same old thing. Our history only begins to make sense when you see that it doesn't move on like Western history – it just goes round and round!'

That was what interested me about the Old Believers. For centuries Russia was a backwater, its peace occasionally disturbed by elites bringing modern ideas, which resulted in sudden upheavals. There was Christianity, there were Nikon's reforms; Peter's determination to turn Russia into a European nation-state, and Lenin's to impose communism. These ideas were all visited on the country top-down, from the centre, and they succeeded in laying down veneers of change. But how much did things change underneath that veneer? And would these present upheavals result in changes that would affect more than an elite?

In the evenings, when we met up for our improvised meal, Vladimir Nikolaevich would talk about life in Burny. While I adored these stories, Alan was growing increasingly jumpy. For he was writing a paper about Burny entitled 'The last medieval village in Europe'. The reality we were hearing about was rather different: yes, in theory the villagers lived off the land; built their houses and avoided machinery and labour-saving devices. But this evening we learned that the men travelled to their distant winter hunting grounds on snowmobiles. 'What's that if not a labour-saving device?' exploded Alan. The students fell about laughing, but the Alekseevs looked deeply distressed.

Day Three. Today Alan blew our cover by ringing the Alekseevs at the airport and asking for them in his few words of Russian. Elena Ivanovna was so angry that she could hardly bring herself to look at him.

Everyone was jumpy. Tomorrow was Saturday. Unless we left then, we would be stuck in Bor until Monday. Each additional day here meant one fewer in Burny, as Alan and his wife had fixed return plane tickets. It was looking possible that we might even find ourselves returning to Krasnoyarsk without reaching Burny. The Alekseevs were looking worn out.

Meanwhile, the restless Alan had found an empty floor of clean rooms with curtains, doors that locked and even bedclothes. They were pitifully cheap by Western standards, but not for the Russians. Alan moved in with his wife, and offered to take rooms for the whole expedition, but Elena Ivanovna refused: this was an instance of the chipmunk flying low. I dithered: I knew I should choose the solidarity of the group. But I was sleeping badly, thanks to a snoring student. Shamefacedly, I joined the Britons.

It was an immense relief to be alone. Now, my only companion was a six-foot balsam whose pink fleshy blooms had dazzling yellow stamens. The fragile branches were suspended from the curtain rail by strands of wire. In this dead-end place it seemed like a vision of Sophia, goddess of wisdom and femininity. I gazed at it, thanking all those lonely men who had resisted stubbing their cigarettes out on her roots, or crashing into her after a night's drinking.

Day Four. Last night, Vladimir Nikolaevich told us we were

not far from the site of the Tunguska explosion of 1908. That
famous event flattened eight hundred square miles of forest and
was heard 700 miles away. The first scientific expedition reported
that huge trees had been uprooted and whole herds of reindeer
killed. One of the few witnesses – from a long away – was so
terrified that he lost the power of speech for seven years.

Finding no crater, the expedition concluded that whatever caused
the explosion it was definitely not a meteorite. By the 1950s, scientists were saying that it looked nuclear: it had devastated an area
twenty times larger than Hiroshima. Could a comet have created
its own, natural nuclear explosion? Still, nothing explained the
size of it. Some suggested that only a black hole could have made
such a bang. Others suspected some lethal combination of matter
and anti-matter. Inevitably, there were suggestions that a cosmic
spacecraft had exploded in mid-air.

Day Five. The Alekseevs had secured transport: a rusting military cargo plane that did a weekly round of isolated forest
settlements. The flying bus rose out of Bor with a deafening roar.
We flew east, following the glittering thread of the Stony Tunguska
River, touching down here and there to collect men going to market.
The plane was soon crammed with men, clucking chickens, a pig
in a crate, kegs of salt fish and barrels of berries.

I had known that we were entering the largest remaining reach
of virgin forest in the world. But only now did the vastness become
real. Undulating over the hills, the woodland looked like the hide
of a sleeping beast: cloud shadows, moving slowly, threw dark
patches over its flanks and gave it breath. Then, without warning,
the pilot looped the loop over a clearing; bodies crashed, barrels
rolled, pigs and chickens squealed. Chuckling, the pilot brought
down the plane and spilled thirteen of us out, dishevelled, on to
a spit of land in mid-river.

THE LOST HEART OF RUSSIA

As the sound of the plane faded an awesome silence settled in. What I had thought of as silence was only ever a muted roar. This had depth and presence. It beckoned, like a new dimension. Shallow water chuckled over the smooth pebbles on that spit of land in mid-river. The fractured surface was flecked with sunlight. Beyond there was only the dappled forest. I knew this landscape from a thousand Russian iterations: paintings by Shishkin and Levitan; forest wallpapers in cramped apartments, postcards, tapestry cushions, plastic trays, poems and eulogies of mushroom-picking. My Russian friends loved the idea of this landscape. But few of them can have been in forest like this. It was their archetypal landscape, however, the ancient place of their belonging.

A flotilla of dinghies carried us up a tributary of the Stony Tunguska. The rippling waterway was refracted into a million fishy scales of light. To one side, the water gleamed darkly purple, on the other it ran chalky green. Standing on the foreshore to welcome us, surrounded by bearded, headscarfed villagers, stood an upright man with bright blue eyes. This was Philimon, about whom we had all heard so much. He was the village's redoubtable lay preacher, and the Alekseevs' special friend.

The headland behind was dotted with log cabins. Across the river reared an escarpment of pink granite. A muddy track wound through the village, with a thin, raised boardwalk. Dogs, cows and children wandered freely, girls in faded print dresses dragging muddy siblings in their wake.

Our hostess, Photinia, blue-eyed with honey-coloured skin, darted round the room, piling the table with food. Next to Elena Ivanovna sat Philimon, Photinia's father. His face, with its blue eyes framed by red-blonde hair, was striking for its air of authority. Two blonde children ran round the table, while in the open doorway a muddy two-year-old was hugging a sheep. By any sociological definition these people were peasants. But in Russia the word does not conjure up a Tolstoyan ideal so much as something narrow and dark. In living memory, Russia's government engineered famines that killed millions of peasants because they were blocking the path of progress. I needed another word to describe these Old Believers. They radiated confidence and intelligence, the assurance that they were anything but marginal, that they lived at the centre of the world.

The Russians have a legend that when the Mongols invaded Russia, the Prince of Vladimir took refuge in a town called Kitezh. A spy gave away his hiding place. But even as Khan Baty's warriors bore down on the town the waters of the lake engulfed it. They say Kitezh is the lost heart of Russia. It seemed to me as I sat round that table that I had found that heart.

That evening I sat on the pebbled foreshore of the River Burny, revelling in the space, after our days of confinement in Bor. The deep green of pines and cedars was broken by paler splashes of birch and hectic rashes of larch. The shallow water chattering over the stones was dark now. From somewhere along the river bank came the sound of shooting. Late though it was, it was light enough for boys to be firing at tin cans.

I had come down here to get away from Alan. The foreigners were lodging in the house of a village elder with a grave, iconic face. Our host Maxim was part of the army which pursued the Wehrmacht out of Russia, right back to Berlin. He was badly wounded on the battlefield: 'in fact, they told my family I was dead, but God watched over me'. Coming home from the devastation of that war with his Old Belief reaffirmed, he had proceeded to make his house and many of the contents too: furniture, cross-country skis, the families' boots. To work with your hands was a kind of prayer, he said.

Next day he was leaving for Krasnoyarsk for an operation, he told us. So if we had any questions, now was the time to ask them. I had asked Alan to hold off posing one particular question, that first evening at least. But being Alan, he could not resist. As the dinghy rounded the bend in the river, he had been the first to spot the satellite dish jutting up over the village. So they'd come to escape from modernity, had they, he gloated; we'll probably all find that they're watching television too.

'Do you have a television?' Alan duly asked Maxim.

The Old Believer drew himself up and said with an air of chilly finality, 'We do not.' After that the conversation froze over.

RUSSIA'S QUAKERS

To be honest, Alan was not the only one who went to bed disappointed: Burny, with its electricity and snowmobiles, seemed much like any other remote village in Siberia.

Next morning, at the service held in Maxim's house, to pray for the success of his operation, I realised how wrong I was. The life of the village was organised around the old calendar of religious and agricultural festivals, with its forty-four saints' days, twenty-seven major holidays and services lasting for hours. We woke at dawn and watched as the red dot of a woman's headscarf appeared, sailing through the mist like a boat. She was followed by a stream of people hurrying along the wooden planks raised above the muddy track through the village. They gathered in Maxim and Galya's largest room, the men in high-necked embroidered shirts, tied with sashes into which their women had woven prayers.

Other branches of the Old Belief had priests, and their services were elaborate, colourful rituals. But this village belonged to the strictest branch of the splintered movement. Russia's Quakers, they had no chapel and no priest, not since their last bishop was killed off by the Orthodox inquisition three centuries ago. Since then they had lived unbaptised, unmarried, unshriven, answerable for their actions only to their God.

The service, which I watched through a crack in the curtain, was a revelation. Ten centuries ago the ambassadors of the pagan Prince Vladimir came back from Constantinople dazzled by the ritual of eastern Christianity. 'We know not whether we were in heaven or on earth,' they said, 'for surely there is no such splendour or beauty anywhere on earth.' Vladimir was converted and the Russian Orthodox ritual has continued to entrance believers ever since with the drama it enacts. But here there was only a lot of men and women praying and singing directly to their God. The service was conducted by a frail, bearded old man who needed prompting now and then by Philimon. All the other elders, including Philimon, had returned too recently from visits to the outside world. Before they could take a service, or be fully reintegrated into the community, they had to undergo a ritual period of cleansing. The longer the villagers spent away from Burny, or the more serious their transgression against the community, the more extreme the spiritual quarantine imposed. This was the community's way of dealing with threats to its cohesion. Sometimes the penance involved a long period of solitude in the forest. The villagers were free to travel out into the world of sin. But afterwards they had to go through this strong, purifying ritual of return.

After the four-hour service, and the communal meal that followed, I went for a walk. The sun had burned through the mist and threads of smoke were rising from the wooden houses. The cows had been let out of their byres and were wandering around, foraging for grass. Yes, that was it. In the Russia I knew, power was imposed from the top. It pressed down on people, filleting them of initiative, determining so much of the behaviour we consider typically Russian. These people were different. They had responded to the schism by taking power into their own hands. In mainstream Russia, there was always someone to blame. These people did not live like that. They could choose to bring in a satellite dish if they wanted to. But they had to answer for that choice directly, to their God.

Just then a middle-aged woman with startling green eyes came running up, pushing her hair under her headscarf: 'Hello! I'm Anfissa, Maxim's sister-in-law. Come and have a drink!' It was nine o'clock in the morning.

'Could I drop by a bit later?'

'No, no. I'm out all day, it's got to be now! It's very important. You see it's my name day!' Traditionally, the feast day of the saint after whom you were named was more important than your birthday. I was making my excuses when Anfissa exclaimed: 'Look, there's your husband!' I turned to see Alan emerging from Galya's front gate, on his own. 'That's *not* my husband!' Anfissa rushed off after Alan and I made my escape. Not fast enough. Alan soon caught up, panting, contrite, trying to be charming: please could I translate?

Anfissa's dilapidated house was furnished only with a metal bedstead, a table and a few stools. The sills were thick with dust. She grinned, following my gaze: 'Why bother with housework? That's what I say. When we were kids our house was swept away by floods not once but twice, but we're all alive and kicking. It's not things that matter, but people. I've always kept open house, like my ma,' Anfissa said, pouring us glasses of her home-made beer. 'The boys come and say "Anfissa, can I chop some wood for you?" As long as I've got enough *brashka* . . . Pity you weren't here a couple of days ago for Stepan Stepanovich's wake. You must've heard – he drowned in the river. Did we put it away! We saw him off well!' The death happened when we were in Bor. Was that the real reason we were stuck there for so long? Perhaps the Alekseevs were worried that we would come here and find the villagers all blind drunk.

'Oh, just lend me your husband for a night or two,' Anfissa was saying. 'He's *not* my husband.' 'We'd get on just fine – don't mind me, it's just Anfissa rabbiting away – I'm all mouth really . . .' A widow, she lived on her own. 'A little top-up? It's good, clean stuff, made it myself,' she kept saying. 'My sister – no not Galya – was staying last night,' Anfissa said to me in a stage whisper. 'You know what she said: "I feel like a good fuck."' She roared with laughter.

By the time Alan and I staggered out of Anfissa's house the village was a blur and our differences were forgotten. A motorcycle was roaring down the narrow mud track through the village. The rider's long fair hair streamed out behind. The track led from the river where we had landed to the far edge of the clearing. Beyond, the forest stretched for hundreds of miles. When the young man reached the end, he turned his motorbike round and raced back again, and again.

IN THE WILDERNESS

News of our drink with Anfissa travelled round the village in no time. Philimon was not amused: Anfissa was the black sheep of the village, it turned out. After that, I had the distinct impression he was avoiding me.

Now I sat with a group of young people on top of the high escarpment, looking down over Burny. From here you could see where the waters of two small rivers flowed together down below. While the River Burny ran purple, the Vel'mo was pale green from gold panning further upstream.

All afternoon we had been picking berries in the forest. From up here you could see how fast the community was growing. A ring of new buildings, bright with freshly cut wood, had gone up round the edge of the village. All over Russia, Old Believer communities were falling apart, but this one was expanding. What was its secret?

My companions could not tell me, for Burny was all they knew. But I learned a lot from them. The village was in fact well connected with the outside world. Three of the fifteen extended families in Burny were not even Old Believers, just refugees from the chaos of mainstream Russia. As for the Old Believer families, ever since they came out of hiding in the 1950s their children had been obliged to attend boarding schools, and their young men to do military service. Other sectarian communities started losing their young to the cities from that time on. But these young people had no intention of leaving. Things were better here, they said.

Some of the children from Burny's secular families were even converting and marrying into the Old Believer families. Grigory, husband of the beautiful Photinia, was a convert, for instance. It had taken him three years to win Philimon's approval for their marriage. Pious and bearded, he looked every bit the Old Believer now and had recently been elected mayor of Burny.

Down below we watched boys spreading grass out to dry on the roofs. Philimon's wife, Natalya Semyonovna, was working her vegetable garden with two of her youngest daughters. Across the street, the convert Grigory was cleaning fish in his backyard. Maxim's wife, Galina, was carrying jars of pickled cucumbers from her summer kitchen in the garden to the storehouse.

It was harvest time. In a few weeks the sun would lose its warmth. Then the permafrost, which had receded enough to till the ground, would grip earth and water again for the next nine months. From first light, everyone in the village young and old was busy gathering food or preserving it. Every hour counted. When the village was still cloaked in mist, a group of the men had set out in their flat-bottomed boats to cut grass. Every household needed a barn full of hay to feed their animals through the winter. In the forest pasture was scarce and for each successive boatload they had to travel further downriver. They would not be back till late tonight.

The village paid their state taxes in kind, and berries would be part of the tithe. We had started by the river, where the canopy of trees was high. Siberian cedar, spruce, larch and birch vied to reach the sun, and the light that filtered through was tinged with green. Boulders and fallen trees made walking difficult. As we progressed slowly up the steep slope, clambering over huge fallen trees, long-legged blonde children bestrode the trees like mountain goats. Gradually, the trees grew smaller and more sparse. We were looking for cranberries, but in the crevices of the rocks there were blueberries, raspberries and blackcurrants too.

When we got back the young men would set off downriver for a night's fishing. 'That sounds like fun,' I said. They laughed; they'd rather stay and watch the Mexican soap opera, they said. But there was no time for that: it was only a few weeks before the river froze over.

On a fallen tree yards away a chipmunk sat nibbling a nut, chattering, watching us unafraid, its striped tail garish. Earlier, while we were scattered among the trees picking berries the silence was broken with little cries. This was how the villagers kept in touch in the forest. Even on a sunny day you could never be too careful. Not so long ago Photinia came face to face with a bear when she was picking berries. When she felt two hands on her shoulders she thought it was one of the boys. She turned round to find a bear standing behind her. If she was terrified, the beast was even more so; it was just a youngster and it wanted to play. It fled, pursued by the hunters. When they tracked it down they found that it had died of fear and exhaustion.

The shadows were long by the time we climbed down the rocks and crossed the river to the village. It had been fun. By comparison with young people from the cities these young seemed so carefree. They promised to take me to the haybarn where they all met up in the evening.

But in fact these Old Believers lived with danger every day. Just the other day, while we were kicking our heels in Bor, Photinia's father-in-law drowned in the river. Maxim and Galya had lost two of their sons in accidents. Even at home they were not safe: for the last two years the snow round Burny was so deep that when it thawed the houses nearest the river, including the one where we were staying, were flooded up to the windows.

Hunting was the most dangerous occupation. When the Old Believers came out of hiding in the 1950s, the state recognised that such skilful hunters could be a valuable source of hard currency. They were offered a deal: if they would sell all the sable they trapped to the state, they could carry on with their lives. This was still their main source of income. The animals had to be trapped in deep winter, when their coats were thick. Temperatures could be as cold as 40–60°C below freezing. Each family had its own hunting grounds, a long way away from the village, and the men would stay out for several months at a time. Every decision, every day was a matter of life and death.

One of the boys who came berry-picking had already started hunting with his father, whose prowess as a hunter had earned him the Order of Lenin in Soviet times. 'When it's really cold you've got to keep moving all the time – you can't sit down, you can't even eat. You'll probably cover ten to fifteen kilometres a day, checking snares all day. The work's too finicky for gloves – you've got to take them off. And each time you do the cold gets in.

'The first few years are the most dangerous for a hunter, Father says. The young are too rash, he says. Like my brother, Ivan. He was just back from military service. He went out with Father and another brother, Peter. They were all working on their own. He'd checked his snares and reached a hut. But it was still light, so he thought he'd go on to the next hut. He wrote a note to Peter, saying catch me up at the next hut. He hadn't realised there were these open stretches, where you sink right into the snow. Anyway, it got dark when he'd gone about halfway. He couldn't see a thing. Kept losing the path, bumping into trees, falling into holes. He was dead beat, so he thought he'd just stop and have a rest. He started making a fire, then his axe broke. I'll just have a little sleep, he thought. It wasn't that cold. What he didn't know was that the temperature was dropping – by next morning it would be thirty below.

'Well, Peter reached the hut and read the note. He was dog-tired, but for some reason he couldn't get to sleep. He got up, thinking I've got to catch up with Ivan, and set off into the night. It was madness. Ivan hadn't even said which hut he was going to. On and on he walked, bumping into things. Then, amazingly, he came on Ivan, fast asleep in the snow. He couldn't wake him up. He had to beat him with a stick to bring him round. Ivan would've been dead by morning.'

THE TIME OF THE ANTICHRIST

A shaft of evening light shone through the window on to Philimon's fair hair, picking up its reddish tinge and the tips of his curly beard, leaving his face in shadow. Today he was much more relaxed. His friendship with the Alekseevs went back many years. They were more than scholars of the Old Belief: they were his allies, guardians of the tradition, mediators between the Old Believers and a Russia which regarded them merely as backward peasants.

Vladimir Nikolaevich was showing me Philimon's collection of books. Some were brilliantly illuminated. Some dated back from before the schism. Many were handwritten, including one, unusually, which was copied by a woman, Philimon's mother's godmother.

Philimon had been talking about the difficulties he was having. There was rising nationalism among the Evenki, native hunter-gatherer Siberians. After the fall of communism, this territory was designated as their homeland. He dreaded to think what would happen if the Evenki started trying to get them out. The Old Believers could not, would not, go out into the world.

The village was also facing problems with the local authorities. The scale of the corruption was new: 'They're squeezing us dry . . . If it were up to me I know what I'd do. I'd just pack up and go. Move on as we've always done, deeper into the forest.' But although Philimon was the chief village elder, these decisions were arrived at collectively. On top of all that, there was the problem of prosperity: the rest of Russia might be on its knees, but here the villagers were managing well, too well for Philimon's liking. Prosperity brought choices like television and snowmobiles.

Philimon sighed deeply: 'We live in a decadent age. All these distractions and labour-saving devices take us away from the physical work which brings us to God. The sins we commit we wash away through work, through prayers and tears.' He sighed and closed his remarkable blue eyes. 'Man cannot serve two masters. This is the time of the Antichrist. We've got to escape from his snares. We will have to do it, before we meet our Maker. It will take fortitude. Determination. Self-discipline.'

Philimon spoke with a peasant burr, but the cadence of his speech and his vocabulary were grand, fashioned by the sacred texts. 'Any day now the Antichrist will come. We have no idea when that will be. We are so wrapped up in our lives that we won't even notice. He will creep up on us unawares. He will be sitting right beside us. We must take ourselves in hand. Repent. But . . .' He paused. 'You mean the community isn't ready?' Elena Ivanovna prompted him. 'That's exactly what I mean. It's the path of the few, I've got to accept that.'

However much they revered their *starets*, their lay preacher, this flourishing community was not going to leave everything behind and follow him. That was the tragedy Philimon faced. He sighed: 'But then again – how could I leave my family?' His face looked tortured.

Philimon had never expected to become Burny's *starets*. His father, who held the position before him, was revered for his piety and leadership qualities. When he resigned the villagers elected Philimon. In those days he was something of a rebel in Old Believer terms. He was, and remained, the best hunter in the region: his average winter harvest of two hundred sables was four times more than most men's. Back then, he read voraciously, and wrote poetry – he used to compose verses for each newly built house and write them on the walls, they told me. The community, who were charged by tradition with arriving at a unanimous choice, hoped he would show his father's talent for leadership. Philimon accepted the challenge. He changed his life to embrace the myth of original purity behind the Old Belief.

All of our cultures were once defined by such myths of purity, I had been reflecting; myths which could not be changed if they were to retain their meaning. But for the Jews, the story of the Garden of Eden was succeeded by the promise of a New Jerusalem. Looking to the future as it did, it unlocked the concept of modernity for us.

Yes, I reflected, this is it, the secret of Burny's success. It is vested in this man with his blazing commitment to his faith. He asked a lot of the villagers. But he did not do so by telling them what to do so much as by challenging them to live up to the example of the books. Philimon was a long way off retiring, but I wondered who would succeed him. Might it even be his madcap oldest son Ivan, the boy racer with his motorbike? More unlikely things had happened.

These Old Believers saw their lives as a gradual spiritual progression, as I now understood it. Little was expected of the children and Burny's teenagers danced, smoked, drank and loved rock music like their counterparts anywhere. Only once they married, which they did early, were they expected to start taking their inner life seriously. From then onwards, it occupied a progressively more important role in their lives, until in the end the serious men – the women did not appear to have this choice – retreated to a hut in the forest to devote themselves to the life of the spirit. That is what Philimon's father did when he retired as the village's *starets*, and Philimon himself would doubtless do the same in due course.

I took my leave and walked back along the raised boardwalk to Maxim's house. Over the fence, Ivan was taking his motorbike to bits. A group of children in rubber boots were driving cows home through the mud. Photinia was taking her washing off the line.

Sociologically, Philimon was just a peasant. Yet, in respect of everything he valued, I was the primitive one, and in his presence I felt it. He had turned his lively intelligence inward and developed resources in himself which were mysterious to me. Philimon was not in a confrontational mood this afternoon, but face to face with him I felt him measuring my spiritual poverty, and that of my world.

PHOTOGRAPHY IS A SIN!

Disaster. On our last night in Burny Kirsty, Alan and I were invited to attend a special five-hour saint's day service at old Anisim's house. The service was due to start at 4 a.m. The room was packed. I felt honoured to be included. We had come a long way since that first service glimpsed through the curtain. Alan was particularly pleased, as he had been given permission to photograph the service.

But at the first click of the camera – he did not even use a flash – Philimon stopped the service and thundered at Alan, eyes flashing like a prophet from the Old Testament: 'Photography is a sin! Get out!' I reeled out into the night along with Alan and Kirsty. What had Alan done wrong? As we edged our way in the dark back to Maxim's house along the narrow wooden boards Alan was fulminating.

For the rest of the night he stormed up and down Galya's front room, while Kirsty and I tried to calm him down. Had Vladimir Nikolaevich given Alan the go-ahead without checking with Philimon? By the time the sun came up we were all exhausted. I sat around at Photinia's, pretending to help make jam, while Kirsty shuttled back and forth between the Alekseevs and her husband, trying to broker a peace.

Picking over the berries, I came to my own conclusion about Philimon's outburst. Whatever misunderstanding there may have been over the photography, he was angry with Alan for other reasons. Ever since he arrived Alan had been asking the villagers about television: did they watch it, did they own one and so on. He discovered that, although there was hardly a set to be seen in Burny, most of the villagers loved television. They just kept their sets well hidden from the village elders. One of Philimon's sons had gone so far as to hack out a hole in the frozen ground and lower the television into it when it was not in use.

Philimon must have known about those televisions. My hunch was that he was in a rage with Alan for undermining the community with his questioning. The young people had been telling me about the community's attitude to rules. 'Imagine a full glass of water,' one of them put it. 'You can tip it this way and that as long as you don't break the skin. But if you break it, the water'll be gone! It's your own business how you behave – what you mustn't do is upset the community.'

This was it, the elusive, almost mystical concept of *sobornost'*, togetherness. A crucial element in the social DNA of Russia, it often lurked behind those things Westerners took to be a charade in her political life: those Soviet elections which voted in leaders by 99 per cent, or the value people placed on political stability at the expense of individual rights. From Philimon's point of view, as the community's *starets*, Alan was creating mayhem by pointing a spotlight at the village's secret vice.

Later on Philimon did invite us for supper. The sun shone low through the window on to a table heaped with blueberries, pine nuts and honey, fresh jam, smoked grayling and aromatic grey bread. The scene looked as tranquil as a Dutch still life. But pull back the focus and the faces were troubled. Philimon was telling hunting stories, making an effort to be hospitable. But the real man had retreated inside. Elena Ivanovna sat frowning. Alan displayed his injured pride like a war wound. Kirsty's eyes were puffy from tears. Vladimir Nikolaevich was cracking pine nuts in his teeth, shelling them and adding them to the pile in front of him. Then he sat back and pushed the pile over to Alan.

Philimon's intervention had drawn a line and I was torn both ways. I loved this thriving, iconic community, this buried heart of Russia. Philimon's unyielding authority supported it like a steel girder. But its survival in the modern world was a delicate balance, an act of defiance. The casual curiosity of an outsider could set it wobbling. In my world, however, curiosity was no sin. How pleased Philimon would be to see the back of us.

MUSIC OF THE FOREST

The last dinghy had just disappeared round the headland on its way back to Burny. We were standing on that island of pebbles in the middle of the river, waiting for the plane to pick us up. It rose out of the forest around us, a sustained chord that appeared to come from an immense choir hidden in the trees, a choir that never drew breath. Soon the air was ringing with sound. It was growing louder all the time. It filled the sky, sonorous as the Om of a cosmic Buddhist meditation. The lowest notes of the chord rumbled darkly, as if a host of great Russian basses were hidden among the trees. The high tones piped childishly true and clear. The forest was ringing with song, the music of the spheres.

'Listen!' I cried. 'Listen!' My companions paused only briefly before resuming their conversations. Then I became very afraid. They could hear nothing. What did that mean? This trip to the Old Believer community had been my fairy-tale wish. I had willed it into being. But it had been difficult. Perhaps it had all proved too much? Had I become a tuning fork for the tensions in the group? Was this glorious music the sound of my madness?

As we travelled back to Krasnoyarsk the memory of it did not fade. It rolled on and on inside me. But I locked it away and told no one about it.

1995

THE DARK SIDE

In Moscow, appearances had always been deceptive. In Soviet times the unifying idea was equality. Now it was prosperity. Only a few years back, I was giving my second-hand clothes to Ira's mother, Elena. Now she was the one mocking me for wearing the same shabby clothes year after year.

Apartment blocks and garish billboards were springing up in the city centre. The streets were vivid with glamorous women. When Ira stepped out wearing her Garbo hat, thigh-length black boots and long pale blue coat with velvet cuffs no one would have guessed that she and her new partner Sasha were living in a cubicle in a high rise a long way from the city centre. The couple were on their way now. They had bought a house in Hungary, and were at the heart of Moscow's new, smart cinema set.

Yet that year there was fear in the air. It was hard not to be infected by it. I kept reminding myself that it was probably nothing but the fear of fear. Still, it was hard to be sure. Everyone had a horror story to tell. An epidemic of robberies had broken out on the long-distance trains. Someone knew someone who had lost everything after being knocked out by an odourless gas in their locked compartment. A friend gave alarming detail about a spate of murders in which bodies were bundled off trains at the dead of night. To be a woman travelling alone was bad enough. To be a foreigner too, well, that was courting danger. Everyone had been warning me against the trains. So by the time I boarded the sleeper for Saratov I was feeling more than usually anxious.

I need not have worried. A stout woman with crimson hair was travelling from Ukraine to a factory in Saratov in the hope of getting her hands on the billions owed to her factory. A balding, unemployed doctor was retraining as an *extrasensor*, or healer. As we pooled our picnics, the talk was of everyday horrors like

cholera, which had surfaced again; of meat infected with tuber-
culosis; of the dangers of depositing money in the country's
unscrupulous banks.

On my way through Saratov I usually stayed with Vera, who
befriended me when I arrived off Benya's boat. But when I rang
from Moscow this time a drunken voice, presumably her husband,
told me she no longer lived there. She must have made her escape,
joined her cult somewhere in the wilds of Siberia. I was delighted
for her. But Saratov would be a sadder place without her.

It was too sad already. Unlike Moscow, no veneer covered the
city's wretchedness. People looked hunted and shabby. Plastic shop
signs dangled, street lamps did not work, rubbish overflowed and
now and then a cavalcade of Mercedes limousines sped down the
rutted streets, carrying the city's mayor, or a mafia boss.

Natasha and Igor had finally managed to swap their house in
Marx for a one-room flat in Saratov. But they seemed strangely
reluctant to meet up. When we did, I understood why. Natasha
was thin, jumpy and so distracted that I was not sure she really
knew who I was. Igor looked crushed.

They were trying to sell the flat and move to Siberia. This was
a terrifying business. With privatisation in full swing, the property market was dominated by thugs. Many had connections high
up in the administration. People who had sold a flat were being
found mysteriously murdered. For my friends, every encounter
with a potential buyer was another round of Russian roulette.
There was no way of knowing whether potential buyers were
genuine or not. 'I somehow thought it would be all right once we
got out of Marx,' Natasha admitted, close to tears, chain smoking.
'But we're having to go through the whole thing all over again in
Saratov. Seven years of my life it's cost me.'

They had presumed it would be a matter of weeks before they
could move back to Siberia, and the protection of Natasha's
powerful father. But weeks had turned into months. They had
run out of money. Ever since I first met Natasha she had been
telling me grandly that she was 'done with possessions', that she
'didn't want to be weighed down by furniture and all that clutter',
that she just wanted to be free. Now anything saleable had gone
long ago.

When the couple moved to the city, Anna took pity on Igor
and secured him a job as a photographer on her newspaper. He

took wonderful photographs, but the job did not last. As usual, he had turned quarrelsome. 'I told him to give in his notice at once,' Natasha confided. 'He just can't sustain normal relationships – he's either got to be in control, or utterly dependent.' Since then, they had survived on the English lessons that Natasha's advertisements brought in. Now that summer was here she was down to one pupil. During lessons, Igor sat in silence on the bed, behind the partition.

Under a white cloth in the corner of the room stood Igor's invention, that machine for making shoulder pads. He was about to deliver it to his ex-wife when a gang searching for her Chechen lover broke into her Moscow atelier and smashed up everything. She had to flee for her life and was hiding out somewhere in the Caucasus.

Hoping to cheer Natasha up, one of her ex-pupils organised a picnic and asked Tatiana and me to come too. On receiving this invitation, Tatiana rolled her eyes, but refrained from further comment.

We met up at Tatiana's flat in Marx on a cloudless, sunny day. Natasha, mercurial as ever, looked like a different woman: her broad-cheekboned face, with its upturned nose, gleamed with excitement and her curls stood to attention. We were being driven by a tow-headed trader called Volodya with bright cheeks and hands like hams, and his business partner, a solemn young Dagestani.

Natasha contrived it so that she and I would travel on our own, chauffeured by the silent Dagestani. On the way, clinging on to my arm, she confided the saga of her many marriages. Igor was her fourth husband. She had bolted from the first three and now she was about to leave Igor. As soon as they sold the flat she was going to Canada to join her childhood friend, she boasted. She was longing to start a new life.

The more wonderful and talented her husbands were, the faster she ran away from them, as far as I could see. Her first, whom she had married when she was in her teens, was an artist, handsome and clever. 'Sasha taught me how to live. He painted and sculpted and to this day when I see something beautiful, I long to share it with him.' So why had she left him? She brushed off the question: 'He wasn't made for marriage.' She paused. 'Anyway, he committed suicide a bit later – and no,' she said, anticipating

my next question, 'not because of me. Sasha was his own man.'
Husband number two was a successful businessman in St Petersburg
now. 'I got bored,' was her only comment on that marriage. Her
third husband was a cripple with 'a talent for attracting pity'.
Then there was Igor.

Natasha's account raised more questions than it answered. What
lay behind her boredom? There were so many things about her
that did not add up. She talked a lot about her father, for instance.
A construction boss, he had been part of the inner circle of the
Communist Party that ran Siberia's capital, Novosibirsk. She clearly
adored him; he was the kindest, most able man in the world, she
kept telling me. So why did she exchange her gilded life for penury
in Marx? Was it just too easy? Did she need to load herself down
with handicaps in order to feel alive? The more I saw of her, the
less I could fit the pieces together. When Natasha was in high
spirits, like today, she was great fun. But I had caught glimpses
of another woman altogether, a black star who ate the light.

After a while, the car swerved off the road, following Volodya's
down an undulating track. We passed an old couple piling grass
on to a wooden platform fitted to the sidecar of an ancient motorcycle. For them, summer brought no days off; every fine day, they
would be out collecting hay to feed their livestock through the
long winter.

As the car wound through a woodland of scrubby birch and elm,
we passed quiet inlets of the Volga, fringed with yellow irises,
where the odd fisherman was sitting. After driving through some
rusting gates, our chauffeurs left us and drove off again, muttering
about 'fetching some stuff'. The place was an abandoned holiday
camp. Before the fall of Soviet power, it would have been crowded
with holidaymakers at this time of year. Now there were no awnings
on the sunshades; the paint had peeled off the pedal boats, and
the rusting swings lay upended by floodwater. Straggling birches
were pushing the camp into the water.

Natasha raced down to the white sandy beach, dancing wildly:
'Hooray! I've left my cage and the horrible beast I'm condemned
to share it with! Who needs men? Anna's not to be pitied – we're
the pathetic ones, the ones who've been imprisoned by men. I've
done with them! From now on I'm going to live alone!' 'Don't
believe a word of it,' muttered Tatiana, 'she'll never leave Igor'.

The water stretched out like an inland sea to distant white cliffs on the far side. The scale of the Volga never ceased to take my breath away. A breeze puckered the green surface of the river. Huge dragonflies with blue bodies and iridescent wings hovered overhead. A heron rose up from the bullrushes. We sat on the white sand and talked. Slowly, the shadows of the poplars lengthened over the water. Still, our cavaliers had not reappeared. Desperately thirsty, we explored the camp, looking for drinkable water. We found taps. But when turned, they emitted only faint groans and scratchings, as if water sprites long trapped in the pipes were making their escape.

Finally, as dark fell, Volodya and his silent companion turned up with meat and alcohol in vast quantities, but no water or soft drinks. The bonfire flared up and we threaded chunks of lamb on to branches of willow, drank sweet Caucasian wine and settled in for a catastrophic night.

Each time we tried to draw the silent Dagestani into conversation, Volodya would cut across whatever he was saying with a boast; about his car, his trading, his three pigs, seven hens, five sheep and wife. Whatever anyone said, Volodya could do it better; whatever anyone had to offer, he had a better one. As he turned up his tape recorder, filling the silence with thumping pop music, I escaped into the water, swimming out until the group around the fire were swallowed up in darkness.

Mother Volga, they called it. Longest of Europe's rivers, she flows through the Russian psyche, provoking her people to song and revolt. Russia's expansion into the steppes had been one long story of ambition and insecurity. The Volga proved the key to controlling that steppe, as the Mongols showed when they set up their capital on its banks to the south of here, commanding trade routes in all directions. Muscovy's control over the vital trade up the river remained precarious well into the sixteenth century. Samara and Saratov were originally built as fortresses. Pirates, runaway peasants and sectarians would seek refuge from the state down here. The greatest of the peasant revolts were mounted from this river, Stenka Razin's in the seventeenth century, Emilian Pugachev's a hundred years later.

Long before I ever saw it, I got to know the Volga through Gorky's early stories. In its heyday as a trade route, it was heaving with life, crowded with sails and steamers; barges loaded with wheat and timber for the northern cities, dragged by lines of men; rafts carrying whole peasant households, complete with huts and cows. Today, thanks to the economic collapse, there was not a boat on it.

When I climbed back out of the water, Volodya was stripping off his shirt, challenging Natasha to armwrestle him. Tatiana and I walked off along the beach: 'I'm so sorry about this,' she said. 'It's just what I was afraid of. This is what passes for Having a Good Time here. It's unbearable – people with no education, no conversation, who can conceive of no way of enjoying themselves that doesn't involve booze.' It was obvious by now that Volodya had no intention of taking us back that night. I unfurled a damp, stinking mattress on a double-decker bunk in a beach hut which our Dagestani politely broke into for us, and went to sleep.

I woke from a dream that I was at sea in a storm, sinking in a small boat. It was dark outside, and the bunk was rocking to and fro, springs groaning. Below me, a man's voice, thick with drink; a woman's giggle. It was Volodya, but who was with him? Mosquitoes were devouring me. Burying myself in the fetid blanket shut out the insects, but not the squeals from the bunk below. There followed a crash and peals of laughter. It was Natasha. She had put her elbow through the window pane. Later, they both ran off into the night. In the silence I heard a quiet sigh. I was not the only witness of this scene.

Next morning, I found Tatiana sitting alone on the beach, arms round her knees. There was no sign of Natasha and Volodya. Here and there on the bushes bits and pieces of clothing were draped. We looked at one another and burst out laughing. 'Volodya's car's gone.' This was more worrying, for Volodya had been far too drunk to drive. There was nothing we could do but wait, and nothing to drink but sweet wine; we preferred to go thirsty.

Tatiana sighed: 'There you have it – the two Natashas, each devoted to different ends. Last night's Natasha was not an aberration. That destructive force is real enough. It's shaped her life, and it may well win in the end. Then there's the other one, the one who can do anything, who is confident, generous with herself, who knows exactly what she can and what she can't give. Perhaps in the end she was just given too much.

'You can't pity her, though. Whatever she has, she's chosen for herself. She started with everything – a powerful father who adored her, an education, a position, choices. Did you know that she was a brilliant mathematician too? Why did she divorce Seryozha? Why did she leave Sasha? Don't ask me. To spite her father? To spite herself? Who knows?' A long silence followed. 'Have you noticed what they've all got in common – Anna, Natasha and Igor, Misha? Suicide. Natasha's mother killed herself. So did Igor's father. Misha's grandmother and Anna's grandfather . . .'

Some hours later, I spotted two faces peering out of the greenery. Natasha's hair stood up like Medusa, and her face was white: 'How wonderful people are! What a miracle!' she said, and her voice seemed to be coming from a long way off.

Volodya: We couldn't find anyone.

Natasha: We were so frightened. Was there anyone left in the whole wide world?

Volodya: And how did we get here?

Natasha: And why were we naked?

Volodya: It was all so strange!

Natasha: Were there people left, I wanted to know.

Volodya: We wandered and wandered.

Natasha: Or were we the only ones in the whole wide world?

Volodya: And wandered and wandered.

Natasha: . . . then suddenly – a person! (looking at the smouldering fire) – Ah, a fire, I remember a fire.

Volodya: What can have happened?

Natasha: There were others.

In the course of this performance, our Adam and Eve emerged from the greenery, blind drunk, confident that they had never been more entertaining. Natasha was wearing a blanket. Volodya covered his nakedness with a sheet. As we squirmed, Volodya fell on an unopened crate of vodka, while Natasha started, recognising me suddenly. Struggling to focus, to piece events together in her foggy brain, she rocked back and forwards, keening: 'Now look what I've done – I've lost your respect, I've lost it, lost it, lost it!'

My heart went out to her. In a society that cultivated total dependence in its citizens, those who fought for their freedom did so at a terrible cost. Did Natasha have the strength left to realise her ambitions, or would she succumb to her dark side? There was no knowing.

1996

CREEPING FASCISM

—⟫●⟪—

When the overnight train from Moscow reached Saratov, Anna was standing on the platform, waiting to meet me. She was sunburned, and under the monkish fringe of dark hair her large brown eyes were brimming with energy. Her boyish face was almost beautiful. Brusque as ever, she brushed aside my greetings and dodged my embrace: 'It's terrible, this capitalism of yours. But I still prefer it to the old regime. The city's like Palermo now.'

Then she was off, striding through the large covered station. It had changed utterly since my last visit. Before, it had always been fairly empty, orderly and clean. Now it was milling with beggars and homeless people with bundles. The stench of poverty hung on the air. Anna seemed not to notice. She was talking intensely, volunteering information, filling me in on the highlights of the past year in Saratov, the old closed city. Gone were the defiant silences. Somewhere in the course of the last year, she seemed to have decided she could trust me.

The city's mayor had committed suicide and two of his assistants had been arrested for taking bribes, she told me. Now, the deputy mayor had taken control of the administration, as well as the local 'mafia'. 'And don't think it's just Saratov,' Anna continued. 'It's like this all over Russia. I don't know what we thought was going to happen after those elections. I suppose we thought things would change overnight. But it hasn't. Fascism is on the way, but it's creeping in quietly.'

Anna had come through a tough winter. Her newspaper, Saratov's one liberal voice, ran out of money and she lost her job. She proved unable to adapt to the life of a freelancer. She was incapable of selling herself. The trickle of work she did have was not enough to feed her and she was too proud to ask for help. 'I don't know how I'd have managed if it hadn't been for my father.

I didn't say anything, but he must have guessed I was in trouble – one day he turned up with a bucket of potatoes. He'd travelled all the way in by bus to give it to me.' A few months later her paper found a new backer and Anna got her job back.

Riding the tram in from the station, we bowled through the tree-lined neoclassical streets of the city centre. The buildings were more decrepit than ever, the roads more rutted, but here and there the bright plastic of a new shop-front gleamed. The girls were looking prettier, better dressed. But the biggest change was the expression on people's faces. They no longer wore that shuttered look which so oppressed me when I first arrived in the city.

Anna seemed happy and excited as I had never seen her before. Though Saratov always struck me as an oppressive city, for her it was a liberation after life in the countryside. She had been at university here, and after she was sacked by the newspaper in Marx her reputation landed her a job.

She invited me to stay with her at the hostel where she lived. While she went to collect sheets for me I took stock of her modest room. As ever, she lived like a nun. Her walls were unadorned, except for a few small Impressionist pictures cut out of a coloured magazine. There was a shelf of books, a kettle and a couple of plates and mugs. Her cupboard contained nothing but a spare pair of trousers and a winter coat. There was more to this than poverty, I realised. She had been downright rude when I showered her with presents: 'Give them to someone who needs them,' she growled. 'I like to earn everything I own – and I hate having anything extra.'

This was her very personal reaction to the fabulous thieving going on all around her. Stealing had always been a feature of Russian life, but never on this scale. After the Party's failed attempt at a coup, giddy sums from Party funds were found to have disappeared into numbered Swiss bank accounts. The greed of the nation's rulers was Homeric. Where once they stole building materials and labour for their dachas, now the new 'democrats', top officials, generals, bankers and heads of industry were pocketing IMF loans, army pension funds and whole factories. All those years of badly cut suits and cramped apartments had left an insatiable appetite for consumption. For people like Anna, Russia's liberal intelligentsia, the result was tragic: 'freedom' and 'democracy' had become synonymous with corruption and chaos.

When Anna came back with the sheets, she was laughing. The

laundry woman was outraged at the idea of my using 'her' sheets: 'These foreigners, they behave as if they own the place!' The woman bought some Western cakes for her daughter recently which had made her ill. At least the packet looked Western; it was probably one of the home-produced fakes which now filled every kiosk in the city.

As we picnicked in her room, Anna kept talking. Journalism was now a dangerous profession. One of her closest colleagues had just been spirited out of the country after two assassination attempts, the last in the crowded main street, where he was hit over the head with an iron bar. He made the mistake of investigating corruption in the administration. Anna, ignoring all warnings, was picking up where he left off.

A nation-wide grab for property was under way, thanks to Yeltsin's privatisation programme. In Saratov, thugs were putting pressure on pensioners and single people with flats in the city centre to swap them for places in high-rise blocks out of town. Those who resisted were sometimes found dead. Anna had taken up the case of an elderly man who refused to be intimidated. Some heavies tried to force him to swap his music store in the city centre for one on the outskirts. He collaborated with the police, and the men were arrested. However, shortly after, he arrived at his shop to find that new locks had been put on the door: it had been taken over during the night. Anna's investigations led back to the deputy mayor, who was consolidating his grip on the whole administration.

She was outraged when her editor spiked her carefully researched story. Only then did she find out who the paper's mysterious new owner was: the deputy mayor himself. The editor warned her to back off. 'But I'm not giving up,' she said, the battle-light in her eye. Ah, so the truth-teller, the *pravednik*, had found her cause.

Worried though I was for my friend's safety, I was proud of her. This tradition of self-sacrifice went back to the early days of Christianity in Russia, to the example of the princely brothers Boris and Gleb, who submitted themselves to death at the hands of their brother's hired assassins. It was present in the tradition of Russia's holy fools, who arrogated to themselves the right to speak freely when others could not; and in the tradition of the Old Believers who committed suicide rather than submit to the power of the state.

But a few days later when I took the bus to Marx to stay with Tatiana and Misha, I was surprised to find how deeply they disapproved of Anna's new-found sense of purpose. Tatiana's view was gently cynical: 'She's courting danger because she's bored – she needs to feel she's alive.' Misha went further: 'The risks Anna's running are a waste of time! Her problem is that she's lost her role. In the past it was different – there probably was a place for people who wanted to sacrifice themselves. But now no one needs that sacrifice! All she sees is horror and chaos. She doesn't understand that it's all happening under her very eyes! Of course it gets rough, but it's fine as long as you don't lose your head.' Misha and Tatiana may not have been right that the risks Anna was running were pointless, but the danger was real. Russia had become one of the riskiest places in the world for journalists, particularly investigative ones. Some forty-two, at a conservative estimate, would be killed in the 1990s.

For the first time a real difference in perspective had opened up between my friends. Misha, as a businessman, was confident that given time the corruption and chaos would die down and a new order would emerge. Anna, more political in her instincts, was in despair. Yeltsin's having stolen the election might be good news for the new economy, but it had doomed Russia's hopes for democracy.

BANGING THE TABLE

When I first arrived in Marx the place felt downright sinister, as if it had a hex on it. But now it was just an ordinary, messy, urban/rural mongrel of a place again. Little metal kiosks had sprung all along the streets, selling brightly coloured 'liqueurs' and other dubious goods. There were cars too, including a surprising number of dusty Mercedes limousines which looked as if they had probably been liberated from the Berlin streets.

To my surprise, Misha's old electronics factory was still staggering on. The half of the workforce who had stayed on were only turning out toy cars, or so they said. Since there was precious little market for these toys, this did not make sense. When I pressed him, Misha just snorted and said that it was 'all too complicated to explain'.

It was indeed. In fact, Yeltsin's government had still not succeeded in breaking the power of these factory managers, who had controlled the old Soviet economy. They were still being subsidised by the Central Bank. The toys, or whatever they were really selling, might be unsaleable, but they were not useless. They were part of a virtual economy, which worked like this: the factory director would slap an arbitrary price on them (the higher the better) and fob them off on his workers in lieu of wages. The workers, who stayed on because they could not sell their flats, used these as barter, to 'pay' for other unsaleable objects produced elsewhere.

Meanwhile, Misha's business was starting to take off. The family were still living in their shabby little flat and driving the same old Zhiguli. But Misha was a manufacturer now. The seed processor was working night and day, producing virgin sunflower oil. It was not yet a profitable business, since inflation was still too high for production to make economic sense. But Misha's partners were underwriting the loss through their trade in soft drinks and chewing gum.

The blue-eyed, fair-haired sportsman had thickened out. A knot of problems sat on his pale forehead, and his style had become more patriarchal. When he heard me talking in an obliging way to the woman in the ticket office at the bus station he told me off: 'You just can't go talking to people like that! It may be all right in the West, but here it's an expression of weakness – it means you've surrendered. You've got to behave as if you owned the place. No, don't laugh! I'm serious. We're living in a dangerous time in Russia. You've got to learn how to bang the table, or they'll eat you for breakfast.'

Misha had learned how to bang the table. But this did not entirely explain the steady progress of his business. When I first met his partner, Pasha, I was slightly puzzled. He had a bullet-shaped head and boxer's body and at his heels trotted a fierce little Rottweiler. It was not just that he was so unlike the gentle, clever Misha that puzzled me. The relationship between them seemed so unequal. Misha seemed utterly devoted to his friend, while Pasha seemed insufferably condescending to Misha. Now I realised why.

Pasha was a childhood friend of Saratov's two most famous godfathers, the brothers Sasha and Lyosha. As boys, they spent their time hanging out in Saratov's boxing clubs. Using these clubs as their power base, the brothers went on to build the most efficient, and violent, of the region's early trading networks. Misha and Pasha were not directly part of their outfit, but they enjoyed its protection.

One of the brothers, the handsome, charismatic Sasha, had recently been murdered on a street in Saratov, in broad daylight. Thousands turned out to mourn him. The city was carpeted in flowers. Violent he might have been, but he was already a legend. Brother Lyosha went round with no fewer than four bodyguards wherever he went.

Misha was more consumed than ever by his work. In the past, he visibly depended on Tatiana to give him the confidence to pursue his business: she was his Beatrice. Business and the cult of male friendship had claimed him. Home was the place he came to eat and sleep.

Now that her daughter, Polina, was older, and very independent, Tatiana had more time on her hands. Natasha had encouraged her

to take a job, as a journalist perhaps. But without Natasha there
to push her, I doubted whether Tatiana would pursue her own
interest at the expense of her family.

Natasha's departure left a gaping hole in Tatiana's life, as it had
in Anna's. Meeting a Soviet aristocrat like Natasha in Marx was
providential for them both. In the rigid, authoritarian atmosphere
of the little town Natasha's irreverence about power and her intellectual confidence cleared a space within which these bright young
provincial women had started to find themselves. 'I don't know
about Anna, but as far as I'm concerned, it's probably a good thing
Natasha did leave,' Tatiana admitted bravely. 'I'd fallen so firmly
under her spell that I've been having difficulty pulling myself
together, learning how to live without her.'

Tatiana was more beautiful than ever, with her mane of fair hair,
pale face, grey eyes and sensuous lips. But more remarkable than
her beauty was her normality. Alone among my friends, she appeared
to be untouched by the craziness of the time.

She had just told me the story of her great-great-aunt, who was
famously beautiful, with fair hair down to her waist. Although
only a peasant, the local landowner married her off to his ne'er-
do-well son, hoping she would be able to redeem him with her
love. She did indeed fall deeply in love with her husband. But he
remained indifferent and never consummated the marriage. Finally,
in a bid to win his heart, the girl set off from her home in the Ural
Mountains for the great monasteries of Kiev. She walked all the
way across Russia and back, on foot. Her pilgrimage took two
years. She failed to win her man back. But when she arrived home
she had acquired the gift of healing. So famous did she become as
a healer that for the rest of her life patients came to consult her
from all over Russia. She passed the gift on to her niece, Tatiana's
grandmother, who enjoyed a similar fame. 'I used to love being
with my granny,' Tatiana said. 'I would sit with her while she
worked at her spinning wheel. I never needed to tell her what I
was thinking – she would tell me.' Her grandmother wanted to
pass on her gift to Tatiana. But Tatiana was young and modern
and had no time for such mumbo jumbo.

Now, as I struggled to find redeeming features in that mongrel
town, Tatiana's gentle radiance, her undamaged sanity struck me
as some sort of miracle. It was almost as if the gift of healing had
come down to her after all.

1997–1998

Following Yeltsin's re-election, the charismatic General Lebed, an outspoken opponent of the war, had finally brokered a peace agreement with the Chechens. The appearance on the political scene of this military hero boosted people's hopes. Here at last was a credible, democratically committed successor to the failing Yeltsin. But Lebed's political career was cut off by the same arbitrary methods that rescued the election for Yeltsin. Acting on the Kremlin's behalf, Gusinsky's NTV television channel aired old footage purporting to show Lebed's links with the extreme right. Lebed was fired and disappeared from the political scene.

After the election, there was no stopping the oligarchs. Boris Berezovsky boasted that seven tycoons were controlling 50 per cent of the Russian economy. Even if not strictly accurate, this was a fair measure of their political influence. Their deal to bankroll government in return for shares in key state assets had given them a controlling interest in Russia's oil and gas. One of them, Vladimir Potanin, was now deputy prime minister, while Berezovsky was handling relations with Chechnya.

The honeymoon between the government and the oligarchs proved short-lived, however. Early in 1997 Anatoly Chubais (the one economist of Yeltsin's original team still in power, and effectively running the country) decided to end the preferential deals which they enjoyed in the ongoing privatisation programme. When Russia's phone system came up for auction, Chubais tried to ensure there would be no insider trading. This led to all-out war, between the oligarchs, and between them and the government.

Meanwhile, Western finance was flooding into Moscow. Now that hyperinflation was over, the stock market was booming. But the results were not reaching beyond Moscow or trickling down to ordinary people. Bureaucrats were still holding back salaries for months and using the money for their own purposes. Some three-quarters of businesses in Russia were still being conducted by barter.

The financial crash that followed in August 1998 was avoidable. But the government and oligarchs were so preoccupied by their ongoing row that they did not heed the warning signs. Russia was spending more money than it made: taxes were not being collected, and the old habit of subsidising Russian industry had continued. The government was financing its deficit by borrowing short-term bonds on the capital markets. Indeed, it was so deeply in debt that it was paying back more than it was borrowing. The solution was devaluation, but the Central Bank was set against that.

The oligarchs' political meddling further weakened the government at a critical moment. They engineered the sacking of Chubais. Then, with an eye to controlling the choice of Yeltsin's successor, Berezovsky instigated the removal of Yeltsin's heir apparent, Prime Minister Chernomyrdin. Yeltsin then asserted his independence and replaced him with Sergei Kiriyenko, an honest young banker. But Kiriyenko's political weakness and inexperience made this a fatal choice.

Then came the crash. First, the West stopped lending Russia money. Next, oil prices fell. Finally, the Asian financial crisis caused foreign investors to draw back. With the Central Bank determined not to deflate, it was inevitable. The government had been in such a hurry to break up its command economy that it had not created the institutions needed to regulate the wild new market.

The financial crisis ruined those whose business was money – including the bankers among the oligarchs. It also destroyed those who had been borrowing. This included a large part of Russia's struggling new middle class. Overall, 30 per cent of small businesses folded. Living standards crashed by 40 per cent.

But it made the fortunes of those, including oligarchs, who owned assets.

1997

IN SEARCH OF THE RUSSIAN IDEA

All afternoon the train had been travelling through a forest of birches. It was mid-May, but the branches were still bare. I was on my way east to Siberia, in search of Natasha and Igor. Whether they would want to see me was another matter. Two years had passed since they left Saratov and Natasha had long ago stopped answering her friends' letters. Anna could not forgive Natasha for turning her back on their friendship.

I must have dozed off. When I woke the light was beginning to fail, but still the forest went on and on. Mile on mile of wild cherry trees in bloom edged the wood like a trimming of lace. I was also going to try to track down Vera, the tiny woman who befriended me when I stepped off Benya's boat. She had left home to join the prophet Vissarion somewhere remote in southern Siberia. Before the Revolution, the outlying parts of Russia harboured many such home-grown sects, as well as the Old Believers. Now this seemed to be happening again. Thousands of people seemed to have joined Vissarion's sect, but it was under heavy attack in the press.

The birch forest had ended and the steppe stretched away to the horizon, flat and featureless. Back home in Britain, the very contours of the island's landscape instilled a sense of beginnings and endings. Here the space just went on and on. The émigré philosopher Nicholas Berdyaev maintained that the essential quality of his people, their aspiration towards the infinite, echoed the great expanses of the steppe. Like Dostoevsky, he believed that when this spirituality, 'the Russian idea', was tainted by Western rationalism, the result was demonic. Berdyaev believed his people had been crushed by the energy it took to claim so much land. The damage I saw everywhere around me, the punishment that industrialisation had visited on the land, the neglected state of everything that man built seemed to bear out his judgement.

Russia's history also suggested that its people traded space for freedom. The bigger the country grew, the less free her people became. Serfdom came quite late on. Western Europe was releasing its peasants by the mid-seventeenth century. But that was when Russia's great expansion east and south was taking place. Her peasants moved often, for the soil was poor and quickly exhausted. These movements felt threatening to the tsarist state, so it tied them down with serfdom. And communism kept them there.

Today it was different. Now it was poverty that held people in place. You would not have thought it if you looked at Moscow. Over the last five years the skyline of the grey, balding, dewlapped Soviet city was transformed. Post-modern turrets, smoky glass cathedrals to capitalism, thrust their way through the concrete. It looked as if a team of make-up girls had done over the old buildings. On what once appeared to be featureless blocks Art Nouveau detail and tendrils of exuberant ironwork were now picked out. Churches were spruce, their onion domes gleaming blue and brown with spangled stars. Neoclassical façades were burnished in raspberry pink, ochre and rust. As for Stalin's skyscrapers, clever lighting added what looked like a hint of irony to their domineering style, by night at least.

Zurab Tsereteli's kitsch statue of Peter the Great, 96 metres high, bestriding the Moscow River, left no doubt as to who was the role model for the new Russia. Thanks to the city's wily Mayor Luzhkov, the transition from state communism to state capitalism appeared seamless. The pompous edifice of the Church of Christ the Saviour, blown up by the Soviets, was rebuilt. Construction took five years, as opposed to forty-four originally. Luzhkov had cleansed the city of Chechen traders and deported the homeless from the city.

The train passed a man on crutches, walking slowly, swinging his dead leg. There had been no buildings for a long time. I watched, expecting to see a house, a village perhaps. Where had he come from? Where was he going?

In Moscow I asked around about Benya. No one had seen him. Someone said he had been kidnapped by the Kirghiz yet again. His friends seemed strangely unworried: he probably spread the rumour himself, they said, because he could not deliver the money he had promised to various artists. He had left a film unfinanced, and a cruise down the Volga that had to be cancelled.

An ample, motherly woman in charge of our carriage brought me tea. The hopes with which I set out on my travels seemed grotesquely wishful now. The transition from communism was conforming to the pattern of Russian history established by Peter the Great. Each attempt to impose Western forms of development clapped on a veneer of modernity. It did not change the nature of power. Indeed, through modernisation, it only threatened to make it uglier.

Authoritarianism was acquiring a new intellectual respectability, thanks to the Eurasianists. Strangely enough, it was my Westernising friend, Anna, who first made me aware of them. When I last stayed with her, she was talking enthusiastically about Lev Gumilev, who was one of the more liberal. Son of the poet Anna Akhmatova (the honour earned him two stints in prison camp), he had acquired cult status since his death in 1992. Inspired by émigrés like Nicholas Berdyaev, the Eurasianists were searching for a Russian identity that did not look to Europe. Their starting point was the country's physical geography, which was more Asian than European. Their ideas were prompted, like fascism, by the humiliation of a nation deeply imbued by a sense of its historic destiny. In their view liberal democracy, with its enfeebling relativism, its incontinent consumerism, had failed as an idea round which different cultures could unite. Russia could offer the world a finer model, spiritually strong, not sapped by individualism.

Gumilev had his own bio-geographical theory: every ethnic group had its historical rise and fall, after which decline set in. But those charged with a sense of national mission could reverse this decline. The great changes of history in the northern hemisphere depended on charges of cosmic energy inspiring ethnic groups with *passionarnost*. The strength of this innate drive was what divided people untouched by greatness from a 'superethnos', like the Russians. It enabled the divided Slav tribes to come together to overthrow Mongol rule, and it could make Russia rise again today.

In Gumilev's theory a decisive role was accorded to these *passionari*, the exceptional individuals who elected to sacrifice themselves for the greater good. When I read this I understood why Misha and Tatiana so deeply disapproved of Anna's crusade against Saratov's corrupt officialdom. Despairing of political reform, unable to see a way forward for her country, my friend had cast herself as one of Gumilev's *passionari*.

For all the romanticism of his engagement with business, Misha was a pragmatist. Given time, he believed that the activities of businessmen like him would bring about changes in Russia which would irrevocably alter the nature of power. He was confident that on the level of the individual, where the patterns of history are made and broken, people were already beginning to slough off their totalitarian conditioning. They were liberating themselves by learning how to work for themselves. I so wanted this to be true. I worried about Anna, though.

The train stopped at a small station. Walking down the train, I passed a woman selling hot pies: 'Hot manty, bi-ri-shi!' Her five-beat call with its rat-a-tat ending was as distinctive as that of any thrush. On the platform a flurry of trading was under way. A deaf and dumb boy was doing brisk business in fluorescent red and orange drinks. A fat woman in a flowered dress and white kerchief was filling a passenger's newspaper with potatoes. Where the platform ended the grass strip by the railway tracks was planted with rows of potatoes. For much of the rural population, potatoes were still the staple diet.

The train was due in at Novosibirsk at four o'clock in the morning. I twisted and turned on my bunk. Natasha and Igor did not have a telephone. By the time I heaved my bag off the train at Novosibirsk station, I was jumpy. What was I doing, on a wild goose chase across Russia in search of people who might have forgotten all about me? The station was bleak. The massive cube of a female guard with a megaphone stood on the platform in a cone of light. I settled among the shabby crowd in the waiting room to wait for morning. The hard seats had fixed arms. A man in a worn suit sat slumped over his bag. A boy was scrunched up in a foetal position. A girl with a mop of peroxide hair hung over the metal arm like a cloth doll.

I must have nodded off. I dreamed about Natasha: the new beginning she had longed for had happened. She was living in an improbable Palladian stone house. She welcomed me absently and walked out into the garden, where a three-legged tomcat was dipping its paw in an ornamental pond. Beyond, in a beech grove, she was embracing an impeccably dressed English gentleman. In the dream, there was no sign of Igor. It was possible that I would not find her there at all. She might have taken up her admirer's invitation to join him in Canada.

I went out to the hall in search of coffee. The real poor, who could not afford the price of the waiting room, were out here. As I waited in line, a man who looked like a dried chilli walked up to me: 'Where is it?' His shiny blue eyes were rimmed with red. 'We had order, Soviet order,' the man's words were slightly slurred. 'We were great. Where's it gone?' He looked at me reproachfully, as though I had taken it.

He was off to the Tyumen oil wells for another month's work. 'It's a bag of shite, everything smells of oil . . . But there's this old place I go past every day – they say it's full of babas praying – wazzit called?'

'A nunnery?'

'Nunnery, that's it. Weird idea – these babas, all locked in together, praying . . . But it makes me feel better . . . .'

His journey would take a day. It was the only available work since Novosibirsk's factories, which were largely military, closed.

'War's the only way out,' the pickled man confided, tears in his eyes. '"S the one thing we know how to make.'

'Against whom?' I enquired.

'My pal's a lathe operator – he'll make us all guns—'

'But who are you going to fight?' I insisted. He focused on the question slowly.

'We'll start with the government, I'll cut Yeltsin's throat myself. Lining their pockets, squeezing the money out of us like blood – it's a bear pit. They'll fight it out, fight for power till there's only one left. Just let me get my mitts on 'em – I'll kill the lot. They've sold great Russia for a bag of gold! It'll never recover! Smashed. There's no putting it together again.' He paused. 'Bloody woman! Got to keep a tight rein!' He made a fist. 'A woman's got to obey a man! She should obey me. They're all the same, good for nothing but fucking and flogging.'

I kept quiet, with an effort. 'Don't look at me like that. Your eyes – they go right through me. Have I said something wrong? Our women, I'm talking about our women . . . well, maybe not all our women. Come on, I didn't mean it.' Pathetic now: 'I'm going to die soon. I'm only in my forties. It's been foretold.'

'Cheer up, it's up to you.'

'No, it's been foretold – I've got five more years.'

I headed back to the waiting room, anxieties blown away by this exchange. I chose to be here, after all. The chilli man was probably right about his death, too. Life expectancy for men had fallen sharply. More men had died prematurely in the last few years than were lost on all sides in the Chechen war. Drink, drugs and suicide were the immediate causes. But it was despair that was really killing them.

THE PRODIGAL RETURNS

I reached Natasha's sister on the phone in Novosibirsk before she left for work. Yes, she assured me, Natasha and Igor were there, and still living together, somewhere on the outskirts of the city. When I asked how they were she sounded guarded. As for finding it on my own, that would be impossible, she said flatly: she would take me out there after work.

Memory had softened the brutish scale of the Siberian capital. The massy Soviet blocks and bullying scale of its streets and squares reflected an ideology which had little place in it for the individual. These undulating reaches of asphalt were intended for parades of military strength. In Lenin Square a huge statue of workers wielding weapons and tools was still striding into its radiant future. But gusts of wind were blinding them with wild cherry blossom.

The grim cityscape was softened by the sight of young girls wearing the latest fashion, spotted platform heels. The girls trod the wavy asphalt tentatively, like escaped giraffes. People were buying bananas and eating them there and then on the street, as if to make up for years of lost fruit.

Natasha's sister was right. I would never have found the couple's flat without her. They were living a long way away, in an old industrial district built by German prisoners-of-war and deported Russian Germans. Walking from the tram, we passed rows of arms factories. When the Wehrmacht invaded, the Soviets had been utterly unprepared for war. They were dismantling arms factories only just ahead of the advancing armies, hastily re-erecting them here. Now those buildings stood derelict, windows broken. Two men were dragging equipment out of one of them.

My friends were living in two rooms on one of the elegantly proportioned, intimate courtyards in the workers' suburb adjoining these factories. Designed in the Stalinist neoclassical style, all ochre and white, there were palaces of culture, playgrounds and bakeries. Crumbling now, lost in thickets of lilac and straggling birch, it was an elegy to that failed attempt to build a workers' paradise on earth.

Natasha and Igor greeted me as if it was perfectly normal for me to turn up unannounced after two years. The contrast between them was shocking. Natasha looked wretched, thin and pale. But Igor was transformed. The discontent which had marred his handsome mustachioed face was gone. His dark eyes had lost that bloodhound droop. He looked plump and prosperous, though this was clearly not true. But he was working. Now he had started, he did not seem to want to do anything else. Later, when Natasha and I went to bed in the couple's double bed, we left Igor writing a business plan for some company. When we got up in the morning, he was still at his desk. After years of treading water in Marx, he was now in love with work.

The couple were living austerely. Their three rooms were furnished only with an iron bedstead, a desk, two chairs and a fridge. Here and there laths were exposed where the plaster had fallen away. Igor's computer was their only possession of value. I went out and bought armfuls of food to celebrate our reunion.

When they started to tell me how things were I understood why Natasha had not been in touch with Anna and Tatiana. By the time they reached Novosibirsk, Natasha's father was ill with cancer of the throat. He greeted his prodigal daughter affectionately. But he refused to help her. He had his own troubles, and clearly felt that she had received enough help already. 'I don't blame Father – he couldn't trust me. I've behaved too wildly,' Natasha said bravely. But she had been counting on his help, I knew.

That first Siberian winter they found a room in some cellar, a refuge for winos and prostitutes. There was nowhere to cook, and nowhere to wash but in the street. One day they returned to find their front door stolen. From then onwards they defied the temperatures of below 30°C by wearing all their clothes at the same time. They could not find work. They spent their time reading books on marketing, requalifying themselves for this new world.

Natasha visited her old gang, the golden boys of her schooldays, to ask for help. Their fortunes mirrored that of the country. Ivan, who proposed that she join him in Canada, was back. 'He did nothing but complain about the Canadians and their materialism!'

Through his words, she heard the lament of a man who, when faced by the confident, bright surfaces of North American culture, had been undermined by a deep sense of inadequacy.

Another friend had also emigrated to the New World. Ilya had done well in Washington, working as a consultant. But he was back home too, health shattered, after developing a brain tumour. He spent all his dollar savings on an operation to save his life.

With each visit her hopes faded. Vasily had become a civil servant, an important figure in the power hierachy of Novosibirsk. Solemnly he advised Natasha that if she wanted to earn good money she should go to the oil wells of Tyumen, live in a barracks and turn her hand to manual labour. The cleverest of the group, Mikhail, an ex-physicist, was designing furniture for prison workshops.

The worst fates, the ones that broke her heart, were reserved for the two most gifted young men of her privileged gang. Anatoly married a woman so eaten up by greed that for love of her he had taken the short cut to wealth and joined one of the city's criminal gangs. He was the charming, quietly spoken blackmailer in the well-cut suit whose task it was to visit factory directors for a cup of tea and deliver the ultimatum: hand over your profits or else.

Natasha's closest friend, Yury, fell victim to just such a gang. He was that rarity, a successful businessman doing his best to be honest. Two men on a motorbike, hired killers, gunned him down with a sub-machine gun in broad daylight after he refused to bow to blackmail.

Statistically, the fates of these two were not so surprising. According to the official estimate of Russia's Chief Procurator, half the country's economy was in the hands of organised crime by now.

After each visit, Natasha would return to the cellar and take out her bitterness on Igor. Mostly, he took it patiently. He loved her dearly and understood what she was going through. But one day the torrent of blame became too much and something snapped. He hit her. It was not a hard blow, by her own admission, but it struck her full on the ear.

She lay in hospital for a long time. Her eardrum appeared to be broken; she was badly bruised and suffering from concussion. She could not talk properly and the rushing in her ears drowned out every other noise. She lost so much weight that she could barely lie down because her bones stuck into her. She promised herself that if she ever recovered she would leave Igor.

Only when the doctors gave up on her did she take herself in hand. She started asking around about doctors. There was only one who could help, they said. He was a brilliant man who had studied in China. But he took only private patients, and they paid him fairy-tale sums.

Using her last strength, Natasha pushed past all the people whose job it was to protect him, into the doctor's office. His chilly gaze froze her. 'If you ever wondered whether there was a God, help me now,' she lisped, this wisp of a woman who could no longer even talk properly. He accepted her as a patient, on one condition: she had to obey his every instruction. After the third session, the rushing sound in her ears began to die down. 'It wasn't your eardrum that was broken,' he told her, 'it was your psyche.'

Jogging up and down the hospital steps, forcing herself to eat, Natasha began to mend. 'I realised I was crazy to think of leaving Igor. Who for? My "golden boys"? Igor was worth a dozen of them.' She returned to the cellar to find Igor living off tins of cat food. But he had landed himself a job – as a lavatory attendant. It was there that he made his first business contact, with the director of a building firm. Igor convinced the man to let him do the marketing.

Natasha and Igor both ended up working for the man he met in the public lavatory. He ran a fine company, building blocks of flats for ex-army officers, using their redundancy money for capital. It did well, in fact too well, for it attracted the attention of a man called Kibirev, 'Novosibirsk's largest rat of all', as Natasha put it. Kibirev took over the building firm and ousted its director. He stole its capital, and poured it into the election campaign which General Lebed was mounting to oust Yeltsin from the presidency.

Natasha and Igor were admirers of the popular General Lebed, who had negotiated the end of the Chechen war. But from the vantage point of the asset-stripped company, they watched in horror as sinister power blocs lined up behind the general's election campaign. They knew that they had to leave the company. But it was winter again and the prospect of living among the winos again was more than they could bear. Despising themselves, they kept on working for Kibirev.

There came a day when they could take it no longer. Natasha staged a spectacular public row. She vented her contempt on Kibirev and taunted him with her freedom, the freedom of those who have nothing left to lose. After that, things became hard. But by then they were at least beginning to understand something about business.

BUILDING HEAVEN OR HELL

Natasha's father was holding a birthday party. I had heard a lot about him over the years: the charmer, the great builder, member of Novosibirsk's old Party elite. She never mentioned her mother, and something about her silence deterred questions. It was her father who brought her up, and she spoke of him with love and pride. She was clearly his darling. But I still had no idea why she fled from him, and from all the privileges that came with that background. In Russia, it was far riskier to throw away such advantages than in the West. What made her leave her first happy marriage, to rush hither and thither across Russia, from one husband to the next, only to end up back home in a basement with winos and drop-outs?

Natasha's father and stepmother lived in a flat in the city centre. We travelled in on the tram. Despite their penury, Natasha and Igor were smartly dressed in clothes from a shop which imported second-hand clothes from the West.

The front door was opened by a vivacious, nut-brown man with a vigorous mane of curls, the spitting image of his daughter. Gallantly, he kissed my hand. The flat was light and airy, but perfectly modest. Had Natasha's father's savings gone in the inflation of those first post-communist years, I wondered? Or was the opulence of Natasha's childhood, which she recalled so vividly, only relative?

Despite the cancer that had struck his vocal cords, her father seated me beside him and regaled me through the long summer evening with whispered jokes and stories. But his efforts and his gallantry could not disguise the sadness which hung over the occasion. His much younger wife, a broad-hipped doll with a round, painted face, produced a sumptuous birthday meal. She hardly spoke all evening, but her face wore a martyred smile. 'What about me?' it seemed to say. Even as she netted her big boss, he had turned into a sick old man.

Natasha fussed around her father and me like a nanny. She was nervous, and it was no wonder. For while we were changing for the party she dropped a bomb into our conversation: her father had spent his life building those arms factories which dominated the city's skyline. 'One made nuclear weapons,' she said in a horrified whisper, holding my gaze in the miniature mirror in which she was making up her eyes.

'My sister and I grew up knowing nothing – we thought he just built houses.' In fact, of course, most of the city's economy, and 40 per cent of the Soviet empire's, was military. 'It wasn't Papa who told me, but Sasha.' He was her first husband. 'He didn't want to. He knew what it would do to me – I bullied him into it.' She turned round and looked at me directly. 'I adored Papa so much. He'd been my idol – I felt betrayed. I couldn't forgive him. He belonged to that world – he knew all about it and he never told us, never prepared us. How I used to laugh when people used to talk about psychotronic weapons! I thought it was pure paranoia! They counted on that, on us thinking it was too far-fetched! But when I asked him about them recently, he said he "knew the factories well"!' Before I could ask her any more, Igor interrupted us, hurrying us off to the party. In the tram coming in Natasha would not look at me, but stood gazing out of the window, frighteningly pale and still.

Natasha's anxiety rubbed off on her father. Even now it was clear how close the two were. When everyone else was in the kitchen fetching food, he whispered hoarsely in my ear, out of the blue, as if he knew what his daughter had been telling me: 'It wasn't right what we did.' At that moment Natasha walked in from the kitchen bearing a steaming plate of *pilau*. 'You were only the builder – it wasn't your fault!' she protested, rushing to his defence. 'Well, what's done is done,' sighed the old man, reaching up to the top shelf of the cupboard for his best bottle of Armenian brandy. 'Let's be grateful for small mercies – the Armenians still love us,' he smiled bravely, filling my glass.

As we sat back, sated with delicious *pilau*, the old man turned to me: 'I don't believe in God – I won't have that,' he rasped in the shell of my ear so that no one else would hear. Even behind these words I heard an uncertainty: had he been wrong about that too? 'Let's drink to peace,' said the old cold warrior.

Natasha's confession about her father had been prompted by her seeing the book I had been lent that morning. It was about psychotronic weapons. I had not heard the term before.

Apparently, they inflicted damage at long distance. They could implant thoughts in people's minds without their knowing it. Oh dear, I thought on hearing this, here we go, back into that unmapped territory, among the monsters. Back home, I would have laughed. But the man who pressed the book on me, a scientist, insisted that these were no fabulous monsters. There was a reason why they did not appear on my mapped world, he was saying: the secret had been too well guarded by governments. It was the dark side of the science he worked in.

Natasha was nobody's fool. She had been like a cat on a stove since seeing that book. Her reaction was what made me really want to know more. When we got back home from the party and she was asleep, I started reading the book.

Psychotronic weapons were no futurologist's idea, I read. They already existed; they were capable of destroying command systems at long distance. The information they transmitted could kill troops, and potentially whole populations. They worked by manipulating the electro-magnetic force-fields around living organisms . . .

I looked at the sleeping Natasha. Was it possible that her beloved father, builder of the arms factories, had built a factory for psychotronic weapons? Was that it, the shock that had destabilised her life, sent her spinning round Russia pursued by furies, ridding herself of the antiques, the crystal, all the finery bought with her father's money?

TOUCHING THE COSMOS

It was on a hunch that I had rung up Professor Kaznacheev's laboratory. Having heard that he worked with shamans, and was a leading figure in an alternative tradition of Russian science, it seemed possible that he might be able to shed some light on the mysterious behaviour of the community in Zarafshan.

So that morning I had made my way up to Akademgorod, the privileged settlement built for Soviet scientists on the wooded hills above the grime of Novosibirsk. The professor's laboratory was housed in a prestigious building, the headquarters of the Soviet Siberian Academy of Scientists. It was a tall tower block set in a forest of birch trees. The foyer was clad in marble, and had a fountain in it, but the tiles were coming loose and the fountain was long dry. Upstairs, floor after floor of long corridors connected the laboratories and offices. But the doors were closed. Somewhere in the building, a window was banging. The place seemed abandoned.

One of the doors in this rabbit warren carried the intriguing title International Institute of Cosmic Anthropo-ecology. I knocked on it. Kaznacheev's deputy gave me a guarded welcome, sat me down and talked. He talked not about science, but philosophy.

The branch of science they were pursuing belonged to a different tradition from that of the West, he explained. It was the result of a uniquely Russian conjunction of scientific thinking and religious philosophy which went back to the nineteenth century. These philosphers disagreed with the way the Enlightenment had displaced God from the centre of the intellectual world. They believed that the West's unswerving attachment to rationalism had led Western philosophy to be obsessed with a false set of problems, the need to demonstrate the existence of external reality. What mattered, of course, was the relationship between people. Western philosophy had lost sight of this self-evident truth.

I was aware that there had been a great revival of interest in Russia's religious thinkers since the fall of communism. Their work had been banned in the Soviet Union. But the professor's assistant was saying that scientists who belonged within that tradition had continued practising right through the Soviet period.

It was when the professor's assistant started talking about the nineteenth-century philosopher Nikolai Fedorov that the gap between the two worlds yawned again. I knew about him. A great librarian, the illegitimate son of a prince, he lived in one room, wore the same clothes all year round, and gave his salary away to the poor. Fedorov fascinated his contemporaries, including Tolstoy and Dostoevsky – *Brothers Karamazov* was said to have been inspired by his ideas. But for me he was just an amusing footnote in the history of Russian philosophy. Deeply Christian, he took the notion of 'the brotherhood of man' so literally that he proposed mankind stop procreating and study how to resurrect the dead. He believed it was man's task to orchestrate nature and the cosmos in order to create paradise on earth.

Now here was the professor's assistant, telling me that Fedorov's grand vision had captured the imagination of a whole tradition of Russia's natural scientists. The philosopher had dreamed about the colonisation of space generations before anyone else. That was Russia's destiny. That was where man's path to immortality lay. Fedorov taught the man they call the father of Russia's space programme, the rocket scientist Konstantin Tsiolkovsky. And through this hero of Soviet science the philosopher's mystical and messianic view of space passed into popular consciousness in the Soviet period. Tsiolkovsky also wrote science fiction, and in his stories he developed many of Fedorov's ideas about the colonisation of space. Tsiolkovsky shared his mentor's belief that the universe was constantly evolving, and full of intelligent life. He maintained that man needed to develop his telepathic abilities in order to open up the secrets of the universe.

Among the scientists who shared aspects of this resistance to the Western scientific approach was the celebrated earth scientist Vladimir Vernadsky, said the professor's assistant. While Western earth scientists tended to study separate elements of the natural world, what mattered most was their interrelationship, Vernadsky maintained. Long before James Lovelock's 'Gaia', Vernadsky not only coined the word 'bio-sphere' to describe the unified view of nature and the cosmos towards which he believed the natural sciences should aspire, he also built on Teilhard de Chardin's notion of a 'no-osphere', where man's thinking became a force that interacted with the 'bio-sphere', changing its chemical structure.

Since the fall of communism such concepts had become part of the wider currency of intellectual and spiritual thinking in Russia. Its adherents, who called themselves Cosmists, maintained that this 'no-osphere' was growing more important all the time, particularly thanks to the Internet. Professor Kaznacheev was one of the pillars of Cosmist thought.

Having sketched out this grand framework, the professor's assistant proffered an invitation which I later realised was a test, a way of determining whether I should be allowed to meet the professor. His laboratory contained a device they had developed that allowed ordinary people like me to understand what it meant to be in touch with the cosmos. The device suspended the magnetic field which covers the earth's surface, he explained. By so doing it allowed ordinary people to share the experience of shamans and psychics. Would I like to try it out?

Having come this far, I was hardly going to refuse. I followed him down flights of stairs, to a damp room in the basement guarded with triple locks. There, he invited me to crawl inside a fur-lined sleeping bag in a huge metal cylinder.

What happened next takes me to the very edge of the sayable. After lying in the dark for a while, my heart started leaping about like a cricket in a box. Then everything went calm and the images began. A dark column seemed to rise out of my forehead. I found myself standing in a deep, dark canyon. This canyon came and went, alternating with a spiral. When that faded away, a brightly coloured fairground carousel appeared. There were people riding the whirling wooden trains, cars and animals. It was a merry scene, at least it was to start with. But even as I watched, something started going wrong. The movement of the carousel became chaotic, alarming. The painted wooden animals and engines were slipping. The centre was not holding; it was falling apart.

Then this sequence faded and I found myself back at the bottom of that great dark spiral, which in turn evolved back into a crevasse.

Black rocks rose up on either side and there was light streaming down on me. I basked in that light. This, this I wanted never to end. But eventually this image faded too. I lay not knowing where my body finished and the world outside began. Everything around me seemed to be spun out of light. The rhythm of my breathing seemed to have changed. It was as if I was learning to breathe for the first time, learning to support this lightness of being through the way I breathed.

I climbed out of the cylinder reluctantly. When I described this magical experience to the professor's assistant he seemed delighted. He not only asked me if I would like to meet the professor, he even offered me a lift back to Novosibirsk in the Institute's chauffeur-driven black Volga. He also lent me that book about psychotronic weapons.

The prospect of trying to explain any of this to Natasha and Igor was more than I could face. I asked the driver to leave me at the city's picture gallery. I sat among the pictures for a long time, trying to hold on to this luminous void, which seemed so vivid with energy and meaning. Only once had I experienced anything similar. Not long ago, after falling seriously ill on a skiing holiday in the Alps, I floated up and soared over the mountains, leaving my body behind on the bed in our chalet. Looking down on the places we had skied that day, I surveyed the distant valley below, with its neat arrangement of toy houses, fields and roads. It seemed as if I was a particle of light, travelling through the air, free even to pass through mountains. It was enough for me to think of a place to find myself there. On my favourite Dorset hillside I planed the air currents, imitating the buzzards I had watched there over the years. I had come back from that experience reluctantly.

All afternoon I stayed in the gallery. When I returned to Natasha and Igor's I said nothing about my day, and tried to hide that book. But Natasha, noticing my furtiveness, became inquisitive.

RIDING TWO REALITIES

The following morning I tip-toed out of the flat while Natasha and Igor were still asleep and waited outside a gutted arms factory for the Institute of Cosmic Anthropo-ecology's black Volga to pick me up.

I was caught in the Slavic version of some Whitehall farce. It was not alarms and assignations I was dodging between, but different realities. On the one hand, there were Natasha and Igor, struggling out of the lower depths of Natasha's self-imposed purgatory. On the other, there was the magic cylinder and this parallel reality up the hill in Akademgorod. Where Natasha's father, the builder, fitted into this farce I dreaded to think.

We drove up out of the stacks and grime to the professor's house in Akademgorod. A pretty wooden dacha, it stood in a clearing surrounded by pines. The garden was a sheet of white and blue – drifts of flowering lilies-of-the-valley and clouds of brunnera. The scent of lilies was heavy on the air. It was sunny, and as we drove up the professor was standing by his front door, hand in hand with his little daughter. His face was rugged and his white hair stood up in a tuft in front. He stood with his feet well apart, as if braced for shocks.

We settled in his study on the top floor, looking out over the tall trees. I apologised for being scientifically illiterate. 'Oh, don't worry! I much prefer talking to writers and other artists from the West – your scientists are so conditioned by their tradition that they think I'm talking rubbish.' Had it not been for my experience in the cylinder, I would have thought so too.

'My research belongs to a very Russian tradition which goes back to philosophers like Khomyakov, Fedorov and Soloviev,' he said, referring to leading nineteenth-century Slavophiles. 'What they all had in common was that they refused to believe you had to choose between religion and science – theirs was a God-centred universe. A whole line of natural scientists in Russia have maintained that tradition – men like Vernadsky and Tsiolkovsky. We call it the cosmos, they called it "the divine" – they're much the same.'

Then he smiled: 'I gather you had a good time in the hypomagnetic chamber? What you experienced is fairly typical. The chamber allows people to undergo the experience of shamans. To communicate with the cosmos. Let me explain . . .' The professor's intellectual mentor, he went on, was a brilliant astrophysicist called Nikolai Kozyrev, whose career was destroyed when he was sent to the Gulag. From the sky over his prison camp Kozyrev observed that some of the stars seemed to be interacting with each other. It seemed to him that Einstein's Theory of Relativity and quantum mechanics were not sufficient to explain what was going on. The universe seemed to be communicating with itself. Kozyrev proposed that there was a third force at work, a carrier of information. He called it 'time-energy'. Kozyrev concluded that the universe was a single, conscious system within which living matter was constantly exchanging information on every level from cells to stars.

'That's where my own research as a biologist began,' the professor went on. 'I designed a series of experiments to find out whether, at the cellular level, it was possible to prove Kozyrev's theory. I set out to try to isolate this dimension which, if it existed, was operating beyond the biochemical, and the cybernetic too. Could cells communicate information to one another holographically, as Kozyrev was suggesting? I found that they could – and I repeated these findings in more than three hundred experiments. I found that one group of cells could transmit a virus, a toxin or radiation to other healthy cells of the same type. They could do this over distance, in conditions where this could not have happened through infection or contamination. I also found that healthy cells could "protect" themselves from long-distance penetration from damaged cells by means of a field immune system.'

The professor proceeded to tease out the implications of Kozyrev's proposition. If all matter was constantly exchanging information, how about man? Why did he seem unable to do this? Or at least why was this capability limited to a few rare individuals, whom we called shamans? He found that at places on the earth's surface where the electro-magnetic field which covers the earth was at its thinnest, people's ability to communicate at long distance was much stronger.

Indeed, sacred sites all over the world were always located in such places. That was why civilisations all over the world always congregated in sacred spaces, he concluded: they went there to reinforce their direct contact with the cosmos. His theory was that consciousness had originally been communicated to proto-man from the cosmos. Kozyrev's mirror, as he called the hypo-magnetic cylinder, reproduced conditions similar to those found at these sacred sites.

In the course of our evolution, Kaznacheev explained, this original capacity of ours for communication with the divine became overlaid by the development of speech and reasoning skills. But it surfaced still in exceptionally gifted individuals, he said, and in times of crisis, too. 'What do you mean by that?' I asked, thinking of Zarafshan. 'Well, we found that ordinary people, often whole communities, rediscovered that capacity in times of emergency. In the last few years we've noticed it happening quite a lot.

'Do you understand what I am telling you?' the professor said, suddenly excited. 'It's really important! We probably understand less than 1 per cent of what there is to know about living matter on the planet. Ninety-five per cent of what we know is about inert, non-living matter – chemistry and genetics. The irony is that just as all these things, like information technology, transport and migration, are bringing our world together, we're facing an intellectual black-hole, a crisis in the state of knowledge!

'If we're going to survive the crisis, we've got to understand that we're part of a living cosmos, one informed by a higher consciousness. Our planet's evolving – it's facing a crucial stage of transformation – one which is only going to come about through mankind's positive intervention.'

The professor's mood darkened, and he became visibly upset. 'The role of "time-energy" in this transformation is crucial. It's a power that can be used for good or ill. That's what I need to talk to you about . . .' Russia had been in the forefront of research into psychotronic weapons, he explained. But ever since Soviet funding had dried up, this information had been in danger of falling into the wrong hands. The Americans had invited him over, rolled out the red carpet for him, he said darkly. But it soon became clear that it was the military potential of his research that interested them. He refused the funding.

The money was all in the West now, he went on. But people in the West were so far away from understanding such matters that they could not even take the prospect of psychic weapons seriously. The West's military was pursuing its own researches, of course, but so successful were they in keeping it secret that few people had any idea how close they were to being able to exploit its full 'diabolical potential'. The dangers of nuclear power paled by comparison, he hinted ominously.

In Russia, some of his former colleagues in this field had solved their financial problems by selling their knowledge, and not just for military purposes. The technology also had enormous therapeutic and healing potential. Every day people came from all over Russia to ask for his help. He was happy to give it, he said, but he would not accept money: to do so was to start on a slippery slope, to make himself vulnerable to all sorts of pressures. The question he had to ask me was this: did I know of any safe sources of funding in the West?

This time I refused a lift and travelled back down the hill to Novosibirsk on one bus after another to get back to Natasha and Igor's. I needed time to think. I liked the professor. He was an endearing figure. With his tanned face, and strong, stocky figure, he looked less like a scientist than an explorer from another, more innocent age. I had enjoyed hearing him talking about his intelligent universe. I had listened as if to a bedtime story, happily, uncritically.

But when I realised why he was talking to me so urgently I became worried. He was in trouble. He needed funding, and he really hoped I would be able to secure it for him in the West. But how? I tried to imagine how it would be if I went home, rang up my few rich friends and asked them if they would like to invest in a device which would connect them with the divine.

The professor was not asking me to understand, but to make a leap of faith. Had I lived in Russia (and not the Russia of Moscow and Petersburg, but this other Russia) I might have been able to. But I belonged in a different reality, as did Natasha and Igor. It was that problem of the golden woman again. As long as I was with the professor I almost believed that there was a golden woman hidden in the forests of Russia. But by the time I got back to London, she would have vanished, become the stuff of legend again.

Speaking Russian was one thing. Reaching across this gap between the two cultures – that I did not know how to do.

TICKET TO THE END OF THE EARTH

This morning I finally heard from Vera. As soon as I reached Novosibirsk, I sent her a telegram. I had not rated my chances of being invited highly, as Vissarion's community was notoriously secretive. But a week later I received a message, via Natasha's sister, that I was welcome.

Igor was working quietly at his computer. Natasha was visiting a friend in hospital. I took out a map of southern Siberia and considered the journey. First, I would fly to Abakan, a town on the River Yenisei south of Krasnoyarsk. Kuragino, where Vera was living, was the very last place marked on the map east of Abakan. I would have to travel on by a combination of bus and train. Beyond Kuragino the map showed no towns or roads, nothing but the wilderness of the Sayan Mountains.

Natasha had been begging me not to go. It was dangerous, she said. At first, I took her warnings seriously. After all, she was born and bred in Siberia. But when I pressed her, I could get nothing sensible out of her. 'It's just – it's the end of the earth. Daddy says that there'll be nothing but tractors out there! Stay here instead,' she wheedled. In Marx she had been a proud woman and guarded. Now she was clinging and slightly pathetic. The last thing I needed was Natasha's anxiety.

Another friend had just shown me an article about Vissarion's community in a national newspaper. It was an interview with a Petersburg woman who murdered her husband to escape from the community. She said her husband had fallen under Vissarion's spell after losing his job; that her only hope of keeping the family together lay in following him. Things had gone wrong from the start. The woman's teenage son had taken one look at the community and gone back home. She had not been able to stand the hard labour and the brainwashing. Why she had not just left was unclear. Instead, with money from the sale of their Petersburg flat, she hired two local men to kill her husband. There was a photograph of the murderer, looking young and vulnerable. I did not know whether to trust the story. It might be a pack of lies, but it was unsettling.

When I first met Vera in Saratov, the newspapers were sympathetic to Vissarion. But latterly, the coverage had turned nasty. The idea that Russians should be free to choose their form of belief was deeply alien. Until the Revolution, Russian nationality and Orthodoxy were considered synonymous. Now the Church was trying to reclaim that monopoly. Press reports usually bracketed Vissarion's cult together with one called the Great White Brotherhood. In the early nineties, the Brotherhood's undernourished, white-clad teenage converts were a common sight on the streets of Russia's cities, importuning passers-by. Its fate was comical and tragic. Its 'living god', an ex-Komsomol girl who called herself Maria Devi Christos, was rash enough to predict that the world was going to end on 24 November 1993. When it dawned, ten thousand of Devi's stripling devotees converged on the sect's headquarters in Kiev, causing mayhem in the city. Devi and her Svengali were imprisoned.

When Natasha arrived home she looked at Kuragino on the map. 'No, you absolutely can't go – you'd be mad! The tics are breeding! It's really dangerous! They're hungry for blood! I wouldn't go if you paid me!' The friend she had been visiting had come back from holiday in the Altai with a suspected tic bite. He was waiting to hear if it was infected.

'I'll be fine,' I reassured her. But her news worried me. I had forgotten about the Siberian tic. Over the last few decades an encephalitic virus was spreading through the tic population in Siberia. One bite from an infected tic could be fatal, they said. Every year, hundreds of people were paralysed and reduced to idiocy. For much of the year the tics did not bite much, but at breeding time they were dangerous. Briskly, I reminded myself that Vera was the most impractical person I knew. If she could keep out of the way of the tic, so could I.

All the same, by the time I went to buy my ticket to Abakan for the journey next day, I was rattled. Novosibirsk's airport for local flights was a grand neo-Stalinist building with outstretched wings and a classical portico. The May breeze blew a drift of white cherry blossom across the deserted asphalt. In Soviet days it might have been a hub of activity, but now flights were few and far between. The ticket office in the marble hallway was empty, and my appeals for help echoed round and round. Finally a young woman of enormous girth emerged from a back room. 'Come back on Monday!' she said, taking one look at my passport and shaking her frizzy head at me.

'Why not now?'

'It's impossible.' This was the old Soviet answer. Usually, it meant 'I'm in the middle of lunch.'

'I can't wait – I've been told that there are only two seats left.' This was actually true.

Then I realised what the problem was: she had never issued a ticket to a foreigner before. So I tried charm. It took her half an hour to make out the ticket. When she handed it over triumphantly I saw it was made out in the name of Mrs Smith. 'But that's not my name,' I observed mildly. The pleats of white lard round the young woman's neck suffused with pink. 'The form is correctly filled out!' she barked. I took a look at the dummy form from which she had been copying. The name on it was Mrs Smith. Patiently, I explained the problem. 'Don't worry,' she said, trying to sound in control. 'I'll be on duty. I'll get you through.' 'But what about my return journey? How am I going to explain that I have a ticket belonging to Mrs Smith?'

There was a long pause. I watched her struggling to come to terms with a world in which foreign women were not going to stand for being called Mrs Smith. In the end, she wrote me another ticket. It had taken an hour, but we both emerged triumphant. I had my ticket for tomorrow's flight. She had crossed her Rubicon into the new Russia.

What is more, the whole transaction was so funny that I had forgotten to be anxious.

THE RUSSIAN ORESTES

When Natasha told me how her father had made his living I thought yes, this was the source of her distress. But there was more to it than that, as I found when I returned to the flat from buying my ticket. Igor opened the front door a crack and peered out suspiciously. 'You! Natasha said you wouldn't be back for a week!'

Natasha had forgotten I was not leaving until the next day. This confusion was new, and alarming. While Igor sat working, she would be sitting around in a distracted state, chain smoking. Now she was fast asleep in the bedroom, breathing strangely. Igor admitted that once she thought I had gone she took four sleeping pills and washed them down with a bottle of brandy. She had been feeling unwell, he said.

That was how I discovered about Natasha's drinking. All that time in Marx she was drinking secretly, unbeknown even to Igor, who thought that she had given up. So that was what used to keep her out of the house all day in Engels Street. No wonder I found her so unfathomable. She really was a person in hiding.

Late that night, when she finally woke up, Natasha seemed almost relieved that her secret was out. While Igor kept working at his computer, she sat on the floor, pale and intent, her little-girl act forgotten, stroking her pregnant cat, telling me about her mother. A beautiful woman, she committed suicide when Natasha was eighteen. 'She's the forbidden subject in our family. But when I came back to Novosibirsk I wanted to know about her – to lay the past to rest. So I went round to see old family friends. What they said was terrible. "She was the curse of your father's life," they told me, "a horrible wife and a dreadful mother." I'd blanked her out – couldn't even remember what she looked like. Then I found some photos in Papa's flat – I was shocked to find how beautiful she was. She'd made our childhood into hell – one long series of rows, threats and ultimatums. She was convinced she was too good for my father and for the world she lived in. My father put up with it all, covered up for her. He felt we needed a mother – that even a mother like that was better than none at all.

'My sister had this lovely friendship with a boy of the "wrong type". Ma was convinced he was going to take her to some horrible cellar and rape her. She forbade my sister to see him. Then one day she saw them together in the street. That was it – she came home and made this ghastly scene – lying on the floor, banging her head. I was terribly rude to her. I couldn't stand her. Papa said, "You mustn't be rude to your mother!" He smashed his fist down on this glass table and broke it to bits.

'After that, Papa and I left. We looked for my sister everywhere, but she'd run away. Papa told my mother we were leaving. He said she could have the flat and everything in it, but we weren't coming back. I remember praying for her death.' There was a long pause. 'A week later she killed herself. I remember the tremendous sense of relief. But I knew I'd done it.'

So that was what was festering inside Natasha. She had killed her mother. Beside this, the discovery that her father had built arms factories paled. This was the guilt that pursued her like the furies, right across Russia. Even in her dreams her mother still followed her, Natasha confessed, beautiful and hateful, promising never to let her go.

Next day, Natasha came to see me off at the neoclassical airport. We had an hour to wait. We sat on a bench. The sun was shining and a brisk wind blew gusts of white blossom across the ravaged tarmac. The drivers were asleep in their cars. After last night's confession, Natasha was helpless and clinging. She was also coughing and had a temperature. I hated leaving her in this helpless state. I urged her to give up smoking, just for the week.

'Promise you'll do it.' I wanted more than that, of course. I wanted to jolt her into facing the trauma of her mother's suicide, which still seemed as fresh after twenty years as if it were yesterday.

'I can't,' simpered Natasha. She had told me that after her mother's suicide, her father behaved as though nothing had happened. I found that extraordinary. But perhaps he had no choice, belonging as he did to the city's Party elite? Part of the rationale for the state-controlled terror of the thirties was to shock people out of their private lives, so that the New Soviet Men and Women could advance into their radiant collectivised future.

'Come on – promise,' I said, referring to the smoking.

'What's the point?'

'Don't wallow.'

'What's the point of my working on myself? I'll become fat and healthy, full of energy, but what's the point of that? I don't believe in God – I can't think of any good reasons for going on living. You tell me why!'

'Why should I? Right now you wouldn't recognise a good reason if I gave you one.'

'You're horrid.' Natasha was simpering again.

'And you're a coward,' I retorted. 'Once you've faced your past you won't need me to tell you. You think you're clever, but you're just a bloody fool.'

'You're a sort of anti-Mephistopheles—'

'You think a bottle of brandy is some kind of answer.'

'Don't be beastly – it doesn't suit you—'

'Don't simper – it doesn't suit you. You're a strong woman – act like one.'

'You're after my soul!'

'Rubbish. Give up smoking – just for a week.'

As the little plane took off, Natasha stood on the asphalt waving. I hated the hectoring role I had taken with her. I felt as if Natasha manipulated me into it, as if she were using me as a catalyst for a process she could not manage on her own.

As the plane headed south-east, towards Abakan, I considered the other crisis Natasha and I had not been talking about. Natasha was not the only one who was feeling ill. I had also been having headaches and feeling sick. The reason was almost certainly a leak at the plutonium factory somewhere near the couple's flat. I heard about this only yesterday, from friends on the other side of town. There was nothing on the news, of course, and no one was being evacuated. But apparantly, when a Japanese group of scientists took their Geiger counter downtown the needle leapt so high that they refused to go any further. When I told Igor and Natasha they just laughed and changed the subject, rather too quickly.

Now, recalling that laughter, there was a steely edge to it. It sounded like stoicism, but it was despair. They had nowhere else to go. One reason Natasha had got drunk yesterday, I guessed, was that here in Russia alcohol was regarded as an antidote to radioactivity.

No one was planning to close the leaking factory, far from it. It was the one arms-related factory still operating in the city, kept going by orders from France. No one was even complaining. In fact, everyone seemed to agree that the city was a good deal safer than before: until recently, radioactive waste was still being taken away in open lorries, through the densely populated old industrial area where Natasha and Igor lived.

That leak loomed in my mind, becoming a grotesque manifestation of all those corrosive secrets which had been kept for too long, the city's and those of Natasha's family. Natasha's father might even have built the leaking factory for all I knew. Perhaps the leak had already begun, even as we were lifting our glasses and toasting the old man's health in his finest Armenian brandy? I should have drunk a lot more of it.

A COUNTRY DOING COLD TURKEY

I was not looking forward to catching bus after bus for the next stage of my journey, from Abakan to Kuragino. But when the little plane touched down at Abakan airport Vera was there, to my amazement. Her heart-shaped face had filled out. She was plump and brown as a freshly baked bun. The ethereal radiance which once lent her a special beauty was gone. Instead, she looked happy.

She had made the long trek in by car thanks to a towering, red-cheeked, laughing young man with gladiator's shoulders and hands the size of boxing gloves. The gladiator's long-legged wife stepped out of the car and stood appraising me with amused curiosity, graceful in her cotton print frock.

Around the airport, the wide green plain bordering the huge Krasnoyarsk reservoir was studded with clumps of purple iris in full flower. We headed east, up wooded slopes and grassy hills towards the Sayan Mountains. Vera and I sat in the back, holding hands, hardly talking, for there was too much to say. I gathered that she had married again. Our companions were her new step-daughter and her husband. All three were in a holiday mood. They joked about Vera's hopelessness as a housewife. I had not known what to expect, but this cheerful normality came as a surprise.

'That's Shushensk, where Lenin married Krupskaya,' remarked Vera's stepdaughter as the car, innocent of brakes, sped past a church with a little spire. Lenin was exiled to Shushensk after being arrested with the proofs of a clandestine newspaper on him. He was still young. Reading about his life, you get the feeling that the beauty of Shushensk had tested his iron will as no punishment could have done. He even tried his hand at poetry. 'In the village of Shushensk, beneath the mountains of Sayansk,' the poem began. But he never got beyond that first line. Lenin swam and fished. When Krupskaya joined him, they hunted together and seem to have enjoyed something like an ordinary married life. Lenin took up chess, and played with his neighbour. So obsessed did he become with the game that when his exile ended he forced himself to give it up altogether.

Poor Krupskaya. Across Russia that summer the gossip was that her autopsy had revealed she was still a virgin. My Russian mother Elena's friend Rosa had heard this in circumstances which made it almost believable. After the war, when she was only eighteen, the KGB officer in charge of her at work used to offload on her the secrets it was his job to collect. 'He would come at night – no, there was nothing sexual in it. I suppose he chose me because I was so young and innocent, so much under his control. He knew most of it would make no sense to me. All I do remember was that story about Krupskaya's autopsy. Even I understood how dangerous it was. I was appalled – to have to carry that around with me, know-ledge that could wreck the life of anyone who heard it! I couldn't tell my friends, my family! He'd taken that into as account as well.'

On top of the hill above Shushensk, we got out of the car. In European Russia what oppressed me was the relentless ugliness. But this – this was altogether different. To the south and east, where we were heading, mountains stretched away as far as we could see, the far peaks capped with snow. I breathed in the pine-sharp air. Overhead the song of a lark reverberated as if we were standing under the cupola of some vast building. What if Lenin had gone on playing chess, I reflected? If he had succumbed to the beauty of this place? How different might Russia's fate have been?

Several hours of bowling over green, undulating hills brought us to a broad, brown river, still turbulent from its descent from the Sayan Mountains. We waited for the rusty ferry, which twisted and bobbed like a paper boat as it carried us over to Kuragino.

The town was built on a grid of streets lined with low wooden houses, each with its garden enclosed behind high fencing. As we pulled up outside one of these houses, a man with the face of a rural philosopher strode out to meet us. Volodya welcomed me kindly, but his eyes were wary.

In itself, their house was unremarkable, consisting of two large, light rooms looking on to the street and a mass of outhouses and storage rooms behind. It had electricity, but other than that it was unmodernised, having an outside privy, no running water and a large clay stove built into the walls between the rooms. But I could not believe my eyes. The contrast to that cluttered, dusty flat in Saratov could not have been starker. Here, everything was in its place, scrubbed and immaculate. The large vegetable garden behind the house was freshly dug and pale green shoots were already beginning to appear in the meticulously planted beds.

Vera and Volodya laughed at my amazement. When I arrived in Saratov, I remembered how Vera had taken me home and swept a path through the dust as she offered me her son's bed. How determinedly she had battled against the claims of domesticity, clinging on to music and poetry as if on to a life raft.

Now the couple gave me their living room to sleep in. As I went in to unpack I caught sight of Vera out of the window. She was in working clothes, planting out lettuces in the garden. I did not presume to join her. I had a feeling that I was very much here on approval, from Volodya's point of view. All afternoon Vera went on working in her vegetable garden. Yes, I got the point: this was how you achieved order, through sheer hard work. But it was tantalising not being able to talk to her.

I went out for a walk. It was a sunny evening. The dust roads were covered in drifts of apple blossom. Here and there cows with calves were grazing on the broad verges. Kuragino was a charming, sleepy town. Unlike Marx, it was not disfigured by neglect and shoddy workmanship. The carving above the windows of the wooden houses was elaborate and in good repair. Here in Siberia, unlike European Russia, that popular tradition was still very much alive. I thought of Natasha and her father in that radioactive hell, imploring me not to come here because it was too dangerous. The contrast to the decaying, dirty, dysfunctional ugliness of Novosibirsk was stunning. Small boys were herding the townspeople's cattle back into town. The herd walked down the broad main street, raising dust, each beast peeling off one by one as if in a slow, ritual dance, making its way down a sidestreet, waiting outside the high wooden gates of its home for the owner to let it in.

Russian writers have often evoked the delights of the countryside with sentimental eloquence. Usually they were city people, writing about summertime at the dacha. In practice, metropolitan snobbery about the provinces had always been corrosive. But since the fall of communism a few quite prominent literary figures had chosen to move out of the city into deep unspoiled countryside. Perhaps these were just individual choices. But there were deeper factors pointing towards a revival of interest in the great, neglected landmass of Russia. For a start, climate change was making Siberia more productive agriculturally. And of course the key to Russia's future revival, her great mineral wealth, lay not in the west, but here.

There were political undercurrents too. Leading nationalist figures were saying that the country's centre of gravity today lay not in European Russia but in Asia. They said that Novosibirsk should become Russia's new capital; that Moscow had sold out to the world order. The idea was being trailed that a partnership of second and third world powers, led by an Orthodox and Islamic coalition, should challenge the domination of the rich Western powers led by America. As yet, most people were too preoccupied by survival to be interested. But if Russia were to turn back towards autocracy, this might be the direction in which an ambitious future leader looked for a 'big idea' round which to rally people.

Vera kept working through the long summer evening, until we all met up for supper. The food was delicious, the vegetables so freshly picked that they tasted of the earth. Vissarion's people were not just vegans, I learned, they ate no meat, fat, dairy food, drank no alcohol, tea or coffee. When I congratulated Vera on her domestic skills she cast an agonised look at her husband's severe face. 'Volodya's the one you should be congratulating. He's the one who's had to put up with me – he brought up his family in a house which he built entirely himself.' She paused. 'He's been terribly patient, but when we were first together I went through this phase when I was even more hopeless than usual. I can't tell you, Susan – I nearly burned the house down. Twice . . .' Volodya's stern expression softened and he looked at his wife adoringly: 'In the end, I realised there was no point in shouting at her,' he said. 'I'd just have to take her as she was.' 'After that it passed,' Vera concluded. 'I can't explain it – it was as if he had to love me at my worst!'

Silence fell round the table. There was so much I wanted to know about Vissarion. But beyond explaining the community's dietary rules, no one had mentioned his name since I arrived. However, on the wall in the room next door hung a kitsch icon which boded no good. It was a framed photograph of Vissarion sitting against a studio backdrop of Tiepolo clouds, wearing a red robe, shoulder-length hair and a saccharine smile.

When the light began to fail we went to bed. Vera and Volodya were sleeping in the kitchen, leaving me the large room next door. There, the only signs of Vera's old life were a couple of small paintings by her talented son. There were hardly any books, and no sign of a tape deck or record player. Did Vissarion disapprove of music and books? If so, it would be a shame, as I had brought my hostess all the songs that Elena Kamburova had recorded since Vera left Saratov.

Soon, the sound of snoring came from the next room. But I was programmed to Natasha and Igor's nocturnal habits by now. On the window sill, a vase full of purple lilac filled the air with sweetness. I lay looking out of the window, luxuriating in the bright starry night over the Sayan Mountains, thinking about the craziness I had left behind me in Novosibirsk.

I thought about all those secrets which were leaking out there, and about the strange science which had been pursued on the quiet through the Soviet period by people like my professor. More than once on my journey I had felt as if my sanity were under assault. Now, gazing into the night I felt clear. At the moment, things were inside-out and back-to-front in Russia. But the craziness was not to be found in the obvious places. The people seeing those visions in Zarafshan were not the really crazy ones. Nor were the Old Believers, even if they did bury their televisions in the frozen earth. Nor was I, despite the fact that I had heard the forest singing. I knew little as yet about Vissarion's sect, but whatever the newspapers were saying, these sectarians were going to have to be very dotty to compete with the madness of life in mainstream Russia.

The true insanity had been there in that awesome experiment which Russia and its colonies had undergone, that imperial mission to collectivise the human soul; to own and control everything, from the natural world to every last word printed in the empire.

Today this was a country doing cold turkey, drying out from that experiment, from an addiction to control, to secrets, secrets, secrets. Things might seem to be all over the place, but people were recovering. Before the country could start to develop the first vestiges of a civil society, or institutions which respected the concept of the individual, much more time was going to pass and many more of those toxic secrets were going to have to be drained out of the poisoned body of the state.

THE SOCIETY OF ORIGINAL HARMONY

I was woken at dawn next morning by a loud thrumming outside the window. It was coming from a wooden box strapped on to a long, spindly pole. When a starling flew up to it, beak full, I realised what it was. There is a word in Russian meaning 'starling box'. I came across it as a student and remember wondering why on earth anyone would go to the trouble of building a nest for such noisy, intrusive birds. Now it made sense: the busy, gossipy sound was a rural alarm clock, a summons to get going, use every hour of daylight in this brief Siberian summer.

Outside the window stood an apple tree in full bloom. Recalling Vera's old life, cooped up in that dark, cluttered flat with a drunkard, I was happy that she had found this peace and beauty. But the kitsch photograph of Vissarion hanging on the wall was a reminder that I still knew nothing about this man and his cult.

Underneath the flowered curtain covering the doorway to the next room Vera's slippered feet were padding to and fro as she clattered around, preparing breakfast. Yes, she really was domesticated. It had rained overnight, and the air was sharp. I washed my face in rainwater from the tub and listened to the neighbours' pigs grunting behind the high solid wooden fencing.

Vera and I walked to the market. On the way, she pointed out a wooden house: 'One of the Decembrists was exiled here – that's his house.' Even here, on the edge of the wilderness, you could not quite escape the heavy boot of the Russian state. The moving spirits behind Russia's first attempt at revolution from above were officers. After driving Napoleon's Grande Armée out of Moscow, they ended up in Europe in 1814, parading in victory down the Champs-Elysées. Their tsar had gone on to preside over a Congress of Vienna which convened to stamp out the bacillus of revolution everywhere. But these young officers were already infected. Most were aristocrats, pampered young men who imagined that if only they could kill the tsar, 'justice' and 'freedom' would break out in Russia. Their rebellion in 1825 was an amateur affair and easily quelled.

Once their prison sentences were over, the rebels were consigned to perpetual exile in Siberia. Most made the best of it, starting schools where there were none, experimenting with crops new to Siberia, writing books and painting pictures. And Siberia rewarded them by adopting them as its very own aristocracy.

Kuragino's Decembrist was not like that. Alexei Tyutchev was not cut out for heroics. As a young man he belonged to Petersburg's elite Semionovsky Regiment. They mutinied because of intolerable conditions and were dispersed among other regiments. In the south, where he was sent, Tyutchev joined another secret organisation, the Society of Original Harmony. Its members were not aristocrats, but penniless country landowners, provincial civil servants, and officers like him. Had it not been for Tyutchev, the Society's members would have grown old talking freedom in their cups. But grander Decembrist friends from the old regiment got in touch with their old mate, and they all became embroiled in the Decembrist plot. In exile, Tyutchev married a local girl, took to drink and eked out a living on hand-outs from richer Decembrists.

That evening Vera, her husband and I walked across town for supper at the house of Vera's new stepson, Viktor. A modern bungalow, it stood on the edge of the town, looking out over a grassy plain that ended in an escarpment of sheer rock. Viktor's pretty young wife and Volodya's daughter, who collected me from the airport, had invited friends over. The house was tumbling with little children. Listening to Viktor's friend singing to the guitar, watching Vera dancing with the little children, I relaxed. There did not seem to me to be anything particularly cult-like about these people. No one had mentioned Vissarion all day, although the young women were keen to show me how well you could eat on a vegan diet. Perhaps Vissarion's community was more a 'lifestyle choice' than a cult? If so, it seemed like a sensible one: rarely since the fall of communism had I been anywhere in Russia where the mood was so carefree.

Only one person looked out of place. Viktor was pale and cadaverous and his head was shaved. Surrounded by these brown, happy people he looked as if he had just been released from prison.

Through the meal he kept up a morbid silence, his deep-set tormented eyes trained on me. As the women cleared away the dishes he moved closer: 'I was the first in the family to join Vissarion.'

'Really?'

'I wasn't even searching. A man at work left me Vissarion's *Last Testament*. The strangest thing happened. I just picked it up – I can't explain. I was filled with a kind of ecstasy – as if I recognised it all. Later, when I got to know more, I realised that I'd been alive in an earlier incarnation, when Christ was.' Viktor's father snorted and left the room, but Viktor was unperturbed. 'Do you know why I shaved my head? I wanted to be loved for the right reasons. All my life people have found it too easy to love me.' I tried to avoid looking surprised; there was little that was lovable about him now. He looked desperate, unattractive, a man trapped inside his skin.

'Russia is the most holy place in the world at the moment,' Viktor went on. His earnest tone had emptied the large, sunlit room. 'I know that in the West you think we're wild, and perhaps we are. But that wildness has protected our spirituality. In the West you have everything too easy. Outwardly our lives here are just like everyone else's. But what's going on inside – you've no idea. Time has changed pace – it's moving at a tremendous speed. The world is going to end. And only those who are completely open to God will survive. Those who are not will perish.' Viktor fixed me with his mesmeric unhappy eyes: 'Remember: there can be different paths. But there is only one Way.'

An uncomfortable silence followed. Unable to bear Viktor's tortured gaze, I looked out of the window. On the grassy plain a rainbow rose like a column into the sky. The rocky escarpment was glowing crimson in the evening light. There was something aggressive about Viktor himself which was not in tune with his words, or anything around him.

On the way home Volodya vented his irritation: 'Viktor's full of hot air. None of them were ever nobodies in their past lives – there were no shepherds or peasants. They were all Napoleons!' I liked Volodya's truculent response.

When we got back home, the sun was low over the crimson cliff that hung over the town. Volodya heated up the bathhouse.

As Vera and I sat in the sweltering heat of the wooden room she apologised for Viktor. 'Poor boy. All his life he was the golden one. Now he's suddenly turned out to be as mortal as the rest of us. The Teacher warned us about this. Once we got here, He said, our hidden faults would come to the surface. We have to face up to them, He said, if we're to move forward. It's not easy. Viktor's got a woman,' she whispered, as though whispering would lessen any betrayal of the family trust. The bathhouse, which was built out of railway sleepers, smelt of wood and tar. 'She has two children and she's left her husband. Viktor knows that if he leaves his wife he'll be giving up his children, whom he adores. He'd also be breaking the Teacher's fundamental rule: children have a right to a father and a mother, He says. How can Viktor, the golden boy, break up the family?'

There was so much more that I wanted to ask her about Vissarion. But we were both treading carefully. In the silence that followed the only sound was the creaking and sighing of the wooden sleepers as they swelled in the heat. Vera beat my back with birch twigs and the bathhouse filled with the smell of the forest after rain. No luxury that the new city Russians could buy could compare with this ancient delight devised by people contending with the harshest of climates and unremitting physical work.

We wrapped sheets around ourselves and ran outside to watch the sunset over the crimson cliffs. The sky round the crest of the hill was orange. A row of small grey and white overlapping clouds stretched across it like tutus in a corps de ballet. The brown eagles had flown back to their nests in the taiga and the starlings were quiet in their high-slung boxes. I breathed until my head swam.

That night, Vera and Volodya gave me a copy of Vissarion's *Last Testament*. I read late into the night. The style was high kitsch, the olde worlde language, with its numbered verses, a parody of the Bible.

So Vissarion was not just a prophet, or even the founder of a new religion. He was actually the Second Coming.

EATING CHILDREN

On Sunday, Volodya's daughter and son-in-law, the laughing young man with hands like hams, arrived early to collect us. We were going to spend the day in the heartland of Vissarion territory.

The community had its own spiritual geography, I was learning. Kuragino was where new arrivals and the faint-hearted recruits lived. The more committed people were the faster they progressed eastward, higher up the mountain. As they did, they acquired the skills required for their new life. This was one where they would live in harmony with the natural world, eating only what they could grow, wearing only what they could make. The heartland lay in virgin forest, at the furthest inhabitable point on the slopes of the Sayan Mountains, by Lake Tiberkul. There, beyond reach of roads, electricity and state hand-outs, Vissarion's men were starting to build his New Jerusalem, a wooden town whose radial design would eventually lead to a temple of white marble.

Our day started peacefully enough. We drove through valleys where red granite cliffs that fell in starched pleats alternated with grassy hills and birchwoods. The sun shone and the woods were a haze of flowers and blossoming shrubs. Standing on the edge of the trees I was tantalised by drifts of white spiraea, blue brunnera and lungwort. In the woodland clearings, the grass was speckled with pink peonies, white lilies, mottled fritillaries, sun-bright euphorbia and orange kingcups. Vera stopped me venturing further, on account of the Siberian tic, which was breeding and hungry for blood. The fields and villages were safe, but the woods were dangerous.

We drove over tumbling rivers, through ramshackle, dying Old Believer villages. Vissarion's community belonged to a vivid non-conformist tradition in Russia which went way beyond the Old Believers. Ever since the eighteenth century, such outlying regions had been a refuge for non-Orthodox believers. Some, like the Mennonites, Baptists and Adventists, were Western in origin. But there was also a profusion of home-grown sects, like the Dukhobors, Molokans and Sabbatarians. From the Tsarist Russian government's standpoint, the problem with these groups was that, like highly motivated minorities everywhere, they tended to thrive. Alexander Rozen, one of the Decembrists, records a striking instance of this in his memoirs. Exiled to Central Asia, he came across a group of sectarians who had set up a community called Outskirts in the province of Baku. Converts flocked to it. The government became so alarmed by its success that they founded a rival village nearby, which they called Orthodoxy. They offered people subsidies and tax benefits, cattle and agricultural machinery to settle there, and many did, including soldiers hand-picked for good character. Ten years later, as Rozen noted, Orthodoxy was a poor village, while Outskirts was thriving.

After a few hours' driving we reached Cheremshanka, the last settlement before the real wilderness began. The little village of wooden houses was framed by wooded slopes and steep green pastures. It was a spectacular site. The snow-capped mountains behind were much closer now. From here on, the taiga stretched unbroken for hundreds of miles.

We had arrived in time for the service at the little wooden church Vissarion's people had built. It was packed with handsome young people and children. They were dressed in colourful, idio-syncratic clothes, home-made fancy dress. The men, who had shoulder-length hair and beards, were wearing high-necked tunics and boots. The women wore long, bright dresses and elaborate hats. The service had a new age, ecumenical feel to it. Thankfully, there were no images of Vissarion; no one seemed actually to be worshipping him.

All might have been well had we not met up with two recent converts as we left the service. A queenly professor of folklore and her journalist daughter, they also lived in Kuragino. A lively conver-sation sprung up about the place of nonconformist religions in Russia's history. I did not notice that Volodya had dropped back. 'People talk as though spirituality died out in Russia during the Soviet period,' the professor was saying: 'That's not true, it just came out in different ways – love songs, for instance. They may be addressed to some Nastya or other, but they're not really about that at all.' As Vera responded excitedly, I caught a glimpse of the woman I had first met in Saratov, one who for all her unhappiness was alive with poetry, music and ideas.

The professor offered to show us a place which gave an idea of how Vissarion's New Jerusalem was going to look. We drove across the village with her and her daughter. Volodya stayed behind with his daughter and son-in-law. The little street of wooden houses took my breath away. We had stepped into an illustration from a book of Russian fairy tales. Vissarion's people were building in the traditional way, using whole trunks of bright birch wood. Every gable, ridgepole and window was encircled with exuberant carving which stood proud, like starched lace. Even the outdoor lavatory was built with the same virtuosity.

A handsome, deep-chested man with a long curly greying beard and hair emerged from a half-finished house with an axe over his shoulder. He showed us the community's first purpose-built workshop; by the autumn it would be full of wood carvers and women making Palekh lacquer boxes. In the New Jerusalem, he boasted, every man would build his own house, and live by his craftsmanship. As we returned to the car, the folklore professor told us that this *bogatyr* was a lieutenant colonel, an ex-Party man who had been pressured by his wife into joining Vissarion's people.

We arrived back to find Volodya in a deep sulk. Vera and his daughter cajoled him, trying to draw him out of his shell. But he had retreated into silence, refusing even to accept food. Sitting in the back of the car, shoulders hunched, long face shuttered, it looked as if his skin had shrunk, trapping the real Volodya somewhere out of sight.

On the long drive home, his daughter and son-in-law did their best to pretend nothing had happened, chattering brightly. Vera sat looking agonised while I cursed myself for not having been more sensitive. I had drawn Vera back into her old world, one where Volodya did not belong. When we arrived back home in Kuragino, Volodya refused to eat supper with us. In fact, as Vera admitted with pained amusement, he announced that he was not going to eat until I left. We agreed that this was not going to do him much harm, as I was catching the train back to Abakan next morning. But I felt helpless to close the rift that my presence had opened up.

For all that, it had been an extraordinary day. After Novosibirsk, with its abandoned factories, leaking plutonium factory and desperate people, Vissarion's people seemed like another race. Mostly, they were professionals – doctors, professors, army officers, artists and even a choreographer. Their faces were bright and open, alive with energy and excitement. Young and old, they looked healthy and handsome. So much for the rumours of malnutrition. The oldest man we met, a retired compressor operator, was the guardian of the new wooden chapel. With his gentle face and grey beard he looked like Tolstoy's ideal peasant. All these people had thrown up their jobs, sold their flats, cars and televisions, to start their lives again here.

Vissarion seemed to have taken bits and pieces from all the world's great religions. His was an apocalyptic creed: only by abandoning our aggressive materialism can the End be averted. No wonder he was anathema to the Orthodox Church: he was actually asking people to live out the ideals which the Church preached.

In Cheremshanka, we stopped at the house of a young couple with a large house which they built themselves. A slim young woman wearing army trousers and an improvised turban stopped her planting and asked us in for blackcurrant leaf tea. As she unwrapped her head to reveal a neck and shoulders covered in red bites, I asked whether those were tic bites. She laughed. How many people had died of tic bites in the community? 'None! I should know,' she said, 'I'm a doctor. Tics are the least of our problems.' The real menace came from the endless official commissions which trooped out to investigate them. There were parliamen-tarians from Moscow; local government officials, delegates from the Ministries of Health and Education. Each group came with its own remit, to examine different charges brought against Vissarion. 'Some are reasonable enough. They want to check that the kids aren't malnourished and that they're receiving a proper education. But most are quite mad. They rant on about us being kept here by force, being brainwashed. If anyone's brainwashed it's them. One lot came to investigate whether we were eating children!

'We had another "commission" just the other day. The man who came first must've been from the FSB,' as the KGB was now called. 'We asked him in but he was in a real state, sweating, eyes all over the place. So we stood by the gate and talked to him. In the end he ventured in, but he sat on the edge of his chair, ready to bolt at any moment. Later on, when he'd relaxed, he told us they'd warned him not to step into any house and on no account to accept anything to eat or he'd be poisoned! They'd shown him pictures of the rapids up there and warned him that we'd try and take him there.' Above the village the road came close to a sheer rock fall. We had stood there to enjoy the view of the white water breaking over the stones as it hurtled down from the mountains. 'They said that was where we pushed people off! So dumb – yet not quite so dumb. They knew we were bound to ask them up there as it's such a great view!'

She sighed. 'It was brave of him to drink tea with us – it's so easy to frighten people in Russia. When the others arrived he ran around like a boy with a new toy. You'd have thought he'd invented us.'

That night I lay awake, breathing in the lilac, struggling with my judgements. Vissarion's community was fundamentalist. He demanded total obedience. The urban, middle-class men and women who followed him had reverted to a pre-feminist view of the roles of men and women, and a conventional division of labour between the sexes, as they learned how to build houses and grow their own food. Worse still, Vissarion, this ex-traffic policeman, expected his followers to believe that he was the son of god. As for the red robes, the quaint olde worlde language and other kitsch trappings . . .

The issue of power was what bothered me about established religions, as well as gurus and spiritual leaders. What I had found so appealing about the Old Believers' relationship with their God was that, in Burny at least, it was direct, unmediated by priests. But ever since the schism, the dominant model in Russian culture had been different. Here, the tradition of power, whether secular or spiritual, was absolutist and centralised, and Vissarion belonged to that tradition.

On the other hand, this was only the second time in my travels through post-communist Russia that I had come across a community where people were not just happy and healthy, but basking in an overwhelming atmosphere of love. Everywhere else, people were fearful, crazed by the effects of social collapse. Except for the greedy few who got their hands on a fat slice of state assets, most people were living in an ever-anxious present, in a land where the future had disappeared.

Vissarion's people were inspired by purpose, too. They had accepted the challenge which mainstream society had yet to address seriously: they were exploring ways of living with nature. In this respect the market economy which won the Cold War was only marginally better than the communist model. Both treated the natural world as if it were an adversary, to be 'dominated'. Perhaps it was a distraction to snipe at the style and beliefs of Vissarion's community. This was an experiment which deserved respectful attention.

I feared for the community, however. The anxiety of the Orthodox Church at the notion of any kind of free market in spirituality was about to result in a Law on Freedom of Conscience and Religious Association coming on to the statutes. The main thrust of this measure was to confirm a special status on the Orthodox Church, along with Russia's Buddhists, Muslims and Jews, and to deny legal rights to any religious associations that could not prove that they had been based in Russia for at least fifteen years. Decisions on these issues were put into the hands of unknown bureaucratic committees against which there was no appeal.

The move was driven by an established Church which traditionally enjoyed a virtual monopoly over Russian 'souls'. The law was calculated to hit foreign faiths and home-grown 'totalitarian' sects equally. So far no move had been made against Vissarion's community. But how much would it take for a disgruntled local priest or official to start up a chain of events that would wipe out this latest attempt to build the New Jerusalem?

I woke up to a blinding light. Someone was dragging off the bedclothes, pulling up my nightdress. Through a haze of sleep I saw Vera leaning over me in her dressing gown. She was barefoot, her hair loose, furrows between her eyes. It was dark outside. She was feeling me all over, between my legs, under my arms, in my hair. 'Don't worry,' she said.

She was looking for tics, she said. In the middle of the night, a tic had bitten her on the neck. I was suddenly awake, heart pounding. Was Vera's bite encephalitic? Only time would tell. As usual she was blaming herself: 'It's my fault. I'm so careless. I didn't search myself before going to bed, or you . . .'

After that, I lay watching Volodya's shadowy figure through the cloth that hung over the doorway. He was busying around in the kitchen, tending to Vera. There was nothing I could do to help. He had sucked at the bite and smothered it in sunflower oil as thick as duck fat. She had drunk her urine, which was said to help combat the poison.

We lay in the dark in our adjoining rooms. The minutes passed with excruciating slowness. Soon, the dawn would come, and the paralysis would either set in or not. The town seemed to be held in a spell of silence. There was no known antidote to the bite of the encephalitic tic. Now and then Volodya and Vera whispered to one another. As long as Volodya stays in bed, I told myself, she's all right. By breakfast time we would know.

I understood the facts by now: this spring the local radio warned people that there were more infected tics than ever. No one was to go into the forest in the breeding season. More than 300 people had died this year . . . three hundred out of what, I found myself wondering. The community, Kuragino, Siberia?

It was growing light now. The starlings were chattering in their high box. In the room next door, nothing was stirring. Volodya was right to blame me; I had distracted Vera. She was a city woman and living, just living here, required every bit of her energy and attention. Vera would never have gone near the woods but for me. She came after me, to fetch me back. But I had not been able to resist the beauty of those flowering shrubs, so many familiar from my garden in England. If anything happened to her it would be my fault.

SINGING CEDARS?

Next day, Volodya came with Vera to see me off at the station. The tic bite was not malignant. Volodya was so relieved that, once he could see that I really was leaving, he had forgiven me.

The train from Kuragino back to the lowlands was crowded. In the hard-class carriage, men lay on the high bunks like fallen statues. On the seats below, people sat crushed together in silence, shoulders sagging, faces set in masks of resignation. After the pure mountain air, the fetid air of sweat and dirty hair in the compartment was a shock. The contrast to those handsome people up in the mountain with their pink cheeks, fancy dress and improbable beliefs was even more of one. Outside the train windows the snow-capped Sayan Mountains danced in and out of sight. Escarpments of crimson rock reared up. The river water hurled itself over the rocks towards the valley below. But none of my companions so much as glanced out of the window.

Everyone in the carriage was eating. In contrast to Vissarion's people, they were all too fat. They ate ritualistically, at every opportunity. They ate in order to forget what they had just been doing and in order not to think what they were about to do. The offer of food was a ritual of seduction whose origin was lost, overtaken by the urgent need for solace. These days they ate wherever they were, on planes, on buses, on the streets, I had been noticing. At bus stops they ate sweets. Walking down the streets they ate bananas. Once they reached the sanctuary of a bench they whipped out a little cutlet, a sausage or a boiled egg, wrapped up and brought from home. And through long days that lurched between being too hot and too cold for comfort, they heaved their heavy white bodies, vanity overtaken by a more deeply rooted yearning.

In the corridor, a group of young girls in platform heels were playing pop songs on a tape recorder. I thought about the new songs by Kamburova which I brought Vera. I knew how much the singer's music meant to her. But she had tucked the tapes out of sight, and not mentioned them again. At first I assumed that Vissarion disapproved of such music. Then I blamed Volodya's touchiness. But perhaps there was another explanation.

Last night Vera told me how hard she had found it to adjust to her new life. 'But the longer I spend here, the crazier life in the city seems to me – all those people buying labour-saving devices so that they can rush to work, sit out their time there and rush back home exhausted to their families. What's it all for? Here the rhythm's different.'

Watching Vera kneading dough, her forearms covered in flour, I understood why she no longer needed Kamburova's music. Beautiful though they were, the songs were all about loss and grief, and she was happy now.

Her days were busy with the very chores she used to hate so much. They were no longer a distraction, but a discipline. That was the secret at the heart of all contemplative religions. Did it matter what Vissarion called himself if he brought about that kind of change in people's lives?

Back in Novosibirsk, I climbed the dark staircase to Natasha and Igor's flat uncertainly. I was not confident of my reception. I regretted having taken such a high-handed tone with Natasha, my Orestes, in flight from her furies.

I need not have worried. The cat had not yet given birth. But apart from that, it might have been a year, not a week, since I had seen Natasha. Her broad features had cleared. Her snub-nosed, high-cheekboned face looked vivacious, younger. She brushed aside my apologies. 'Nonsense – I'm glad you were so rude. It's just what I needed.' She was still smoking. But she had taken more drastic action. She had tracked down a therapist whom she had known since she was young. 'He was a star, quite different from these quacks with their miracle cures. He was dedicated, a sort of holy man. I found him terribly aged. He was only nine years older than me, but his beard and hair had gone grey. He'd used himself up helping his patients.

'Amazingly, he even remembered me. He said I'd have to let go of it all. He tried hypnosis and it all came pouring out. I could see it all so clearly. I could see you too – you were everywhere. You were right when you accused me of being afraid. I've been running away. And suddenly I can face it. I see why you wouldn't tell me what the point of living was. You were right. I've kept thinking about the word for 'fate' – *sud'ba*. I used to think it meant what's been doled out to you – lifeline, stars and all that. But that's wrong. What it means, quite literally, is God's judgment.'

Natasha had actually been quite ill, Igor confirmed. 'And while I was in bed I had this frightful dream,' Natasha said. 'I was surrounded by bears with great black auras. They were like the bears in the fairy tales. They had people inside them. But there was nothing sweet about them.'

After her first session with the doctor, she tried to persuade Igor to visit him. He refused. He too, she told me now, was haunted by the ghost of his mother. She had also been a raging beauty, cold as sin. Behind her back everyone had called her 'Mme SS'. She refused to divorce Igor's father, who loved another woman. In the end his father escaped by committing suicide. Instead, Natasha dragged a young friend of theirs to the doctor. 'He's another victim of the mothers. His is psychotic – she's sucking the life out of him. He's handsome, talented and decent. But she won't even let him go out with a girl!' The doctor agreed. 'He said the woman should be put away and never let out. They should all have been locked up, the mothers – Igor's, mine and that lovely boy's. The deadly mothers. The boy's life'll improve. But can he ever be normal? Can Igor and I? That's the question.'

Next day, I travelled west again, leaving Natasha, that talented, dynamic woman who had spent years destroying herself. I was hopeful. For the first time all those different Natashas – the golden one, the dark star and the pathetic little girl – had a chance of coming together. With the help of her holy man she might even be able to confront her past.

Natasha had other news for me, too. Before leaving for Kuragino, I told her about our expedition to the Old Believer village, and about the music I heard in the forest. She was visibly struck by what I said. It reminded her of something, she said. While I was away, she had remembered what it was. She had read an interview in the local paper with some old woman called Anastasia who lived on her own for years in the Siberian forest. Every now and then she would hear the Siberian cedars 'singing' to each other. The music was her delight, her reason for living in the forest. What's more, 'She said that only some people could hear it!'

That was all Natasha could remember. She did not even know what paper the article was in. But what she told me was enough. So I really had heard the cedars singing.

THE TWELVE-STEP CURE

On my way back from Siberia I passed by Saratov to visit my friends. Last time I saw Anna she was in an exalted state, acting the *passionara*. Despairing of democracy, she was bent on exposing the corruption of Saratov's deputy mayor, whatever the danger to herself. Now that I knew more about the Eurasians whose thinking inspired her I had come to share Misha and Tatiana's concerns.

Every time I arrived in Saratov, my heart sank. The old city centre was looking more dilapidated. Rubbish overflowed the bins, the streets were all holes and the appearance of the odd new shop mocked the surrounding shabbiness. Most depressing was the contrast between the shabby, sad-faced pedestrians and the ebullience of the men and women I met in Vissarion country.

For all this, my friends were surprisingly buoyant. Tatiana had just given birth to a baby daughter, whom they christened Nadezhda, which means hope. The family was living in Saratov now – and the rift with Anna was a thing of the past. Indeed, Misha and Anna were closer than ever.

By way of celebrating my arrival Misha took Anna and me, his daughter Polina and her friend out of town for a picnic by the Volga. There was a new authority about Misha. Business was booming. Having taken the risk of going into manufacturing before inflation was low enough to make it profitable, the gamble had paid off. His virgin sunflower oil cost twice as much as anyone else's, but it was good. It tasted of sun and nuts and people were prepared to pay. With sixty people on his books, Misha was now Marx's biggest employer. Although he had started without capital, he had a head start on his competitors.

Anna had been through a tough time. Her newspaper, *Saratov*, was in serious financial trouble. She was put on short-time and forced to take work wherever she could find it, collecting material

for opinion polls. Her outgoings were minimal, since she lived a
monastic life in her hostel. But she admitted that sometimes she
was barely able to keep herself fed. That period was clearly over
now, though what caused the change I did not yet know. I was
curious. But I knew Anna better than to ask. She would tell me
what she wanted to, in her own good time.

At a casual glance, she looked little changed: she still wore her
hair in a tonsure which framed her grave brown eyes with their
blue-tinged whites. She still walked as though facing into her own
private gale, head down, striding. But the force-field of tension
around her had died down. It was only occasionally now that I
felt her alarm, flapping like the wings of a wild bird. She was
much better dressed, too. Indeed, all in all, she was looking rather
handsome.

On our way to the Volga we drove through the outskirts of
Marx, through the area they called New Thieftown. Since my last
visit brand-new buildings had sprouted up. They were fantastical
in design, towered, turreted, indiscriminately arrayed with arches,
pillars, dormers, mansard roofs, windows French, oriole and gothic.
'Each time the builders start work on a new building we try and
find out who they belong to,' Anna commented. 'But they put the
builders under oath to say nothing – and the paperwork always
credits ownership to some Ivanov, or pensioner aunt.'

Misha finally stopped the car in a meadow studded with tiny
white and yellow flowers. The floodwaters of the Volga had just
died down. The mass of inlets which fissured the landscape on
this low eastern bank were still full of water. On a finger of dry
land between two inlets, two men were harpooning their quarry
with long-handled forks as the fish spread their eggs in the
shallows.

It was the first picnic of the year. The sun was shining. The
branches of the trees were still bare, but even before the buds
burst, an aura of green hung round them. Although the air was
cool Anna stripped off down to her lime-green bikini and offered
her long pale shanks to the sun. We all wandered around, collecting
driftwood for the bonfire. Above our heads, a cloud of gnats filled
the air with a ringing tone, and from the nearby willows a chorus
of frogs were singing in contralto bursts. Such moments of beauty
were rare in European Russia, where the most beautiful places
had been despoiled by man's messy pursuit of an unrealisable idea.

As we hauled our wood back to the fire I ventured to ask Anna how her crusade against corruption was going. 'I can't bear it when journalists play at false heroics,' she growled, slamming the door shut on further questions. 'There are risks in journalism, of course, but you have to be realistic.' Realistic? Anna? She had taken the job of law correspondent at the newspaper. I understood that she started to thrive from that moment on. Indeed, last year she was voted one of the twenty best journalists in Russia by the Writers' Union. 'I'm not even a member!' she said crossly, and I understood that she was just trying not to sound too proud.

That was not all. *Izvestia* asked her to become their full-time correspondent in the city. She refused: she was quite happy where she was, thank you. What a sweet moment that must have been, considering how some years ago the paper had asked her up to Moscow for a trial, then failed to offer her a job. Now, in her capacity as law correspondent she earned more than any other journalist on the staff. Finally, most importantly for her, her poems were being recognised: the city's literary journal, *Volga*, was publishing them regularly.

At this point, I embarrassed Anna by bursting into tears. I felt so proud. It was paying off, the long, slow bet I had placed on these intelligent, decent young provincial Russians. The way their lives were progressing bore out my growing conviction about the country and its post-communist time of troubles. Despite the chaos – indeed because of it – it was proving an enormously creative time on the level of individual lives. While the country's leaders flailed around, behaving reprehensibly, on the level of ordinary people something important was beginning to happen, something on which Russia's future depended. Anna and Misha did not count as remotely ordinary – they were too smart. But in one sense they were. For they both started with no advantage but native wits and education. Where they led, others could follow. Given time, people who did not have their natural advantages would also start recovering from their addiction to state control. They would lose that terrible obedience to the state which was Russia's curse. The frightened little person who sits inside every Russian was starting to shrink. Russia's people had started their twelve-step cure. It was early days yet, the trees were still bare, but the aura of green was there.

Later on, at Anna's office I would leaf through her recent articles, observing the common thread now running through her work. She was keeping up a sustained attack on the popular sentimentality for 'the good old days' which had started to settle in. She was educating people about themselves and their past. Here she was interviewing an old man who was a prosecutor during the Khrushchev years. He was haunted by the memory of sending a man to the camps for ten years for complaining about bread rationing: 'I knew the worker was right. But I kept my protest to myself . . .' Nothing had happened to change Anna's view that fascism was creeping in. But rather than offering herself as a despairing sacrifice she was working to ensure that if this time came again the Russian people would be better able to resist it.

Recently, when a gang in Saratov gunned down eleven young rival gangsters with sub-machine guns, the shock waves reverberated right round Russia. The national press blamed capitalism, and demonised the thugs, assuming that they belonged to a criminal underclass. But Anna tracked down their parents. She found that these 'demons' were children of the old Soviet proletariat, communism's favoured class. They still lived at home; washed their hands before meals and gave their mothers flowers on Mothers' Day. She wanted her readers to understand what had happened to these young people. When the economy collapsed, their sudden descent from privilege into poverty was more than they could cope with. They responded by helping themselves to what they were brought up to think was theirs by right.

I went out and bought a good bottle of wine: I wanted to celebrate Anna. In the old days, we had both been culpably wishful. But she was now using her journalism to encourage her readers to acquire the basic tools needed if that missing civic space were going to be built in Russia. It was going to take time, a long time. But if politics were going to change here, ordinary people were going to need to develop a new take on individuality, one which vastly increased their sense of the rights and responsibilities due to the individual.

Now, as we sat on the flower-studded water meadows, something began to stir far away in the steppe. Minutes later, the wind was on us, gusting through the trees. The poplars were dancing and the tops of the willows and birches swaying. But here on the ground, the air was quite still. Then, as suddenly as it had come, the wind moved on and a gust of rain swept in, sending us diving for shelter.

The rain stopped as abruptly as it started, and we gathered round the bonfire to drink beer and eat salt fish. On the bonfire, Misha was cooking long kebabs which we threaded on to stripped green branches. His boyish face had filled out and he looked confident and, for a moment, almost relaxed. When we first met, there was little to distinguish him from all the other young men who were trading in anything they could lay their hands on. I did not yet understand what it was in the circumstances of his life, or parentage, that stiffened him for success. His rarest quality, it seemed to me, was his faith in the future. Fortune favours those who can imagine a future when others cannot.

Right now he was in a rage. He had just been turned down by the local authorities for the only loan he could afford. 'They took one look at our application, assumed we were just traders, and turned us down! It's outrageous! I'm just the kind of entrepreneur Russia needs! I'm making something really essential – and my money's all here! But they just treat us with contempt. In fact we're the only source of money they've got to pay all their taxmen and policemen. Do you know we've now got four hundred policemen in Marx – yes, in the town alone! They squeeze us and squeeze us.

'No matter how hard I work, I'll never be able to live as well as the most piddling of these bureaucrats. It's not that they earn much, but boy do they steal! It would be OK if they robbed in moderation, but their greed for other people's money is bottomless. Who is it that lives in castles and drives foreign cars around here? It's the officials. And when they've lined their own nests, they go on to house their parents, to set up their kids, their cousins and aunts! They don't just take money, they take anything – building materials, workmen – anything!'

'Ah well, at least the young don't have illusions any more,' Anna said, looking over at Polina and her friend, who had tuned into some music on the car radio, opened the car doors, and were dancing on the flower-studded grass.

Anna accompanied me to the railway station. It was growing dark as we stood on the platform. A man was going down the train, tapping the wheels, testing for metal fatigue, just as he was doing a century ago, when Anna Karenina watched him before throwing herself under the wheels of the train.

There was no one else in the four-bunk compartment of the sleeper. In the old days, the train would have been full. We would have shared food, stories, jokes and fears. Now only the rich could afford to travel. As the train prepared to leave, my friend who had always seemed so allergic to intimacy was affectionate as never before. She gave me a book, on the first page of which she had written: 'Sometimes you find that you are much closer to a person who was born on the other side of the world and who speaks a different language than to those you live alongside.'

The train set off into the night, over the long-suffering Volga countryside. 'I think that you are a-little-bit-me,' Anna had once written to me, when she barely knew me. I was moved by her words, moved enough to return to Marx. But I did not understand what prompted them. Now I had come to love this difficult, intelligent, intractably honest woman and to share her feeling that in some mysterious way our lives really were connected.

MUSIC OF THE SPHERES

For a long time I barely dared open up the memory of that music I heard in the forest. But it had gone on resonating in my mind, that glorious chord which sounded as if all the choirs of Russia were singing at once, hidden in the trees. Natasha's story had reassured me. It allowed me to own my experience again.

At the start of my journey, I had dreamed about travelling to a strange city full of totemic objects where I communicated with people in trochees and spondees. The reality had been even stranger than that dream. How could trees sing? I made desultory attempts to find out, but I had no idea where to look.

Then, in the course of the winter, I came across a clue in a footnote in a remaindered book. It was about a waterfall in western Mongolia which was said to 'sing'. Herds of wild animals would come there to listen. People came too, from all over Mongolia, students of *hoomi*, the native tradition of throat singing. They came to learn from the waterfall.

Back home, I went to hear a group of visiting *hoomi* singers from southern Siberia. Their wild rhythmic music, the songs of a herding people who lived and slept under the sky, were interspersed with high light ringing sounds that seemed to take on a life of their own. Though the sounds were strange, the intervals were familiar. That was when I understood. The *hoomi* singers had perfected the art of teasing out the harmonics in a single, sustained, guttural note, using the cavities of the head to amplify the sound. What I heard in the forest were natural harmonics.

Pythagoras is credited with being the first to start exploring natural harmonics in a systematic way. After hearing the sound of a hammer striking an anvil, he observed the intervals of the overtones released by that blow. He worked out the mathematics of the ratios involved, and explored their significance for geometry and astronomy.

*   *   *

What was it that had produced the music I heard as I stood in the Stony Tunguska River, with the Siberian forest stretching for miles around? Had the receding outboard motors of the Old Believers' dinghies, or the approaching plane, triggered the harmonics of the forest, setting every cedar for miles around ringing with sound?

I began to become aware of the harmonics around me, aware that everything from planets to plants, wind to engines, was in a state of constant vibration. One night on the radio I heard a snatch of music from Fontenay Abbey, in France. It was a single bass voice, singing low sustained notes. The singer was releasing silvery scarves of sound that floated on the air, bursting into harmonic cadences. That was when I realised that the art of playing with the harmonics of the voice, which those *hoomi* singers had preserved, was integral to the great European tradition of sacred singing in the Middle Ages. So much so that some of the architects of the monasteries had even learned how to build in such a way that the church would act as a resonating chamber, triggering those harmonics. All this we knew once and then forgot.

My travels in the unravelling Soviet reality had taken me a long way off the map of my known world. Again and again I had come up against things I could not describe, because I did not understand them. Doing so had made me despair, for what kind of a writer was I if I could not lassoo the reality around me into words? But now I began to accept that I did not need to understand everything. Even as I grasped what that music was, I also realised how little understanding mattered. What did was the music, those vibrations of the Big Bang, the sound of life itself. Plato and the classical world had regarded it as the music of the spheres. This was where thought and language gave way to silence. But 'For most of us,' as Eliot put it,

> there is only the unattended
> Moment, the moment in and out of time,
> The distraction fit, lost in a shaft of sunlight,
> The wild thyme unseen, or the winter lightning
> Or the waterfall, or music heard so deeply
> That it is not heard at all, but you are the music
> While the music lasts. These are only hints and guesses,
> Hints followed by guesses . . .

1998

LOOKING FOR MOTHER OLGA

———◦————

When I returned to Russia that September, the financial crash had only just happened. I was seriously worried for my friends, whose lives were just starting to sort themselves out. Would this catastrophic blow have sent them flying?

In the event, Anna, Natasha and Igor had no money to lose, as they reminded me wryly. All three were unaffected. As for Misha, the last time I saw him he had been complaining how desperate he was for capital, how no one would give him a loan. But he had come through the crisis precisely because he had no capital, and had borrowed no money.

In Moscow, however, the lives of Ira and her new husband, Sasha, had been shattered. Since they started working together, their production company had been expanding fast, employing ever more people, turning out a stream of documentaries. The couple were a familiar sight on the Moscow social scene, at film premières and chic restaurants. They were successful and glamorous: tall Sasha, his Nordic good looks set off by a tailored Nehru jacket; Ira, slim and swan-necked, flamboyant in a miniskirt and thigh-length boots. They spent their summers in their house in Hungary, on the shores of Lake Baloton, and they were building a fine house in Moscow, in a gated com-munity on the city limits. Sasha was just about to buy his own regional television channel, and had borrowed the money to do so.

The collapse of the market in August left Sasha with colossal debts. Both houses were instantly sold off to pay their creditors, as were all but the couple's most basic possessions. When I stayed with them in the small, dark basement boiler-room where they had found shelter Ira was the one comforting me: 'Look, don't worry – it's only money! We'll pay it back, however long it takes. We're lucky – we love our work.' Her chief concern was clearly for Sasha's health. I marvelled at Ira's stoicism. But Sasha's gaunt face told its own story. It was not just his health that worried me. He was no longer young, and his creditors were threatening him, intimating that they would get their money by fair means or foul. The country was back on its knees again. Now that Chechnya had won de facto independence in the first round of its war with Russia, people were worried about the possibility of Russia breaking up. What if other ethnic minority enclaves, like Tatarstan, were encouraged to secede from the Federation, they fretted? What if Siberia, with all that mineral wealth, decided to make a break for it?

Back in London, I had been reading about the emergence of a different manifestation of regional identity. A Keston Institute report suggested that paganism had survived as a coherent faith in parts of Russia; indeed, that one Finno-Ugric ethnic minority on the Volga near Kazan had even considered adopting it as their official religion after the fall of communism. I wondered whether Anna, who was a journalist in a Volga city to the south, knew anything about this. When we met up, I asked her. She burst out laughing: 'Paganism! What a load of nonsense!'

I was not so sure. I wanted to go there and see for myself. For a start, Russia's peasantry was well known to have clung on to its pagan beliefs for centuries after Christianisation, practising what they called *dvoeverie*, or 'double faith'. Besides, when it came to Russia, I had given up believing that because something was implausible, it was necessarily untrue. No one travelling in Russia since the fall of communism could have failed to notice how, once ordinary people could no longer afford Russia's health service, they had turned back to their traditional healers, the old peasant women, for help. The pages of Russia's newspapers were peppered with small ads which offered to see off your rivals in love or business by means of a good, old-fashioned curse.

However, in the light of Anna's reaction, I told Ira of my plan rather tentatively. Her response was different. Earlier in the year, she had been filming among one of those Finno-Ugric Volga minorities, the Mordvins, and she was amazed to find people so deeply in thrall to the old peasant healers. She even remembered the name of one of the wise women, Mother Olga, whom the locals talked about with particular reverence. Indeed, if I really wanted to go, she would be happy to come with me.

So off we went, in search of Mother Olga. We took the overnight sleeper east from Moscow, heading for Saransk, the main city of the autonomous republic of Mordovia. The Finno-Ugric Mordvins were one of a group of non-Slav ethnic minorities that had been living on the Volga since long before the Slavs came to the steppes. Over the centuries, most of these minorities had eventually converted to Christianity. The Mordvins had held out longer than most, until the seventeenth century or later.

One of the bunks in our compartment was taken by a pale, hollow-chested young lieutenant returning home on leave from Murmansk. As luck would have it, he lived not far from Mother Olga's village, and had heard of her. 'Not my scene,' he said condescendingly. Of course, when he joined the army he left all that behind; became part of modern Russia. But Ira persisted. 'Ma's into all that,' he conceded. 'But you can forget about her – Mother Olga's given up seeing people. Her son was killed in a motorcycle accident – well, they called it an accident.' It happened right after she used her mysterious powers of divination to help the police identify a murderer belonging to one of the local mafias. Before we even arrived, our one fragile lead had broken off.

Did he have any other suggestions? 'Dunno,' he said, turning his back on us. 'But Ma did mention some woman in Chamzhinka.' When the train arrived in Saransk next morning we looked for a taxi. 'Woman in Chamzhinka?' the driver on the platform pondered. 'Must be Alla Stepanovna. Been there with the wife.' Was he playing us along? There was no knowing. As he headed out of town he reminded us that the Finno-Ugric Mordvins belonged to two tribes, the Moksha and the Erzya. Chamzhinka was Erzya country.

After bowling through rolling countryside of fields and woods, we reached the outskirts of a small town. The car slewed off the road on to a mud track flanked by half-built houses, each sporting a comical array of architectural features, expressive of their owners' long-thwarted individuality. The building outside which we stopped was different. It was cobbled together out of bricks and concrete, festooned with trailing cables. There was no placard, nothing to suggest that this was the house of a well-established folk healer. In fact, the place seemed deserted. We rang the doorbell long and hard, but there was no reply. Still, it was only breakfast time. Exploring the building, we opened a door at the side. The dark basement was full of people. They were packed round two trestle tables, dressed as if for church. We waited outside. It promised to be one of those golden September days which often come just before the Russian winter sets in. 'Women's summer', they call it; when it arrives, it is like a consolation, a promise to hold on to through the dark months. In the gardens around us, the boughs of the trees were heavy with apples and cherries. We had come to the *chernozyem*, the belt of fertile black earth which runs up from southern Russia in a broad north-easterly belt.

People were busy harvesting potatoes and fruit. But in the healer's garden there was nothing but weeds, rubbish and a rusting generator. A mongrel bitch and her puppy came and sniffed our legs. Presently a middle-aged man with a cherubic face framed by grey curls came out, peered at us through the tinted glasses on the end of his nose, and went back in.

As the sun moved higher, the people in the basement started to join us, settling on planks, stumps of wood and upturned buckets. We swapped symptoms and troubles, shared food and fizzy drinks from the local store. Some were clearly seriously ill, people on whom the doctors had given up. A sad-eyed woman called Masha, who had brought her tearful daughter, told us about her previous visit. She had slept overnight in the basement with a group of people, waiting for a session. But next morning, Nina Stepanovna chucked them all out: during the night someone crapped on the healer's front door step. 'Who'd have done that?' I asked. 'A sorcerer,' whispered a frail old man who was kneading bits of bread into balls and popping them into his mouth.

'They're always trying to get Nina Stepanovna,' Masha volunteered. 'She's white, they're black,' she said, spelling out the obvious for these outsiders who understood nothing.

'It's war!' said a babushka in a red headscarf. 'Always was – always will be. There's one near me keeps devils under her floorboards!'

The sun was high by the time the healer's cherubic emissary appeared again. Briefly, he sawed at a piece of wood, then lost interest and stood in the sunshine, enjoying his status as 'her' husband: 'Hang on. She's having a cuppa. My advice is – don't cross her. The tongue on her!'

Finally, the healer appeared. She was short and shapeless and wore a flowered housecoat. She had an enormous frog-like mouth. 'Whadda you think?' she said, nodding proudly towards her man. 'Not bad-looking is he, my Yura?' Then she returned to the house. Clutching his grey curls, as if to say 'I've done what I can,' the cherub followed her.

The patience of the waiting group amazed me. No one even ventured to ask the healer why we were waiting. By mid-afternoon one young couple started looking restless; their daughter would be on her own at home. 'Don't leave – you can stay the night in the basement,' said Masha. They were not convinced. The basement was a damp concrete box with a tiny window, trestle tables and a few narrow benches. We were sad to see them go; after the hours of waiting they were no longer strangers. No sooner had they left than the healer beckoned us all into the basement. 'Sorry you had to wait. No way I could see you while *they* were here.' A frisson passed through the group. 'Meaning?' I asked Masha. 'A spell. They'd come to put a spell on her!' she whispered. Ira and I exchanged amused glances: this woman understood about power.

In the basement people were sitting pressed shoulder to shoulder round the table. The room was lit by a single bare bulb. A row of paper icons was fixed round the wall. The atmosphere was charged. The three of us sat on benches at the side with other late-comers.

Half an hour later Nina Stepanovna made her operatic entrance. Gone was the country baba; carrying a huge leather-bound book, the silver threads of her headscarf catching the light, a large brass crucifix round her neck, she circled the tables like a diva. Now and then she stopped to feel someone's head, neck or breast. 'Don't be shy now – pretend you're on the beach!' she clucked, putting people at their ease.

At the end of the table sat Borya. Six months ago he'd been carried in here, unable to walk. The healer had been working on him ever since. She'd taken a curse off him, he said. Now she made him parade up and down the room; he was still limping, but only slightly. They beamed at one another in triumph.

Opposite Borya sat a woman with a corkscrew perm called Valya. All day she was groaning, restless from the pain in her back. Her blond, virile husband had taken her from one hospital to the next, but no one could tell her what was wrong. We were longing for the healer to put Valya out of her agony. But Nina Stepanovna's progress round the table was slow. She would move on, then turn back, as if weaving a web around us.

'Which of your folk was killed by lightning?' the healer asked the red-scarfed baba, after putting her hand on the woman's head. The baba's mouth dropped open. 'That was Uncle Fedya – but how did you . . .?' she gasped. Nina Stepanovna moved on, feeling people here and there, using her cross like a stethoscope. 'My – you don't 'arf nick a lot of stuff!' she commented, rummaging in one woman's hair as if she could feel the booty. The woman hotly denied it. Nina Stepanovna smiled and patted her fondly: 'Can't kid me. I've worked on a farm too. But I never took more than I needed – don't get greedy . . .'. Tears welled up in the woman's eyes: how well Nina Stepanovna understood her!

She might have been reading from some invisible print-out of their lives. When she reached Masha's tearful daughter she put her mouth to the girl's back, walked to the corner of the room and bent over, her body wracked with coughing. The girl started sobbing. 'Cry, doll. Go on, let it all out. You'll feel better soon,' said Nina Stepanovna kindly. 'And when the first frost comes go out in your nightie and lie in a puddle at the nearest crossroads. Don't worry, no one'll see – and you won't catch cold.' The girl hugged Natasha Stepanovna as if her life depended on it.

Next came a well-dressed woman from a long way away. Nina Stepanovna dealt with her briefly: 'As for you, my china doll, why did you sell your wedding dress? Ai, ai, ai – you can't sell wedding things. You can't give 'em away and you can't borrow 'em! You're body's cold all the way down the right side – go to church and confess.'

'It's your thyroid,' she said to the next woman. 'When you get home, take a knife and go like this' – passing the cross over her throat. Then she muttered: 'Leave this white body, leave these yellow bones, amen, amen, amen. And avoid mushrooms.'

Next she came to the old man with the fearful eyes. 'How old are you?' she asked. 'Sixty-five? You look ten years older. Don't worry, it'll be all right – where were you in the army? It's the radiation what done it. Oats and hops – three spoonfuls to a litre of water, strain and drink with fifty grams of honey. And what were you up in court for? I know. You didn't mean it. You were drunk.'

There was no judgment, and no condescension. Like children, her patients showed her their bruises and let her kiss them better again. 'What about kids?' she asked the old man. 'Did you leave it too late? . . . There's an adder hiding under your house. Go home and find it. Kill it, put it on the crossroads and say: "Snake, dear little snake, wherever you came from, whoever put you in my house, I leave you at this crossroads. This is your family, and to me amen, healing and grace" – that's what you must do, dearie!'.

Valya's turn was next. Twisted over in pain, she could hardly wait, and nor could we. But Nina Stepanovna returned to the old man again. 'Are your legs tired?' she said. 'That's the arthritis – is there a birch in your garden? Take the one that buds earliest, cut it down and give away the wood to lonely old women – whatever you do, don't take it into the house. And say this: "John the Baptist, John the Healer, take my darkness, give me your light. Cure my ills, my pains, my nerves and my veins."'

At last she reached Valya. She walked straight past the suffering woman and stood behind her handsome husband. He scowled as if to say: 'Don't look at me, I'm only here for her.' 'Who's Lyuda then?' she asked sternly. Ivan said nothing, but the blood rose to his cheeks. So did our collective anger – the cheat, the bastard! 'Don't go thinking your wife's the one with the problem. It's you, ducky! Tell us about the crash then?' she murmured conspiratorially. 'What crash?' Ivan bluffed. 'Come on now,' she said, a complicit smile on her frog-like face. We hardly breathed. 'You mean on the bike.' He sounded like a boy caught stealing apples. 'The motorbike. You were drunk, weren't you?' Valya was looking on astonished. The healer held up a warning finger: 'Come back and I'll cure you. Till then – keep those flies buttoned up!'

As the healer walked round the room, her mood lifted and so did ours. She touched one person with her hand, another with the crucifix. She blessed jars of honey, tea, towels and photographs which people had heaped on to the table. She muttered prayers and recipes: 'Save me from the Evil One, from war, from thunder and from lightning, heavenly host, despite my unworthiness. Cut up pine needles finely, add water, boil for five minutes, cover and leave till morning. Take with a spoonful of honey three times a day.' She was moving lightly as a girl, gaily, wrapping us in her protection as she went through her own ritual dance.

As she passed Valya, the sick woman grabbed her hand. 'Don't abandon me!' Nina Stepanovna sighed, tipped the woman over her knee and worked her lower back like a skilled chiropractor. Valya howled, but it was relief we heard in her voice now.

Then the diva was gone. As people filed out into the dusk, leaving offerings of money, we sat stunned by the drama we had witnessed.

THE GODDESS AND BABA YAGA

Those of us staying overnight were considering our options for sleeping (a mattress, the table, a concrete floor, some narrow benches) when the healer reappeared: 'You doll,' she said to me sternly. 'Need help. Come upstairs with your friend.' Back in her quarters, Nina Stepanovna gave us blankets and unlocked a door on a fine room, unfurnished except for a chandelier and a few pot palms.

We were fast asleep on the carpet when the light flashed on and off a few hours later: 'Wakey wakey!' Nina Stepanovna was standing in the doorway, frog face lit up by a grin. 'You can sleep when you get back home! Here, I'm the boss!' It was four in the morning. In the kitchen, where dirty dishes were stacked on the side, the cherubic Yura was waiting, bottle in hand. 'Hey, is there really a tunnel under the sea joining England to Europe? Glug! Glug! What's it like going under the sea?'

'You can hear the fishes talk,' I answered, half asleep.

'Hey Nin – let's go visit her under the sea!'

'She can have her England, fishes and all. I've got my love,' she answered, kissing Yura tenderly. 'He was done for when we met. Tell 'em, Yur!'

'She saved my life! I was boss of the *kolkhoz* here. It was December. Terrible frost there was. I skidded. Got stuck in snow. Turned off the engine and went to sleep. When I woke I couldn't move. It was dark. I could see lights out there – it was our guys, stealing bricks in a lorry. Couldn't budge, couldn't shout. By the time they got to me my face was black. Hellish pain. Fingernails came off. Doctors were going to take my arms and legs off. The wife walked out.'

'I took him in,' Nina Stepanovna threw in.

'Do you remember?' Yura asked gently. 'I reached over and

took off your scarf. Turned you into a woman again. After eighteen years.' Nina Stepanovna tilted her frog face and batted her pale eyelids.

'Be a crime not to drink to that!' Yura bellowed.

'How did you save him?' I asked.

'By using God's gifts. My mother had the gift too. When it was dark she'd drop round and treat a sick kid.' Yura was nodding off again. 'It wasn't allowed then. You got prison for it. I knew nothing. But she must've passed it on. After she died, Pa gave me her book. Just a little exercise book. I chucked it in the corner. But later on, well . . .'

'Was Yura your first husband?'

'Oh no! We had four kids when Vasya died. He was a forest guard. Came on a group of 'em stealing wood. They beat him to death. God bless my enemies!' She crossed herself. 'I was just a pig girl. Sometimes I amaze myself. How do I know that someone's fifth vertebrae's smashed. Huh?'

She paused to refill our glasses. What made Yura drunk only tuned her higher. 'I get it from Him.' She threw a glance upwards. 'I was in Sergiev Posad.' The complex of monasteries at the heart of the Russian Orthodox Church was near Moscow, a long way away. 'This priest, Father Naum – he tore into me! "You're a bad girl," he said. "Stop doing spells – start curing people!" So that's what I do. I help people, and it makes me happy.' Yura surfaced from sleep: 'A crime not to drink to that!' he mumbled, and we drank. So that was it – while we were waiting out there all day, she and Yura were sleeping off the night before.

She recalled the day she'd found a handsome young couple sitting in the basement: 'I told 'em straight out: "You're brother and sister." "Oh no we're not," they said. "We're both orphans, but we're husband and wife!" "Go away and find out about your parents," I said. A few weeks later they were back. Turned out I was right. There'd been six of them. Pa'd gone to jail, Ma'd died. Kids shoved in different orphanages.' What should they do, they ask me? They already had kids. "Go to your priest. If he blesses the marriage, well and good," I said. A few months later they were back, with all the brothers and sisters they'd tracked down. "Now we've got a family, thanks to you. You're our mother now."'

'Crime not to drink to that!' Yura surfaced in time for the

punchline. Soon he was asleep again. But was he really? A thought was stirring in his troubled brain, pushing through the slights, the needles of jealousy, foggy lumps of love. He looked across at his wife, sober suddenly: 'I'm a wreck.' He spoke as if the two were alone. 'I'm in the way, aren't I?' 'Shut it, fuck face,' she said, unconvincingly, and put her hand on my head. 'As for you Zina, someone's put a curse on you – kicked sand in your eyes. You probably thought it was a joke. But that was no joke. You were wearing a swimsuit – white with red spots. Remember?' What could I say? She was magnificent.

We had entered a different reality. Here, the air was teeming with good and bad spirits. 'Where's your cross?' were the first words Nina Stepanovna addressed to me. To walk around unprotected, a prey to every piece of passing malevolence was as stupid as going out in snow without boots.

This Russia was new to me. But I would find that scholars like Joanna Hubbs had been piecing together, from legends, folklore and artefacts, fragments of a history of Russia's wise women. All over the Eurasian landmass the mammoth hunters had left behind statues of Ice Age goddesses. Those with heavy thighs and spilling stomachs might have been portraits of Nina Stepanovna. In the steppes, the hunters' goddess had ruled over earth, air and water. But somewhere between the seventh and third millenia BC, as hunting gave way to agriculture, a shift of power took place. A legend Herodotus records seems to capture that transition: the Scythians who ruled over the Russian steppes in the first millennium BC worshipped a goddess, half-maiden, half-serpent, called Tabiti. One day Herakles went to sleep by the River Dneiper when tending his cows. He awoke to find that Tabiti had stolen them. She agreed to release them if he would become her lover. When the three sons she bore him reached manhood, she offered them the bow Herakles had left behind: the one who could bend it would become the first king of the Scythians.

Hubbs points out that when Prince Vladimir of Kiev was baptised by Byzantine missionaries in the tenth century, the prince's warrior elites adopted Christianity. But the clans they protected held on to their female deity. However, by that time the powers of that female deity were greatly circumscribed by other gods. She evolved into the earth goddess, Mokosh, a word that evokes the dampness of Mother Earth in Russian. Her origin was Finno-Ugric, like

Nina Stepanovna's Eryza people, and Hubbs confirms that her cult remained particularly strong among these Finno-Ugric people. Indeed, in that legend of the golden woman which fascinated European travellers, we catch the image of that goddess. It echoes down to us through the painted wooden *matroshkas* in every Russian gift shop.

Christianity found ways of dealing with the tenacious culture of that female deity. It incorporated her into the Mother of God. It co-opted her, as the priest did Nina Stepanovna when she visited Sergiev Posad. It also demonised her as Baba Yaga, the witch of Russian fairy tales who kidnaps children and cooks them for her supper. My Baba Yaga had lured me into her house and she was not going to let me go until she had 'cooked' me.

In the course of our long drunken night, I learned that the Communist Party had also co-opted the wise women. Back in the 1970s Nina Stepanovna was offered brilliant prospects by the KGB in Saransk if she would work for them. She turned them down. She preferred to work with pigs.

LIFTING ZINA'S CURSE

The operation to remove Zina's curse took place in a room which Nina Stepanovna kept for chosen patients. The afternoon sun slanted down on Ira and me, two young couples, a bent old man and two babas in headscarves. Nina Stepanovna handed me a massive, leather-bound volume. 'You, doll, can read to us.' It was a prayer book in Old Church Slavonic, the written language which missionaries had cobbled together for the Slavs after Prince Vladimir's conversion to Christianity. Was she joking? One glance was enough to answer that. The carousing dame of the night before was a stern priestess now.

I ploughed through the prayers, mutilating the mellifluous sounds as she attended to other patients. 'Louder!' she kept saying remorselessly. 'Louder!' Only when she finished with all her other patients did she turn to me: 'You can stop now. You're not very good at it, are you?' I heard the judgment behind her jeering: how dare you patronise me in my own house, crediting my showmanship, but not believing in my power?

Putting a hand on my head, she delivered a scathing report on the state of my internal organs. The questions she asked did not fish around, like gypsy fortune tellers and astrologers. They were precise and accurate. 'You nearly drowned – when was that? Your house burned down recently? What's this dog – black, white spot on chin, not yours, seems mighty fond of you?' It was as if, with her hand on my head, she was reading some holographic chronicle of my life, blurred but accurate.

Before Ira and I left to catch the night train, she repeated her warning: the work she had done to lift my 'curse' would leave me in a bad state. So by next morning when our sleeper pulled into Moscow's Kazan Station I was in a cocky mood: despite Nina Stepanovna's dire predictions I was in the pink of health.

It was still early when I reached the flat where I was staying with Ira's mother, Elena. I tip-toed in, took a shower, revelling in the luxury of hot water, and regaled Elena with stories over breakfast. Then I lay down for a brief rest. An hour later, I woke to find that I could hardly move. I forced myself to get up, and collapsed, as if every muscle and tendon in my body had been cut. Alarmed, Elena rubbed me down with spirit and plunged my feet in scalding water. But I knew that I was not ill, but jinxed.

For the next three days I lay there, unable to read or talk. Appointments came and went, but there was nothing I could do. I was immobilised. Through the window I watched the sunlight on the plane tree in the courtyard. No wonder Yura was wary of Nina Stepanovna. She was a potent force. She did not like my detachment, and she was right, too: it was monstrous of me to have imagined that I could go and observe a wise woman in Russia, and not be observed myself. Whatever she had done to me, it served its purpose: she had forced me to concede her power.

Lying there, I had a strange dream. The house was full of vermin. I was laying poison down on the floor when a mouse with pink punk fur minced across it. The mouse was followed by a hamster with a gold watch chain. A chipmunk gave a speech of interminable length. I was watching a revolution: self-possessed, unafraid, the animals were taking over. As I woke up, the chipmunk's speech turned back into the sound of children playing on the rusty swing outside.

Powerless to move, or even read, I had plenty of time to reflect on why Nina Stepanovna had done what she had to me. I had come out here expecting to be able to understand whatever happened to me in Russia. But the chaos of the times had kept subverting my intentions, reminding me of the poet Feodor Tyutchev's warning: 'Russia cannot be understood with the mind alone.'

What had I really learned from my travels? That was what I was forced to consider as I lay there. Still, my way of dealing with my experiences had remained deeply Western. The stranger my journey became, the harder I clung on to my reason, the Western habit of detachment. Nina Stepanovna, the pig girl, had humbled me, forced me to stop, to recognise a power that I did not understand.

The longer I lay there, the more ashamed of myself I started to feel. Yes, I had always been sympathetic to the people I wrote about. But had I really engaged with the challenge of meeting people like the Old Believer Philimon, and the Cosmist Professor Kaznacheev? In their very different ways, both of them and Nina Stepanovna were militant crusaders against rationality, that progressive force which had displaced God and mystery from the centre of the world. If asked, I knew they would all agree that we in the West were prisoners of our own achievement.

When St Stephen of Perm asked the pagans why they were so resistant to Christianity, they explained that they were a hunting people. They said that if they were converted they would lose their connectedness to the natural world, and to the animals they hunted. We had built the modern world on our ability to detach ourselves, to analyse. But in the course of that we had lost any sense of living in an equilibrium with that natural world. Nina Stepanovna's question hung in the air: was I happy to remain the prisoner of my own detachment? Where did I want to belong now?

When Nina Stepanovna was laying into me during that final session she asked me: 'Why did you sell your wedding dress?' The question shored up my scepticism, as my wedding dress was in a trunk in my parents' attic. But now that I considered it I realised how shrewd it was. Her patients all came from Russia. When hyperinflation was raging, every married woman would have scanned her possessions for anything of value to sell. She gauged the question wrongly only because she had never met a woman who came from a land so far away that her life was not ruined by the post-Soviet collapse. She was not leafing through some holographic image of my wardrobe. She was challenging me on the subject of power, as she did the other women. Hold on to what is important, she was reminding me: do not think that by sacrificing yourself to your men, your children, you can make up for that abuse of power that is visited on everyone, but on women most of all.

'Give me gold,' she asked me harshly at one stage. I was wearing only my gold wedding ring, and I was not going to give her that. During the long pause that followed I could feel my fellow patients looking at me, thinking how rich I was, and how mean. Well, what the hell? It was just a ring. When I tugged at it, stung by the implication, Nina Stepanovna seized my hand and stopped me.

'Give me gold', she demanded again, more roughly. Again, I pulled at the ring, and again she stopped me.

'Give me gold,' she repeated.

'No,' I said this time, crossly.

At this her pale, frog-like face cracked open in an enormous smile.

'You see?' she said, ruffling my hair. Yes, maybe I was beginning to.

On the fourth day I recovered, as mysteriously as I had collapsed. Only then did Ira admit what Nina Stepanovna had told her in confidence: I would be ill for three days. After that, the curse would be lifted.

1999–2004

Vladimir Putin, a career officer in the FSB (Federal Security Service), became Prime Minister in August 1999. He became acting President when a derelict Yeltsin stepped down at the end of the year. His elevation returned to power a security elite that had been marginalised since the fall of Soviet power. For them, the end of communism was the great geopolitical catastrophe of the twentieth century. Their policies would be driven by a burning sense of shame. The governing idea of the new regime would be the need to restore Russia's greatness.

The month Putin became Prime Minister saw Chechen separatists invade neighbouring Dagestan. A series of explosions in residential buildings across Russia, ostensibly caused by Chechen terrorists, also killed some 300 people and sent shock waves through the country. The vigilance of a local man prevented a further explosion in Ryazan which bore the hallmarks of having been planted by the FSB. Thus was the public prepared for the start of a new Chechen war, together with the emergence of a strong leader.

The failure of the first Chechen war was seen as a shame which had to be avenged. In the course of this new military campaign in Chechnya, Putin started transferring the task of pacification from the Russian army to pro-Kremlin Chechen militias. Akhmad Kadyrov was 'elected' president in Chechnya's first elections in October 2003. After he was assassinated the following May, his son Ramzan, whose militias proved even more brutal than the Russian army, became his de facto successor.

After the second Chechen war began, terrorist attacks inside Russia became a feature of life, heightening people's feeling of insecurity. Strong rumours of the FSB's involvement accompanied some of them. The seizure by Chechen fighters of a Moscow theatre in October 2002 did Putin's popularity no harm, although 129 Muscovites were killed along with the fighters when the building was stormed.

The culmination of these attacks occurred in September 2004, when Chechen fighters occupied a school full of children and adults in Beslan, North Ossetia. Bungled intervention by Russian troops left hundreds dead (officially, 340, but in fact far more), and a stench of obfuscation coming from the Kremlin. Once again, rumours of the state's murky involvement were rife. Putin's popularity faltered, but soon recovered.

From the start, Putin declared it his mission to reassert the power of the state: what was good for the state was a priori good for Russia. On the domestic front, his first major step was to call the regional governors to heel and form seven vast regions, governed by his appointees. Next, he destroyed the independent media empires of Berezovsky and Gusinsky. By the summer of 2001, the old hierarchical state structure was starting to re-emerge.

Putin proceeded to set up a series of institutions which imitated the functions of democracy, while remaining under state control: virtual 'political parties', a 'free press' and an 'independent judiciary'. He encountered little opposition. For most people 'democracy' was by now synonymous with gangs, wild speculation and the absence of regulation. They wanted order and stability.

Putin's popularity was cemented by the buoyant economy: ever since the financial crash of 1998 it had been growing at an average 6.4 per cent a year. This was chiefly due to the price of oil. When he came to power it stood at $17 a barrel, and it had been rising ever since. Other measures helped: non-agricultural land could now be bought. Barter was no longer playing a significant role in the economy. Putin had also succeeded in revolutionising the system of tax collection, and introduced a new flat-rate income tax.

Popular though Putin was, his strategy produced problems. He had come to power as a moderniser. But the regime he introduced was in many respects ill-suited to the task of modern government. There was a price to be paid for having centralised power, for having undermined the judiciary, reined in the press and destroyed the political opposition. Without horizontal supports and counterbalancing powers, the bureaucracy was doomed to inefficiency and, above all, to corruption. Gone was the freewheeling corruption of the 1990s, which had put power in the hands of gangs. The streets were safe now, but the state bureaucracy itself was infected with corruption, from top to bottom.

Western business interests were becoming alarmed about the state's increasing high-handedness. In October 2003 the oil oligarch Mikhail Khodorkovsky was arrested on charges of tax evasion. He was sentenced to nine years in prison and the assets of Yukos, Russia's largest private company, were redistributed to those close to Putin. Khodorkovsky, alone among the oligarchs, had made the mistake of starting to use his wealth to support the development of democracy in Russia.

Once hopes that the West would launch a great post-communist Marshall Plan died, an anti-Western mood began to set in among Russia's elites. The decision by the Western powers not to dismantle NATO fed this mood, and NATO's air strikes against Serbia in 1999 stoked the flames. Russia's new sense of isolation was increased between 1999 and 2004 by the choice of three former Soviet republics and four former satellites to join both NATO and the EU. Their admission directly contravened the agreement between Gorbachev and US Secretary of State James Baker in February 1990 not to 'expand the zone of NATO'.

Putin's decision to support Bush's war on terror after the attacks on New York in September 2001 defied this new anti-Western mood. However, the overture was poorly reciprocated by the new Republican administration: US aid to Russia was cut back. America withdrew from its thirty-year-old Anti-Ballistic Missile Treaty with Russia. Congress confirmed the old Cold War Jackson–Vanik amendment, which linked its trade relations with Russia to levels of Jewish emigration. The US also failed to throw its weight behind Russia's bid to join the World Trade Organisation.

Most ominously from the leadership's point of view, when two former Soviet republics (Georgia in 2003, Ukraine at the end of 2004) turned their faces westward in 'colour revolutions', the hand of the United States was deemed to have played a critical role. Fears of this happening in Russia would become a governing political factor from now on.

One of the Kremlin's responses was to declare its ideological independence from Western theories concerning the legitimacy of the state. Vladislav Surkov formulated the concept of sovereign democracy to describe Russia's autocratic government. This vested the regime's legitimacy not in the people or their votes, but in the strong national identity of its governing elite.

2004

CORDELIA OF THE STEPPES

'There, you see,' said Khanin. 'What's the most important feature of the Russian economic miracle? Its most important feature is that the economy just keeps on sinking deeper and deeper into the shit, while business keeps on growing stronger and expanding into the international arena.'

Viktor Pelevin, *Homo Zapiens*

Lying back on my top bunk, I surrendered to the rhythm of the train. I was travelling overnight to Saratov. My companions were a wiry sergeant-major from Engels and a young couple from Moscow, she pregnant, he pink and porcine, going to visit her parents. Russian Germans by origin, they had grown up in Central Asia and arrived back in Russia with nothing, refugees from nationalism.

In the mid-nineties it was hard not to be infected by the collective anxiety on such journeys – all those stories of passengers being gassed, of murderers bundling bodies off the train at dead of night. Now that seemed a long time ago. The rituals of the sleeper worked their soothing magic: the bulky attendant brought us sheets and tea, and we ate our picnics. Outside, the trunks of the birches gleamed.

The sergeant-major, proud that the army had kept him on beyond retirement age, was poor and lively: a skier, he sailed on the Volga, played the guitar and grew flowers and vegetables. The young businessman and his saleswoman wife had no time for hobbies, they admitted shyly. By the time they got home from work, they had no energy left to do anything but watch television. But soon they would be able to start building their house.

This conversation dried up rather suddenly. I watched my

companions coming up against something which embarrassed them, a line running through our compartment. The young couple belonged to the new middle class, which numbered some 30 million by now. Every day the distance between this new class and the rest of their compatriots was growing. As the train drew into Saratov, I thought of my friends. Misha and Tatiana obviously belonged to this new class. But I was less sure on what side of the line I was going to find Anna.

Since my last visit to Saratov Misha had become Mikhail Ivanovich: an important man. In his early forties now, his face and the curve of his shoulders expressed dogged determination. He had filled out and become self-assured.

With the help of that processor which had sat unused for years in a shed in Marx he had now cornered 35 per cent of the market for sunflower oil in Saratov province. He sold his virgin oil right up and down the Volga, as well as in Moscow and parts of Germany.

The *Solntse* factory was now enclosed by tall gates. A row of tall silos for storing seed had sprung up. The plant employed 180 people; working night and day, it produced some 600 tons of oil a year. When I first met Misha, Rodon, the secret electronics factory for which he once worked, was the largest employer in Marx. Now this role had passed to *Solntse*. Since my last visit, *Solntse* was awarded a prize by an independent panel as one of Russia's 100 finest products.

Misha had started farming, too. Indeed, he was the largest private farmer in the district. Three years ago, knowing nothing about agriculture, he took over a bankrupt collective farm in what had once been a Russian German village. His land now measured 40 kilometres from end to end and encompassed three villages.

He had equipped the room off his own large office as a gym, full of gleaming equipment. He regarded the increasingly anti-Western political mood in Russia as so much posturing. His own horizons had grown along with the business. His family holidays were spent in France now; Tatiana dressed in Max Mara, and he relied on Germany's agricultural fairs to keep him up to date with farming techniques and machinery.

So Misha had realised his dream, become a powerful businessman. Why was it then, I kept asking myself, that I did not feel more like celebrating my friend's success? Something was missing when Misha talked about his work. The zest, the appetite for adventure had gone. He seemed strangely subdued.

Misha's farm manager, Viktor Goldantsev, drove me round the farm in his jeep. An elegant, balding man with gold-rimmed glasses and a well-cut suit, he cut an improbable figure in that rural landscape. He knew nothing about farming when Misha invited him to run the operation. But it was a shrewd choice. Viktor knew how to make things happen: for years he ran a nuclear power plant in the ice-bound north, Murmansk. He was enjoying himself now. 'When we took it over, the place was a wreck,' he shouted as we bowled across the steppe, looking over vast fields of mixed crops. 'The irrigation was broken – everything was. There wasn't a single tractor – and no one'd been paid for two years!' Last year the farm turned a profit for the first time. 'But it'll take a generation or two before people here learn to work again normally.'

Misha himself was making the fifteen-hour trek back from Ukraine. He was driving against the clock, bringing his elderly mother to live with the family in their luxurious apartment in Saratov. Misha's mother had worked the land all her life. Although she was nearly eighty, through the years of inflation, when city people could not manage on their earnings, she had kept her two older children and their families fed from her plot of land. Only when she grew too blind did she give it all to her older children, like King Lear, and go to live with them. Now they had declared themselves fed up with housing her. She was too difficult: her precious Misha could look after her. The old woman was horrified at the prospect of being dependent again, and on a daughter-in-law with whom she had little in common. Tatiana was worried, too. For a start, she could barely understand the old woman's thick Ukrainian burr.

When I met the old woman, Lyuba (short for Lyubov, 'Love') was being entertained by her seven-year-old granddaughter Nadezhda ('Hope'), whose blonde face adorned every bottle of *Solntse* oil. Not much larger than her granddaughter, she wore a white kerchief, flowered housecoat and heavy woollen stockings. Sitting on the edge of her bed in the large flat with its parquet floors, she looked bewildered. Her nut-brown face was ploughed with lines and she gazed out from sightless eyes. 'So good to me, so good,' the old woman kept muttering. Tatiana's kindness had upset all the old woman's expectations.

Lyuba was the reason why Misha had survived in the jungle of Russian business, where so many other decent, clever people failed. She had come through the great famines of 1932–3 as a child younger than Nadezhda now. That genocidal famine killed more Ukrainians than in any war in the country's history. The facts had been so harshly suppressed that no one knew what the toll was – five million, possibly as many as eight. For decades the famines were mentioned in no Soviet book, no newspaper or speech. But Ukrainians understood why they happened, and it was not shortage of grain. It was the result of a policy aimed at breaking the spirit of Ukrainian independence, and the resistance of its peasantry to collectivisation.

Although Lyuba and her four brothers survived, malnourishment left her unnaturally small. Those famine spared, war did not. All the men in the family went on to die at the front, except one brother, who died later of his wounds. Lyuba married at eighteen. After begetting two children, her petty criminal husband abandoned her. She and her mother remained on the collective farm, effectively enslaved. For like all the *kolkhoz* workers, she was not allowed to leave the land; nor paid in money or kind for her labour. In order to feed her family, she had to set to work tilling her own plot at the end of her working day.

A strong woman, she had a fiery temper and unshakeable will. At the age of thirty-seven she met a man older than herself who had fought in the war, been arrested and gone to camp on some trumped-up fraud charge. By the time he was freed his wife had long ago remarried. Misha's father could not have been more unlike his temperamental little wife. He had a saintly sweetness. He never raised his voice, or told his wife off. 'He was so gentle that when he stroked his little son he would go like this,' said Tatiana, passing her hand over her daughter's head a centimetre away, without quite touching.

When Misha was little his grandmother was struck by lightning as she was working in the fields. Had she not fallen into a puddle, she would have been killed outright. The lightning burned her right down her back. So great was the pain that she could not bear it; she hanged herself.

Now, the sole survivor of those years sat in her room missing her own bed, her dog, the cow and hens which her daughter had wasted no time taking over. Misha came back from work late and went into the darkened room where his mother sat alert, waiting. He handed her an ear of wheat from his fields. Lyuba's sight was almost gone and it was dark, but she only needed to feel the ear of wheat: 'Three weeks it'll be ready – not a day before, mind.' Then her youngest child sat on the floor and talked to her as he could to so few people about the difficulties of his day and the toll success was taking on him: 'I can't go on, Mother. I'm just too tired . . . '

'You'll do it, son,' Lyuba reassured him. 'You'll go on.' He would because she had, because he was her beloved son.

FREEDOM IS SLAVERY

As long as I stayed with Misha and Tatiana in their fine new flat, driving in the car, I was insulated from the real Saratov. But when I moved to Anna's I began to appreciate what had happened in the city.

Although Russia's economy was growing steadily, Saratov had regressed to another century. Old wooden buildings were leaning at tipsy angles along the piss-reeking streets. Headscarved women sat begging, intoning interminable prayers. Homeless men with matted hair, faces burnished by alcohol, rummaged through overflowing rubbish bins. Yet every now and then an immaculately modern girl would emerge from one of the topsy-turvy houses and pick her way to work down the ruined road.

At a crossroads, police outriders were clearing the traffic aside for the governor's cavalcade of six black limousines. As they shot by, sirens blaring, I wondered whether the tinted glass in their car windows was dark enough to obscure the disrepair of the fine nineteenth-century buildings past which they sped. Built by merchants flush with money from the wheat and timber trade, those façades with their fine wrought-iron balconies were merely decrepit when I first visited Saratov. Now they were fit only for demolition. The odd new shop-front, chic café or arcade with slot machines had been clapped on. A huge cathedral had also shot up from nowhere. But these bright splashes were like lipstick on the face of a wino; they merely threw the dereliction into sharper relief.

Of Saratov's 1 million population, some 30,000 people were living in high-rise blocks which were condemned as too dangerous for habitation, according to Anna's paper. New blocks were going up all the time. In theory, 15 per cent of the flats in them were allocated to social housing. In practice, these too were being sold off privately. The old ones were just falling down. The month before my visit, two more collapsed. In one, which was fully occupied, an entire side wall fell away at dawn one day. How no one was killed remained a mystery. The residents trooped outside and waited until they realised that, this being Saratov, no one was going to bandage them up and offer them somewhere else to live. So they returned to the ruins and got on as best they could with their lives.

The man presiding over this disintegration was Ayatskov, the notoriously corrupt Yeltsinite governor of Saratov province. Putin's attempts to remove him had so far failed. He was the man whose corruption Anna started investigating all those years ago when he was the city's deputy mayor, before learning that her stories were being spiked because he had bought up the paper she was working for.

For years, the law was after him, but he enjoyed protection high up in the pyramid of power. One prosecutor began a trial case against him for pocketing millions of dollars on some deal involving American combine harvesters. But that was suspended. Meanwhile, every street kiosk in the city paid 'rent' directly to him. The most visible display of his wealth was the Wagnerian castle he built himself out in the country, and the private plane which flew him to it.

Anna, who covered such cases in her capacity as law correspondent, was welcoming. With her boyish figure and monastic bob, she looked barely older than when we first met. She was less awkward and better dressed now. But a light had gone out behind her eyes. She looked huddled over somehow, as if some string holding her up had been cut.

Last time we met, I was so proud of her. She had come into her own. She was using her interviews to explore the extent to which each person is responsible for their past, and that of their country. She was helping her readers expand their sense of the rights and responsibilities which attached to them as individuals, rather than the state. When I left her I was feeling yes, this is how that civic space needs to be built in Russia; it will take time, but one day, surely, it will end up being realised in a new contract between the rulers and the ruled.

That felt like a long time ago now. I knew Anna too well to expect from her a straightforward account of this missing period.

Only when she told me that she had stopped writing poetry altogether did I realise quite how depressed she was. For her poetry
mattered more to her than anything.

One day I went into her office at *Saratovsky Arbat* and sat
reading backcopies of the paper while she worked. The paper was
more than usually parochial. Anna's articles were mostly about
crime, but they were dull, with little of their old ambition.

I tried not to be disappointed. After all, Putin had come to
power announcing in his Open Letter that 'the stronger the state,
the freer the individual'. To anyone old enough to remember Soviet-
speak, the message was clear and only a little more prolix than
the three slogans of Orwell's Ministry of Truth:

WAR IS PEACE
FREEDOM IS SLAVERY
IGNORANCE IS STRENGTH

One of Putin's first moves when he came to office was to close
down Russia's two remaining independent media empires. The press
took the point: as in Soviet days, its role was not to stimulate individuals to think for themselves, but to support central government
in the task of keeping order, making Russia great again.

Anna was living in a couple of rooms in a slum on the city
limits. It had no flush lavatory, no hot water and no carpets. A
dim bulb hung down from a wire in the high ceiling, like an unripe
pear. Lorries shook the windows as they roared out of town on
the main road. But Anna loved her flat, which had enabled her
to leave the hostel and keep a pet at last. Lucy, her black cat, was
her intimate now. When she came home at night, Lucy would
bound out from among the rubble to meet her, like a dog.

Anna had turned her energies inwards. Of an evening, she would
lie on her bed, Lucy on top of her, reading works by Russia's great
religious writers, so long banned. Or she would go and visit Father
Michael and the nuns who ran Saratov's Catholic church. Her face
lit up when she talked about the elderly Irish priest and his group
of happy, dedicated nuns from all over the world. 'They're lovely
people – I really enjoy their company.' There was an unspoken
'but' at the end of this sentence. Although I was curious, I knew
better than to ask.

* * *

Anna's life was beset by problems. She was about to become homeless again, for a start. In her desperation to get out of the hostel she had recklessly traded in her one possession, the flat in Marx, for five years in this slum. Now, long before that period had elapsed, the son of the woman living in her flat had turned up, claiming his legal right to live in his mother's flat. Anna, legal correspondent though she was, had not thought to legalise her house swap.

What was she going to do now? Buying was not an option. Even in the rough part of town a small flat now cost around $7,000. As an experienced journalist, she earned relatively good money – twice as much as a teacher, five times as much as a nurse. But it was not enough to save. Mortgages were extortionate, and to get a loan required two people from the province to stand surety. None of her friends would risk that: what if she fell ill? This was why people took to accepting bribes. But Anna was condemned to honesty.

She had professional problems, too. Some Chechen who lived in Marx had complained about an article of hers, some weapons having been found at his home. The accusation had released her buried anxieties, left her with a morbid fear of misrepresenting anyone in print. No wonder her articles were so dull.

Where was the passionate, eccentric woman I had come to visit? I was sure she had not changed. But she was in hiding. Reading her diary was an act of desperation, though I reassured myself that Natasha had long ago told me how Anna used to leave her diary out, in order for me to read it. When she went to work it still lay there, on her writing table. For three days I just looked at it. On the fourth I picked it up: 'No! I haven't crossed over from Catholicism to Orthodoxy,' I read, 'or the other way round. I remain both, and neither. Catholicism has given me a lot! I feel much more comfortable in the Catholic Church than in the Orthodox one, but when I want to confess I go to the Orthodox Church. And as I wait for my confession I feel tormented, terribly tired from all that standing, from all those hours listening to a language I don't understand a word of. Tired too of taking part in something I don't understand. I feel tortured, angry, but I don't go back to the Catholic Church. Well, perhaps I will, as a guest. That I can do.'

That voice, the voice of the real Anna, was so alive that I felt as if I had been eavesdropping. Guiltily, I closed the diary and put it back. But I had read enough.

I sympathised with the struggle she was having with Orthodoxy. After the end of communism people's thirst for spiritual answers was so apparent: who were they, and what did they believe in, if they weren't communists? The Orthodox Church did not appear engaged with this crisis. Yes, the Church had too few priests, and they were sorely under-educated. But it seemed to me that they could at least have translated the prayers and liturgy into modern Russian, or given newcomers translation sheets. For anyone walking into the church off the street, as Anna had done, the prayers and liturgy were incomprehensible. I tried to find out why the Church was doing nothing about this, but the answers seemed to me unsatisfactory, evasive. All I knew was that a priest in Moscow got into trouble with the Church authorities for holding his services in modern Russian.

However, as I learned more about Orthodoxy I began to see how much my concern with understanding marked me out for the Westerner I was. It landed me in the thick of the great ongoing theological battle between the two branches of Christianity, Eastern and Western. Over the centuries, theologians of the Western Church grew more and more preoccupied by wanting to understand divinity, to grasp it in words. But the Eastern Church insisted that the fact that God could not be understood was the point: rationalism was not an appropriate tool for the discussion of God. Slowly, as my travels brought me up against the limits of understanding as an approach, what once bothered me about Orthodoxy started to interest me more and more. For this Church regarded itself as the guardian of a tradition which was proof against attempts to modernise it. It was a proper mystery, one with which each person had to contend on their own, in their struggle to contemplate the mystery of God.

I could not talk to Anna about what I read in her diary. But next morning, as I got up, I was thinking about the frustration with the language and rituals of Orthodoxy which her diary expressed so vividly. The theological divide between Rome and Byzantium had its correlation in the cultural divide between Westernisers and Slavophiles. As long as I had known her, Anna had been quintessentially a Westerniser. Intellectually curious, she must have begun her spiritual explorations by wanting to understand more about her faith. It was hardly surprising that where the Orthodox Church would not, or could not help, the Catholic Church engaged with her need. As time went on, she must have started to realise that what she was looking for went deeper than understanding. So here she was, caught on the ancient theological divide between Christianity's Eastern and Western traditions; between her need to understand – *kerygma* – and her longing for religious experience, which cannot be grasped with words, *dogma*.

Anna's bathroom was a good place for such reflection. Washing in it involved standing in the bath, leaning over a bucket and dipping one limb after another into cold water. As I dried myself I considered the journey Anna and I had been on since the early 1990s. How dismissive we would both have been if anyone suggested that one day this mystery would come to have more meaning for us than understanding.

Anna broke her self-imposed silence about politics only once. For a moment, her passion flared out like gas from an oil field. We were walking in Saratov's 'Victory Park', a monument to Saratov's days as a hub of the armaments industry. The bluffs around us were adorned with rusting tanks and heavy artillery. 'Make no mistake – what's happening now is the re-Sovietisation of Russian life,' she burst out unexpectedly. 'Take the press – there is no freedom of speech left. Putin's clever – typical FSB man. He didn't make a great announcement that would have brought the intelligentsia out against him. He just set about picking off the independent voices one by one. And people don't react. Partly, they're just tired. Partly, they know it won't do any good. It's not that I don't mind any more – far from it. There was a time when I was almost hysterical. But I've had to accept that nothing I can do is going to make any difference. We were very naive, you know, during glasnost – we really thought we could change something.

'I'd like to think that the next generation'll do better,' she went on. 'You just can't tell. For a start, they're not remotely interested in freedom as an idea. They want to be successful, personally, and they're prepared to work for it. They won't become political until some bureaucrat gets in the way of their ambition – if then. Take Polina,' she said, referring to Tatiana and Misha's older daughter. 'By the age of fifteen she was grown up, focused on her ambition.

She worked all the time – never took days off. At her age I was all over the place.'

No wonder Anna was in despair. The Yeltsin years were now generally regarded as those of Russia's humiliation. But I knew better. She and Misha between them had demonstrated to me better than anyone the way hope ran through that chaotic time like a bright thread. Thanks to them, I had begun to see the 1990s as a time of incubation, when people were starting to think and act for themselves. It had not seemed absurd to imagine that when things finally settled down, the order that emerged might be one where a critical mass of Russians would begin to understand why it was important for Russia to develop a civil society, with an independent press and judiciary, a place where the rights of individuals mattered. Anna had staked everything on that. While Putin's regime had brought stability, it had killed off her hope that she would see a civil society develop in Russia within her lifetime.

I came away feeling wretched about our friendship. In the years after the fall of communism I had felt a-little-bit-Anna. But we had met at a time when the pendulum of Russian history was pointing westward. Now it had swung away, towards autocracy. Anna's life as a prominent provincial journalist was tied to the swing of that political pendulum. From now on, we were going to have to make an effort to bridge the divide. There was the added problem that anything I wrote might make life awkward for her.

MY DREAM HOUSE

Over the years I had sent letters and messages to Novosibirsk, but there had been no response. Natasha and Igor had vanished without trace. I found them through Anna. She had received an email from Igor out of the blue, with some information he thought would interest her. 'And did it?' 'Huh!'

The couple were somewhere in Crimea now, on the Black Sea. I had invited myself to stay with them. The departure hall of Moscow airport was full of Russians who seemed to consider it normal to be going abroad with the family on holiday. They were leafing through glossy Russian magazines entitled *Limousine* and *Property Today* and their children were wearing brand-new track-suits and listening to iPods. But these beneficiaries of Moscow's boomtime were not rich. They worked as bookkeepers, chauffeurs and chefs. Crimea was cheap and did not really count as 'abroad'. Indeed, it had been part of Russia until 1954, when Khrushchev, in a quixotic gesture, bequeathed it to Ukraine, his native land. Until the Soviet Union broke up that had not made much differ-ence to Russia. But now it was a phantom limb: it felt like part of Russia, though it was not.

On the flight I tried to imagine what had become of Natasha and Igor. Would they have joined the thrusting new economy of my fellow passengers? When we last met in Siberia, the couple had come through many an ordeal and equipped themselves with business skills. I tried to imagine them living a prosperous, middle-class life by the sea, but this seemed unlikely. The forces shaping their lives were stormy and unpredictable, and this move suggested that Natasha was still running away from her past, from the mother who haunted her dreams.

Natasha was there to meet me at Simferopol airport. Her snub-nosed Slav face under that thick mop of curls was burnished by sun, and her eyes were sparkling. She was jumping up and down with excitement. By her side was a smartly dressed younger man who walked with a bad limp. Hmm, so she had finally left Igor. 'Oh no, it's not what you think!' she said quickly. 'Meet our dearest friend and colleague – Volodya, hero of the Afghan War.'

As Volodya drove south out of Simferopol, Natasha told me his story. A much-decorated young colonel, he had been brought here straight off the battlefield in Afghanistan, almost dead from his wounds. By the time his convalescence was over, Crimea had become home. The community of retired Russian servicemen was large, for Russia's navy was still based here. After the Soviet Union fell apart, the government struck a deal with Ukraine that until 2017 they would go on renting the facilities of the naval base.

The low rolling hills over which we were driving were so dense with colour that we might have been in a landscape by Derain, or the young Kandinsky: purple fields of lavender, vastly over-grown, gave way to golden slopes of wheat, ripe for harvesting, then to ropes of green vines stretching out of sight. The usual litter of rusting frames and posts, half-built concrete sheds and fencing could not mar the improbable beauty of the place.

Once, said Volodya, the wine was good and the trade in lavender oil lucrative. But the collective farms that had kept the Soviet naval bases supplied had fallen apart. The soil was so rich it produced three harvests a year. The food kept growing, but there was little market for it now. By the roadside men and women were selling tomatoes, raspberries, cherries and strawberries, and vegetables, ridiculously cheap.

Natasha was talking about the politics of Sevastopol and some project that she and Igor were doing with Volodya. As she talked, something fell into place: the same instinct for trouble which led the couple to move across Russia into the eye of a political storm in Marx was surely at work again in their move down here. For Crimea, fought over for centuries, was today locked in a battle invisible to the outside world. It had become Ukraine's Hong Kong: Russia's empire might have fallen, but the Russians were still here, and their navy too.

Such was the political impasse between Ukraine and Russia that no one was in charge. 'We live in the present, a present that's stuck in the past. You can't get anything done – not even buy a train ticket, let alone get a phone line or a passport. Not unless you know someone, or have money to bribe them. There are Afghan war heroes who've been waiting twelve years for a phone line! It was really hard when we came here – we couldn't find work at all. And if we hadn't met Volodya we'd never have managed.'

When the sea came in sight Volodya turned down a track and threaded his way between plots of land lush with flowers and fruit trees. In each, a little house had been cobbled together out of scavenged bits and pieces. The car pulled up in front of a couple of concrete huts with tin roofs, standing in a maze of weeds. Behind the fence, two dogs leaped around, barking in delight. Igor was standing, as upright in his bearing as ever, beaming at us. He was tanned and handsome. The moustaches which still curved down on either side of his mouth were still black and elegantly trimmed. But his hair was white now, and his front teeth were gone.

We sat and drank fruit juice in the shade of a pergola improvised out of army camouflage. After Volodya left, I looked inside the hut. It was simply furnished. To my surprise there was hardly a book to be seen. On Igor's immaculately tidy desk there was a computer, and even an Internet connection. Thanks to Volodya, Igor said with a grin, they were producing a newspaper again – and they called it *The Messenger*, like the last one. This time they were distributing it free.

'As you can see, they've gone, the possessions. It seems we had to lose everything. One more time. We had to learn how to live all over again. The dogs taught us to get up at dawn and go to bed when it got dark. At one point we even had to sell our books – even the English ones. Just to stay alive. We lived on buckwheat porridge for a month. It's funny – food was always something I'd taken for granted. Then we understood how little you need to live on. And how good it made us feel. So light and free!' Natasha's words spurted out like uncorked champagne.

'If we'd stayed on in Novosibirsk we'd never have learned these things. Life was too easy. Yes, we were earning good money. We were living in this nice flat. We had everything a person could want. But there was nothing to do – nothing but drink *kefir* and listen to the air conditioning. Besides, it wasn't really honest, the money we were making there. Do you remember? Igor thought up this brilliant wheeze for advertising the houses the company was building. We set up this competition for children to draw My

Dream House. We used the winners in our ad campaign. The paintings were wonderful. But it wasn't honest – it looked as if the company was really going to build those dream houses. Which couldn't have been further from the truth!'

I was sleeping in a hut across the yard from theirs. As I went to bed I noticed an unopened crate of vodka bottles stashed under a table in the corner of the room. So Natasha was still drinking. How come she was looking so happy, so healthy, then? How come they were publishing *The Messenger*, but giving it away? How were they earning any money? Nothing quite added up.

However, I had cleared up an old mystery. Over supper I asked Igor and Natasha about those rumours running round Novosibirsk when I last visited them. Rumours of a leak at the plutonium factory near their flat. Were they right? Yes, it was a bad leak, they said. Natasha, who was marinated in alcohol, was unaffected. But Igor, who did not drink, suffered badly. His teeth fell out soon after my visit.

After I turned the light off the sound of digging started up, quite close by, in the next-door garden. Now and then a torch flashed. On and on the digging went. What could they be doing, I wondered as I drifted off to sleep.

THEIRS NOT TO REASON WHY

When the cock crowed at dawn next day, the household was already stirring, to my astonishment. My friends had been confirmed night owls. The morning sun slanted through the window into the tin basin as I washed my face. My question about the moonlight digging made Natasha and Igor laugh: 'They must have been burying something they'd stolen,' said Igor. 'You'll soon find nothing here's the way it seems!'

After breakfast, Natasha and I set off for Sevastopol. The couple never left home together now, not since the burglary, when all their computer files relating to *The Messenger* were wiped. It was a warning: someone wanted them to know they were being watched. But Igor was not going to miss us: Volodya had left behind a fat file for him and he sat up late into the night reading it. There was a gleam in his eye; he had his material for the next edition of *The Messenger*.

Heavily laden with passengers, the communal taxi laboured uphill towards the port. As we reached the summit, I could see why this south-westerly point of the Crimean peninsula was so bitterly fought over for the last two thousand years. The city stood on a series of headlands divided by profound inlets. They were superb natural harbours. Along their banks lay the rusting hulks of the old Soviet navy.

From one headland we boarded a ferry to the city centre on the next. Natasha stood in the prow, wind in her hair: 'How good it is to get out. I adore wandering.' Then she thought for a moment: 'Yes, I know what you're thinking – I hope I *have* mastered the restlessness. But I can't be sure.'

In the sea-bright air the low, white-painted buildings of Sevastopol sparkled. Set back from tree-lined streets, garnished with neoclassical touches, they were punctuated by elaborate war memorials and unexpected glimpses of the sea. After the German army besieged it and left it in ruins in 1941 Sevastopol was awarded the status of a 'hero-city'. The architects from Leningrad rebuilt it on the old lines of the nineteenth-century naval garrison. Until the end of the Cold War it was closed to foreigners. Today, its dingy Soviet-style shops were still decked out with obsolete products.

There we met up with Volodya, who showed us round the city. With his old-fashioned military courtesy and self-deprecating competence Volodya was good company, but so unlike Natasha and Igor that it was hard to imagine how life had thrown them together.

We visited the huge stone rotunda which housed a panoramic depiction of another year-long siege of the city, this time by France, Britain and Turkey in the Crimean War of 1854–5. There was little in the panorama's account to remind us that this siege ended in defeat. Perhaps that was as it should be. History called it a defeat. But the city survived and remained a Russian stronghold, home to the imperial navy.

One civilisation after another fought for mastery of this peninsula. The greatest of the caravan routes from China ended in Crimea. It was from this south-westerly anchorage that the cargo was despatched to the markets of Europe. Under the Greeks, the city state of Cherson flourished here. Today people were clambering over its fallen columns, carrying their picnics across its paved forums to the beach beyond. After the Greeks, the city fell to the Romans; then to the Huns, Byzantium and Kievan Rus before becoming a Genoese trading colony. From one of these Genoese enclaves in Crimea, the city of Caffa, the Black Death entered Europe. The Mongols razed the city when they colonised the Eurasian landmass at the end of the thirteenth century. Long after their empire was broken they remained in their khanate in Crimea, continuing to harass Muscovy from the south. It was not until the middle of the eighteenth century that the Russian army managed finally to dispel this threat.

By that time Russia was desperate for an outlet to the south. The empire needed to secure a southern port for trading, as well as a navy to protect itself. When Catherine the Great wrested Crimea away from the Turks in 1783 she had dreams of reviving the Byzantine Empire, with her grandson Constantine as emperor.

The Turks were not alone in being alarmed by those ambitions. The British and French had imperial territories to defend. So in the middle of the nineteenth century, all three powers came together to destroy Russia's Crimean fleet once and for all.

A century and a half later the fleet was still there, if rusty. The big question now was whether Russia's navy really would agree to leave Sevastopol peacefully in 2017. Despite its white paint and brave show, there was an air of tubercular romanticism about the city. Although a mere 1.5 per cent of Crimea's population spoke Ukrainian, this was Ukraine now. The Russian officers, the sailors and the large supporting civilian workforce stranded here with their rusting hulks were pawns in the larger political game being played around them.

The city was virtually ungovernable, Volodya said. The last elected mayor died in mysterious circumstances. There had been no mayor at all since then. To the extent that it was being run at all, Ukraine's President Kuchma and Russia's Ministry of Defence did so directly, but pulling in opposite directions. In the vacuum in between, criminal gangs acted with impunity, running protection rackets, drugs and arms deals and murdering anyone who stood in their way.

When Volodya was brought here from the Afghan front the doctors pieced him together and he re-engaged on this new battle front. He served as the navy's commissar in Sevastopol, in charge of welfare. Being honest and energetic, he was popular, far too popular for the town's administration, who sacked him. So he ran instead for Sevastopol's Duma. The election brought him so many votes that it looked inevitable he would become Chair of the Duma. That was when his chief rival accused him of bribing voters with vodka. This was an unlikely charge, as Volodya did not drink. It was rendered even more implausible by the fact that he was accused of bribing voters in six different places at once, as 120 witnesses offered to testify. He was neither allowed to challenge the case in court, nor take office. As Igor warned me, nothing in Sevastopol was the way it seemed.

It was at this juncture that he happened to meet Igor and Natasha, whose fortunes were also at a low ebb. Igor, observing that Volodya needed a new power base, proposed that they start an organisation to support the welfare of the 'former people', Russian ex-servicemen and women. Many of them were now in desperate straits, needing help to adapt to civilian life. That was how the League of Officers came into being.

This unlikely relationship seemed to work. They made up for one another's deficiencies. Volodya, for all his leadership qualities, lacked a higher education. My clever friends had more education between them than they knew what to do with. In that corrupted scene, they shared one vital quality, honesty.

The League of Officers now had some 700 members, and *The Messenger* was its newspaper. In fact, it was not really a paper, more a series of in-depth *samizdat* reports, a guerrilla publication which appeared irregularly, when something needed saying. Some 5,000 copies would be published, given away free. This way, as Volodya explained, it could not be closed down by having crippling taxes imposed on it. Nor could Volodya be accused of taking bribes.

The Messenger played a significant role in the life of Sevastopol. It was the only publication not directly controlled by the local administration. Notionally, Volodya was its editor. Rumours about the paper were rife: it enjoyed powerful backing and was produced by a staff of thirty. In fact, it was entirely written by Igor and Natasha. Their names appeared nowhere, and they received no salaries for their work, only gifts. This was deliberate. Anonymity was their only protection. For since they had no institutional backing, they ran the danger of being casually eliminated if their identity leaked out.

Here in Crimea, the couple appeared finally to have found a place where their personal dramas were drowned out by the larger crisis going on around them. Yet experience made me cautious. There was always that dark force in Natasha that kept her dancing to a music the rest of us did not hear. That dance had carried her from the inner circle of the Soviet aristocracy to the status of penniless outcast. It had kept the two of them spinning round Russia like tops, full of fine intentions which did not materialise, unable to shake off their trouble, to settle down and become part of Russia's new middle class.

The sun was long over the hills by the time Natasha and I arrived home. Igor was looking pleased with himself: in our absence, he had produced a draft of the new edition. The file Volodya left him contained a record of the correspondence between

a local businessman, an ex-officer and the head of the administration. The businessman wanted to supply gas to Sevastopol,
supplanting the ancient Soviet system, which was in a state of
collapse. The letters documented the bribes that the administration
demanded of the businessman. He refused; he knew that if he gave
in, he would be vulnerable to arrest at any time. From then on,
the administration would be able to milk him dry.

My friends were excited: the new issue of *The Messenger* was
going to be explosive. It was the first time a businessman was
prepared to go public on the issue of bribes. Igor had spent the
day substantiating the story; they had to be totally sure of their
facts, for *The Messenger* was only as good as its reputation.
Tonight, Natasha would rewrite Igor's draft. It would be on the
streets within a few days.

ONE SMALL MEND IN THE PAST

Natasha and I spent the afternoon travelling by ferry and bus around the promontory, exploring the battlefields of the Crimean War. We climbed up to an old Genoese fort on the gentle green hills above Balaklava. Down below, in the perfect little harbour with its graceful swan-necked outlet to the sea, a few old buildings on the waterfront were done up, and people were sitting out in the shade of umbrellas. But this idyllic, almost Mediterranean scene was spoiled by a rusting metal floating dock and a string of rusting naval vessels which hogged the waterfront. On the far side of the harbour you could see the gateway to the submarine base which the Soviets had hollowed out of the rock.

During the Crimean War it was from this little harbour that the British kept their troops supplied. Up that valley in front of us, under fire from Russian guns on either side, the Light Brigade galloped their horses in the charge commemorated in Tennyson's famous poem:

> Theirs not to reason why,
> Theirs but to do and die.
> Into the valley of Death
> Rode the six hundred.

A dishevelled man offered to sell me two buttons he dug up in the valley below; buttons from the coat of a British Hussar who had doubtless died there. 'It is magnificent, but it is not war,' as the Marshal of the French troops described the historic charge with unkind precision. By winning the battle, the Russians prevented us, the enemy, from advancing on Sevastopol from inland. But they had not saved the city for long.

Natasha was fun to explore with, an unending source of

irreverent information. As we sat on the hillside, she expressed her delight at being free of the house, where she spent long days alone with Igor. So I made a suggestion: why not use her excellent language skills to organise English-language tours for school kids around the historical sites of Crimea? The idea appealed to her. But when we got home Igor took me aside and warned me off pursuing it: Natasha was not strong enough, he said. Fleetingly, I wondered what his motive was, but not for long. Igor was the one holding things together now.

When we first met, Igor was a caged bear, maddened, incapable of holding down a job. Natasha seemed like the resilient one. But perhaps that always was an illusion. This gifted woman was a Russian Orestes. She had taken on herself the role of scapegoat, carrier of the sins not just of her family, but of the herd. It was far too heavy for any one person to bear.

When Natasha and I reached home that evening, covered in fine white dust, we walked over the hill to bathe it off in the sea. The late-afternoon swimmers were leaving and the red sun danced on the water towards us. Up on those green hillsides despoiled by the concrete and metal graffiti of state socialism, Russia's great oil companies were stealthily buying up the seafront, erecting forbidding, high-walled dachas, cementing today's national tensions into Crimea's future.

Leaving Crimea was proving difficult. Although I was a legitimate visitor, it transpired that I could not just go and buy myself a train ticket to Kiev: Volodya was going to have to 'procure' a ticket for me. When he did, he refused to let me pay, which left me wondering how to repay his kindness.

I consulted Natasha and Igor. 'It's not things that he needs,' replied Igor. 'But there's something you could do – put the poor servicemen of our League of Officers in touch with some British organisation.' I thought about this. Who to suggest? Language was one problem – few people in Crimea spoke English, and Russian speakers in my country were rare. British servicemen perhaps – but as Russia grew steadily more anti-Western, making that connection might be misconstrued. 'You're telling me there's no one in England who's interested in us?' Igor said provocatively. Nonsense, I told him, and told them about something I had never mentioned before. I described how we had organised Bookaid, how people from all over Britain had given us more than a million English-language books, which we had sent to the public libraries of Russia and its former republics. I admitted that I had not talked about it before because I found it too painful when people ascribed some ulterior motive to us. 'Ulterior motive? Heaven forbid!' exclaimed Igor sarcastically. 'You just wanted to teach us how to live!' Then I got really angry.

The silence that followed was long and awkward. Then Natasha moved the conversation on to safer ground: 'I bet you can't guess the most important thing you ever did in Marx. You probably don't even remember – it was that evening you talked to my English pupils. That evening changed their lives – no, I'm serious. You treated them like equals. It made them see themselves differently. The encounter changed them. Because of you, because you kept their hope alive, they went on to study languages at Saratov University – all of them!'

I was grateful to Natasha for her intervention. In the past, when Igor was in attack-dog mode she would sit back and enjoy the spectacle. She was gentler now.

The following evening, when we were sitting in the shade of the camouflage, the couple finally started talking about themselves.

Natasha and I had just returned from visiting Inkerman, the site of another of the great battles of the Crimean War. There, at massive cost, the Russians staved off what might otherwise have been the allies' easy conquest of Sevastopol. It took a year for our incompetently led, disease-ridden, bloody siege to prevail. At what price? In the end, the Russian fleet lay scuppered, their territorial advances were temporarily halted, as they were today. The French came away with what military glory there was; the Ottoman Empire was shored up for a little longer. But the war cost even more lives than the American Civil War. As for the British, the greatest gain was that the filth, disease and terrible neglect of the wounded prompted Florence Nightingale and her pioneers to lay down sound principles for modern nursing.

When they first arrived in Crimea, Igor and Natasha lived in the village of Inkerman. It lay at the end of a deep inlet whose mouth was guarded by Sevastopol. Natasha and I took the ferry down the inlet from the 'hero-city', along a lovely, rocky coastline despoiled with spent machinery, rusting hulks, abandoned floating docks and gaping sewage pipes. 'We loved it here,' said Natasha as we walked inland from the boat. 'We lived in the dormitory settlement of a power station that was closing down. The buses had stopped – not profitable! So we had to walk everywhere – we developed these Herculean thighs. Our best friend was this great black dog called Jack. It was he who showed us round the Inkerman caves.'

Without Jack they would never have found the concealed entrance to a vast underground military complex which was tunnelled out in the 1930s. The dog led them to it. 'There it was, with all its own factories and houses. We thought it was abandoned at first, but we were wrong! There are people still living down there – whole communities, schools and shops. We got chased out. People say there are vast arms dumps down there.'

Then, pointing up the hillside to a place where the smooth green slope broke up like a cubist composition, Natasha went on: 'And that's where they blew up another underground town in 1942, to stop it falling into German hands – it was still full of people, our own people! They gassed them to finish them off. And it was the Germans, the enemy, who set about rescuing them! Our people only admitted that three years ago. There are survivors still alive – we met some of them.' Yes, this had been a leitmotif of my travels – this daily reminder of the contempt of those with power for those without it.

'We used to spend whole days up here with Jack,' Natasha continued. 'It's been the animals who showed us the way, always the animals. One day when we were walking round here we came on this great big crow, far larger than any we'd ever seen. It didn't fly away, just turned round and gazed at us. When we got home I looked up the crow in a book of mythology. It said that in cultures all over the world the crow means a meeting. What do you know? On the following day we met Volodya!'

Natasha and I walked to another cave community which Jack showed them. This one was in the high white chalk cliffs behind the village of Inkerman. Time and conquest exposed the interior of layer after layer of eroded caves on the pale cliff face. Here and there in sheltered corners frescoes still clung to the rock. People had clearly been living in these caves since long before recorded history. But the visible traces of habitation dated back to the eighth and ninth centuries, when icon-loving monks from Byzantium had fled the iconoclasts and taken refuge here. Following Jack's path, we walked to the entrance to the catacombs, but it was sealed off now with a metal gate. Round the corner a recent breach blasted in the rock led to a white quarry. The remains of searchlights betrayed that it was once worked by the Soviet slave army, part of the Gulag. I went into a small whitewashed working church to light candles for the victims. Natasha waited outside: 'I won't come in – I feel awkward in church. Don't know why.'

Later, when Natasha was telling Igor about our day he interrupted her at this point: 'I know why you wouldn't go in,' he jeered: 'It's because you're cursed.'

'It's true!' Natasha agreed cheerfully. But the way she said it made me hope that however much she once felt cursed, she no longer did: it was a joke now, if an edgy one.

'Yes,' she went on, 'Crimea's been miraculous for us. It's taught us how to live. And each step of the way it's been the animals who helped us. That black dog Jack was the first. He was wonderful – he used to come to our house and scratch on the door, inviting us to come out and play with him. Then he got terribly ill and his owner had to put him down. That same day – it must have been ten in the morning – we heard this scratching at the door and we said "It must be Jack." I opened the door and there was nothing there. I found out next day that he'd died at that time in the morning. His owner said the same thing'd happened to her.' She paused. 'After that how could you fail to believe that animals have souls?'

'And it was dolphins who cured Natasha of the drink,' Igor took over. 'One day I came home and found her lying on the floor in a pool of blood. I really thought she was done for—'

'I'd got blind drunk and fallen down, gashing my head and nearly taking out an eye . . .'

'Volodya came and took her to hospital.'

'What about that crate of vodka then?' I finally asked the question.

'Ah, that – I keep it there as a warning.'

It was Volodya who took her to the dolphins. They were once part of the Soviet navy's intelligence operation. Most had been sold off. The rest were going through a lean time, as they always lived off frozen fish, and now there were none. The woman who trained them went round collecting money for them. She got them working again too, this time not to make war but to heal people.

'There was one in particular,' Natasha went on. 'I'd hang on to him so tightly that it must have been very painful for him. But he didn't object – he'd swim off with me round his neck, and I could feel his power—'

'Their trainer's the one who said to us: "People think of the relationship between man and animals as being like a pyramid, with man at the top. But you should turn that pyramid on its side – that's how it really is."'

Natasha interrupted: 'That's what we've come to learn here – to take animals seriously; to live with them, to live with plants.'

'Maybe that's where you're one step ahead of us,' I reflected. 'After all, communism and capitalism were ever only variations on the same theme. In both of them man's on top of the pyramid. Capitalism may have proved stronger, but it may be doomed too because of just that – our arrogance about the natural world. Look at climate change. There's a chance we'll get through, because the market's inventive. But if we have an economic collapse it'll be much worse for us. At least you've learned how to live with a minimum.'

'Last winter the mice got into our clothes,' Natasha laughed. 'They ate only the very best of them.' 'Only the very finest wool, for their nest,' Igor took over. 'They turned up their noses at the rest.' 'The wise mice,' Natasha added. 'We had to learn not to mind about things. Yes, animals have been our teachers – we had a lot to learn. We were emotional cripples. Take Pasha for example.' Pasha was their mongrel. 'He's the one who taught Igor that he can't do anything with his head alone – that he has to learn how to love.'

The sun had dropped behind the hill by the time Natasha and I took Pasha out for a walk. It was magic hour and the sharp outline of a pale crescent moon hung in the violet southern sky. We walked over the open grassland to the wooded hill and looked down over the coast. 'As soon as I saw this place I thought, yes, I could live here,' she said. 'I recognised it too. I used to have this recurring dream: there was the sea, rocks and a bay. I'd never seen the sea either. But that dream came back again and again. When we arrived here I recognised it at once.' She paused. 'The situation here's bad – but at least there's work for us to do.'

The air was balmy with the smell of growing things. Each

footfall released the scent of bruised wormwood. All along the little river at the foot of the hill the frogs were singing. In this half-light the Soviet detritus of concrete and rusting metal that scarred the landscape was barely visible. 'The Greeks believed that the gates to heaven and hell were in Crimea. Well, they were right – they *are*. Everything that God has made is heavenly, and everything that man made is hell,' Natasha murmured.

As we walked we were greeted by a red-bearded Tatar shepherd. Evdan was grazing his sheep. He was just back from Kiev, he told Natasha with an enormous smile; he became betrothed there. His fiancée was longing to come, he said. This was a lonely place to be a serious Muslim, for few of Crimea's Tatars were interested in religion, but it was even worse in Kiev. All this land was once owned by his grandfather, Evdan explained. That was before Stalin deported the Crimean Tatars en masse to Central Asia. Evdan was an educated man, a mechanic by trade. But when he started taking his religion seriously, he decided to become a shepherd to keep out of harm's way. Walking the land every day with his sheep, it felt like his again.

Dark fell before we reached home. We were noisily greeted by little Musya. Natasha brought out fruit juice and we sat out in the courtyard under the crescent moon. 'When Evdan and I started talking,' Igor began, 'we found that though we had nothing whatever in common, we'd come to the same conclusion: that the world was so multi-faceted, so infinitely beyond our comprehension that all we could do was to concentrate on living as decently, as ethically as possible, and encouraging our neighbours to do the same.'

'Susan, you remember when we first met?' Natasha went on after a long silence. 'We were expecting the worst.'

'Yes, you were pretty unpleasant that night.'

'In the old days you, the West, were a fairy tale,' she continued: 'A land where everyone was decent and true. Trafalgar Square, Hyde Park, we trod them in our dreams.'

Igor interrupted: 'But by the time we met you the foreigners had started coming, and we'd found out that they were just the same little jerks as us, cheap businessmen who despised us, who simply weren't interested in who we were. We'd been brought up to believe that the collective was everything; that there was no such thing as individuality. That's why we're all so riddled with inferiority complexes. And now it turns out that there isn't anything *but* the individual; that all governments the world over are equally awful, that there's only this fundamental principle, the same in religions the world over.'

'This principle you can arrive at in so many ways,' Natasha concluded, 'through nature, culture or education.'

Natasha and I were waiting for the train to Kiev when she asked me: 'What do you think? Is it going to get better here? Or is this just a glimpse of what the rest of the world's going to be like after everything collapses?' How blithely I would have reassured her if she had asked me that at the start of my travels. Now I just did not know.

Volodya must have come by my ticket through a contact in the FSB. For I found that I was sharing a compartment in the sleeper with a friendly couple in the secret service who assumed I worked for some arcane part of the Organisation. I did not disabuse them.

When I opened my notebook out fell an article I had found about the Crimean War. It was from *Flag of the Motherland*, the mouthpiece of the Russian armed forces in Sevastopol. It proposed that we, the British, were still out to punish Russia for our defeat in Crimea, because the war had 'destroyed a significant proportion of the genetic bank of their aristocracy'. I was vastly amused when I read it. But Natasha and Igor ticked me off: I must take it seriously, because of what it had to say about the way Russia's Ministry of Defence was thinking.

When the train reached Kiev, I rang Natasha and Igor to find that, news having got round of the impending edition of *The Messenger*, the businessman who refused to pay bribes had got permission to supply gas to the town. Natasha and Igor were jubilant. 'You're our good angel!' said Natasha. 'After you left we sat down and had a good cry. Now it's raining so everything is in mourning.'

'I love you both,' I told them.

'No, you can't love us – we're revolting. Revolting – but redeemable.'

My visit left me feeling deeply connected to Natasha and Igor, and proud of them: at enormous cost to themselves they had slain the dragons of their past. In the course of doing so they had mended one small piece in their country's torn past. The path they had chosen was fraught with difficulty, for Crimea was too important both to Ukraine and to Russia for either to surrender control. But whatever happened, Natasha and Igor would not lose their moral compass, as Natasha believed her father had done. They would always be on the side of the powerless.

2005–2007

On 1 January 2006 Russia became the focus of world attention when it briefly cut off its supply of gas to Ukraine and Europe. Although the tactic was aimed at Ukraine, it shocked the West. It demonstrated how vulnerable dependence on Russian energy had made it: the state-controlled monopoly provider Gazprom was now supplying Europe with two-thirds of its gas imports, and this was being piped through Ukraine.

Russia's decision to turn off the tap on Ukraine in mid-winter was more than a drastic negotiating tactic. It was an escalation of the power struggle which started when Ukraine went to the polls at the end of 2004. Russia and the United States were both involved behind the scenes in that bitterly fought election. The resulting Orange Revolution shifted the country's orientation from East to West. After that, Ukraine even applied to join NATO, and started permitting NATO exercises on its territory. This was a further defiance of the agreement with Gorbachev not to expand NATO eastwards.

Russia's displeasure was not confined to Ukraine, for Georgia and Moldova had also changed their allegiance. As the year progressed, Russia increasingly reminded them how unpleasant it could make their lives. This strategy came to a head in the autumn of 2006, when Georgia's arrest of four Russians engaged in covert operations triggered the deportation from Russia of thousands of Georgians.

Russia's re-emergence on the world stage was symbolised in the summer by Putin's chairmanship of the G8 summit in St Petersburg. Putin was riding an economy which was growing at over 6 per cent a year. A poll in July showed that 86 per cent of the electorate supported Putin's leadership. The streets were no longer run by gangs; the oligarchs had been brought to heel, and a fifth of the population was now said to belong to the middle class. The president had not merely restored order; he had restored Russia's self-respect.

But this achievement came at a price: in August, the takeover of the newspaper Kommersant *by a subsidiary of Gazprom removed one of the last two independent voices in the press. This was followed in October by the contract killing of Anna Politkovskaya, critic of Putin and tireless chronicler of Russia's behaviour in Chechnya. The last remaining independent paper,* Novaya Gazeta, *had lost its star journalist. Her death provoked worldwide protest, but little in Russia itself.*

Meanwhile, unconstrained by the checks and balances of a free press, effective opposition and independent judiciary, corruption was spiralling out of control. No part of the edifice of state power, from top to bottom, was unaffected.

Over all this Putin reigned supreme. The end of his second term in office was drawing to a close. Thanks primarily to the rise in energy prices, but also to his prudent handling of the economy, GDP had increased sixfold since his accession, and poverty had been halved. According to the constitution, he was due to leave office in the spring of 2008. Would he do so? The pundits thought it unlikely.

2006

FAIRY TALE IN DUBIOUS TASTE

Eight years had passed since Ira and Sasha lost their money during the financial crash. Sasha, who borrowed money to buy a regional television station, was still weighed down by colossal debts. Though the couple remained stoical, Sasha's handsome, ravaged face told its own story. Harassed by creditors, his heart was playing up and he was plagued by insomnia. 'In his place I'd have topped myself long ago,' one friend confided. Well-wishers urged him to declare himself bankrupt, but Sasha was determined to honour his debts.

The icons hanging in every corner of their flat indicated the deep change in their life. Their year now revolved round the rigorous calendar of Orthodox feasts and fasts, major and minor.

Their politics had changed, too: 'The liberals would hate me for saying this, but we're very pro-Putin,' Ira announced a shade defiantly. 'He's given Russia back her self-respect. *The intellectuals* are always going on about the constraints on our freedom of speech – but whenever you turn on the telly there they are, protesting about Putin's authoritarianism! I'm fed up with them – you never hear them saying they're grateful for anything.'

The documentaries they made were nothing like the standard fare of soap opera and celebrity concerts which dominated Russian television now. Made on tiny budgets, the weekly series *More than Love* told stories of ordinary people with inspiring lives: a woman who had chosen to redeem a brutal murderer through her love; a simple couple who adopted the unwanted children in their district. 'We want to increase the amount of happiness in the world,' Sasha declared, smiling beatifically.

For all the pressures on them, they adored one another, and their work. 'The crash was the best thing that could have happened to us,' Ira insisted, refusing my presents. 'We're really not interested in *things* any more.' When we first met, Ira was a talented writer and filmmaker with an acerbic wit, but she was not happy. Though she was a dutiful wife, it was clear she was acting a part. 'You're right,' she sighed: 'I wasn't *born* good. It's been the great labour of my life.' When communism broke down, so did Ira's marriage. Only when she met Sasha did things fall into place for her.

It was a sunny Saturday, and the three of us were heading for the country. Ira, who had only just learned to drive, rode the car as if at any moment it might take off like Pegasus. Bowling along Moscow's new raised motorway in the sunshine, we almost did seem to be flying over the capital. Gleaming mirrored skyscrapers were flashing by on either side; tall blue and yellow cranes showed where more blocks were going up. The dingy old Soviet city centre had become a celebration of capitalism.

Our trip was prompted by a conversation with Sasha the other night. He mentioned an ecological settlement some city people were building near where they spent their weekends. It was one of a whole lot of such eco-settlements that were springing up all over Russia, he said. They were inspired by these books about a woman called Anastasia.

'Books?' I interrupted. 'What sort of books?'

Anastasia was not a common name in Russia. I knew where I had last heard it.

'Well, they're fairy tales really. But the ideas behind them are rather sympathetic. Very ecological.'

'You mean Anastasia's not real?'

'Well, she's supposed to be. This man meets a gorgeous blonde who lives in the forest, and is fed by wild animals . . .'

'Where are these stories set?'

'In Siberia.'

Was it possible? The woman Natasha told me about, who lived in the forest because she loved listening to the cedars singing . . . her name was Anastasia.

When Sasha gave me one of the books to read I saw that it was part of a whole cycle entitled *The Ringing Cedars of Russia*. There was a voluptuous blonde on the cover, rearing her head against a wild sky. It told the story of a trader who, while peddling goods to outlying villages in Siberia, meets a nymph of the woods and they have a romance. She proceeds to bear him a son, and in the course of many volumes, initiates him into her magical vision of life.

The first book came out in 1996, the year before Natasha mentioned the singing cedars to me. Ostensibly, it described events that took place the year I visited the Old Believers. There was a good deal about the extraordinary powers of the Siberian cedar, too. According to 'Anastasia', the trees only 'rang' when they reached old age, and when they did they had extraordinary curative powers. I had to laugh. There I was, still spellbound by the memory of that music in the forest, only to learn that it had been co-opted into some fairy tale in dubious taste.

Sasha and I looked up the website. The author looked a bluff sea captain, with a handle-bar moustache. Whoever he was, he was certainly a canny operator: the books had sold 10 million copies, been translated into twenty languages and inspired some 200 eco-settlements. Sasha got in touch with the friend who told him about the one nearby: perhaps he could introduce us to someone there? I'll do better than that, the friend replied: 'I'll introduce her to Anastasia herself.'

We were well out of Moscow when Ira veered off the country road and pulled up at a tiny, raspberry-pink chapel with a gleaming dome. The chapel had been built, or rebuilt, at the site of the holy spring attached to St David's Monastery. The old chapel had been destroyed by the Soviets. However, all through that period people kept coming, travelling long distances to visit the holy site.

Today the place was teeming with people. Two wooden huts had been built over the broad stream flowing from the spring. Outside both stood long queues, one of men, one of women, among them young brides in white dresses who would once have been posing in front of a Soviet war memorial. When our turn came, Ira and I entered the darkened hut and stripped off, together with women young and old, before immersing ourselves in the icy pool of sacred water.

On the outskirts of Serpukhov, we drew up at a low building bearing a sign that read Ecological Restoration Services. The field behind was sown, rather messily, with flowers and vegetables, studded with greenhouses and odd buildings. While Ira parked, four women appeared, one from each building, as if in a ballet by Pina Bausch. Of different ages, all beautiful, they walked towards us with their backs straight and their heads high.

At the bottom of the field Sasha's friend Alexander Vygovsky was wrestling to heave a tall concrete fencepost into place with the help of a tractor. In his fifties, he was deep-chested, with a grizzled beard and sardonic glint in his eye. 'So you've met the harem?' he said with a grin. There was nothing remotely harem-like about the four women, who were scrutinising me with an astringent air. The first to join Vygovsky was the group's lawyer, a woman with long fair hair and sad green eyes. Her daughter was now the group's garden designer. The other two, dark-haired, amused, were the plantswomen. They ran a consultancy which dealt with everything concerned with land ownership, from the Byzantine legal difficulties of acquiring it, to the design and planting of gardens.

'It's not quite what we came out here to do—' one of the women began before Vygovsky interrupted: 'Russia's facing a disaster. We've got 1 billion 709 million hectares of land, but right through the Soviet years we were ploughing up virgin land at a rate of 10 million hectares a year. There's only 140 million of virgin forest left. Now most of that land's been abandoned, since the collective farms collapsed. People imagine it just reverts to its natural state. But it doesn't. It becomes a wasteland. It has to be reclaimed. That's what we're doing.'

Vygovsky came out here with grand plans. He and his communards were going to buy a huge tract of land, cleanse it of chemicals and farm it organically. Then the local authorities started putting obstacles in their way. It emerged that though the land was notionally for sale, it had been acquired by shadowy interests, along with most of the land worth working round here. They only managed to get their hands on this small field because, being littered with derelict outhouses, nobody wanted it. The green-eyed lawyer sighed: 'How I loathe Russia. I wish I could leave and never come back.'

'Come on, let's go for a swim,' Vygovsky suggested after a pause. 'Then I'll introduce you to Anastasia.' As he drove the jeep along dust tracks between wide fields he pointed out tarpaulins along the side of the field, under which whole Central Asian families were sheltering. After the fall of communism, when the collective farms collapsed and their workforce left for the city, Korean businessmen somehow got their hands on this land, and they now employed these migrants to work the fields for them.

Back at the commune the gates were opened by a stolid woman with a blonde plait and a thin man with a mouth like a letter box.

'Susan – let me introduce you. This is Anastasia,' Vygovsky said solemnly. 'Go ahead – ask her what you like.' The woman blushed scarlet. I looked at the dead-pan Vygovsky and laughed.

It was a good joke, but it never quite got off the ground. Vygovsky was expecting me to be an American journalist, which in his book meant very naive. I would have to have been, for the young woman, a rather earnest Russian German, was comically miscast for the role of magical wood nymph. She did know a lot about the Anastasia settlement, though, as she and her husband had joined it. They were expelled for reasons which clearly had something do with Vygovsky.

'The whole thing's a scam,' Vygovsky fulminated: 'A "brand", a way of making money! Megre's not the real author – he's just a businessman. The FSB's behind it. It couldn't have happened without support high up – they actually *tell* their people to vote for Putin! They've made a fortune out of the books, and from selling those bits of cedar. Then there's the cedar oil, so called – I've had it tested, it's ordinary oil with a few drops of cedar added. And when they join the settlement they have to put a thousand dollars into the cause . . .'

On and on he went. Originally he had been enthusiastic about the settlements, according to Sasha. So when had he changed his mind? And was what he was saying true? He was, as he was telling me in the jeep, something of a Scheherazade when it came to stories. In Soviet labour camp – to which he was consigned for starting an ecological movement – he had survived by telling stories: first he told his inmates every one he had ever read; then he started making them up . . .

'They're trying to provoke this sort of pioneer movement – to recolonise Russia! But the cretins who join up know nothing about the countryside. They sell their flats, buy these animals – they don't even know how to look after them! Even those who do get their act together realise pretty soon that they haven't got a chance of living off the land. Not off one hectare, which is the myth they've been sold! It's just not possible! Ecological communes haven't ever been able to get by without outside help – look at Vissarion's lot, look at your Owenites, Susan – they're all the same. And in the case of Anastasia's, they'll find that the land they've bought actually belongs to some absentee Chechen . . .'

Vygovsky had worked himself up into a passion. It almost sounded as if the man were jealous. As his diatribe moved onwards, outwards, the dividing line between fact and fantasy vanished: the conspiracy was not just the Anastasia books; it was the whole corrupt corporate system that was bleeding Russia dry. The English started it, of course, when America was Britain's colony. Now Blair was America's puppy. Russia had been sold down river – they bought Putin when he was working for the KGB in Germany. The Jews were behind it. The system was rotten from top to bottom. He had friends high up in the *apparat* – they knew what was going on, but the system was too strong for them.

The four women were looking on with Buddhist detachment. It was impossible to tell what they made of this rant. 'What's going on is the destruction of the ethnos, the Russian people. Where are the Real Russians, the ones with conscience? They've been systematically destroyed – look at what *they* did to the Serbs! The Belorussians are the only ones who are still holding out – Lukashenko's a hero! But if Jews like you had their way . . .' For lack of any available Jews, this jibe was addressed to the very Nordic Sasha.

Finally, to puncture this engulfing conspiratorial ectoplasm, Sasha interrupted: 'Tell them what Max is doing,' he said to me. My son was building community radio stations in Africa, Latin America and Palestine, I told them. Vygorsky dismissed my son as an agent of the system, of course. That did it: he was quite entitled to his stale, paranoid opinions, I retorted. He could rant to his heart's content, but not pronounce on the activities of a young man he knew nothing about, one who did more than produce hot air like Vygovsky . . .

'Oh dear, now I've offended the English woman.' Vygovsky was contrite. 'I was only joking.'

Back in Moscow, reading Vygovsky's essays, I felt more sympathetic to him. They were all about the importance of restoring the 'dead' tracts of Russia's countryside. Vygovsky was knowledgeable, a serious ecologist, but the essays made ponderous reading, bristling with footnotes and statistics. However, this scholarship did not quite conceal the fact that the underlying ideas were strikingly similar to many of those in the best-selling Anastasia books. These were familiar from my visit to the guru of Cosmism,

Professor Kaznacheev, he of the magical cylinder. The professor maintained that, for better or worse, living matter, the bio-sphere, was going through a crucial transition, becoming dominated by the noosphere, the layer of human thinking and belief that girdled the earth.

No wonder Vygovsky was angry. As an ecologist, he believed that his contribution in this age of the noosphere was a vitally important one. But he was up against the blockbuster version of Cosmism, aimed at a mass audience. The Anastasia books told the story of a gigantic, intergalactic battle between the forces of good and evil, one which was reaching its decisive climax. Anastasia initiates her businessman-lover into the wildest reading of man's lost magical powers, from long-distance viewing to direct communication with the divine; from astral travel to man's colonisation of outer space. . . . How could Vygovsky compete with that?

THE TWO-PLANK BRIDGE

Anna and I sat in the sparkling new premises of a Baskin and Robbins ice-cream parlour in central Saratov, sipping cocktails from long-stemmed glasses. Outside, the gold stars on the chapel's turquoise onion dome gleamed in the morning sun and the sound of ascending arpeggios reached us from the turreted conservatoire beyond.

Last time we met I feared Anna was losing the battle against despair. But today she looked festive in a flowered summer frock, and her eyes sparkled with amused intelligence. I had often worried about her being lonely, but now I was celebrating her independence. For well over a decade the population had been shrinking at the rate of more than 600,000 a year, and Russia's men were the core of the problem. They were dying of alcohol and drugs, committing suicide, crashing their cars, falling victim to the careless violence of a society which put as little value on the individual as ever. While Anna had to chronicle the effects of this in her journalism, at the end of the day she was free to go back home and write. Yes, she was writing poetry again.

Anna's career had also taken an unexpected leap forward: she was working for the Saratov edition of a racy, muck-raking and extremely successful national paper, *The People's Pravda*. The pressure on her to sharpen up her journalistic style had done her good. She now earned three times as much as a senior surgeon, a museum curator or a teacher.

'Well, what do you make of Saratov?' she asked. I gulped my Martini, playing for time. Saratov had defied my attempts to grow fond of it. Yes, the chapel outside had been restored; some bank had done up a Jungendstil building; a few new housing blocks had gone up, and a glass-fronted shopping mall. But the faces in the street looked miserable, and everything that was derelict two years ago was far more so now. The streets were pock-marked with holes, stinking hills of rubbish baked in the sun – the dustmen, unpaid for a month, having gone on strike.

'I'm sorry, Anna, but it's worse than ever . . .' She sighed: 'Yes – there really *is* something rotten about it! I can't stand it. The business of living here, just living, is too hard. Everyone's exhausted. I'd love to leave, to move up north, somewhere like Vologda.'

'Why don't you?'

'My parents. They're old. Three hours on the bus from here.' She fell silent, before adding: 'Putting up with things, learning not to notice, not to mind. *That's* the life skill you need to develop here.'

Over the next few days, leafing through backcopies of the paper, I started to see what she meant. When Putin came to power, the budget per person in Saratov province was more or less on a par with the country as a whole. Five years later it was little more than half the national average, despite the fact that the country's economy had been growing year on year. In neighbouring provinces, investment had increased between two and forty times, but here in the province between four and five times less was being invested than a year ago. Official corruption had become so bad that the big taxpayers had decamped over regional borders. The province was a black-hole for public money. The region's ombudsman had received more complaints about this province than any other in Russia.

What about Putin's reforms, I asked Anna. 'Reforms?' she snorted. 'Nothing's changed here – they've just got worse. Well, I can't say *nothing's* changed – they did force Ayatskov out in the end.' The fabulously corrupt official Anna vowed to unmask in her *passionara* days had gone on to become the province's governor. As long as he remained in the job, he enjoyed immunity from the law. Even now, he seemed to have cut a deal which protected him and his closest allies from prosecution.

A recent spate of arrests among top officials offered a spark of hope, however. Anna's chronicles of official greed, in her capacity as the paper's legal correspondent, were leavened by flashes of Gogolian farce. There was the city's ex-mayor who buried diamonds and silver spoons in his garden; the ex-Minister of Roads, imprisoned on seventeen charges of stealing staggering sums from his budget. First he beat up a cellmate for smoking. Next, he complained that prison guards had shaved his head against his will and beaten him up. Then, after writing a formal complaint he proceeded to eat – yes eat – his testimony. Now he was claiming that the fabulous sums he stole were not for him, but for key members of Putin's government, one of whom masterminded Putin's presidential election . . .

The present governor was an honest technocrat. But how could he turn this soup of corruption into a viable administration? Months after the arrests of those top officials, many of their jobs were still unfilled. As the province drifted, rudderless, some businessmen were feeling nostalgic for Ayatskov, who at least 'made things happen'.

Meanwhile corruption kept eating its way through businesses and bureaucracies, police stations, tax offices, colleges and hospitals. I had come up against a tragic consequence of this among my own friends. When I arrived, I tried to track down the two sons of Vera Romanenko, my friend who had joined Vissarion's community. After we had drawn a blank, Anna suddenly said: 'Hey, Romanenko – that's not a common name. Was one of them was called Dmitry?'

That was how I learned about the murder of Vera's older son: a gifted goldsmith and painter, he was attacked one night by a gang of drunken law students, celebrating their final exams. '*Law* students?' Well, not real ones, she explained. They were thugs whose families bribed their way through college. It was common practice: while the straight students sat writing their exams under strict invigilation, next door a lecturer would be dictating answers to the bent group . . .

'The corruption's immeasurably worse than it was under communism. Then, people at least knew they were doing something wrong. Now they seem oblivious. I'll give you an example: there's a young detective who was sent to prison for taking an enormous bribe. I wrote the case up. When he came out he got a job as a journalist. Well, I was looking for a job, and this paper called *Reporter* offered me a place. "There's someone on your staff who wouldn't want me around," I warned the editor. "Nonsense! He'd be delighted!" he replied. And it was true! He didn't seem to have the faintest idea that he'd done anything wrong! That's the trouble – we've lost our moral bearings.

'How can you change things? I don't know. I was born in our local hospital, deep in the country. My father carried me home proudly in his arms. He had to cross this river over a bridge which was only two planks wide. The river was in full spate. On the other side the two grandmothers stood watching, praying he wouldn't fall in. Since then Khrushchev has come and gone. So have Brezhnev, Andropov, Chernenko, Gorbachev and Yeltsin. Now we've got Putin. But when I was back for my birthday this spring there it was – the same two-plank bridge. What kind of leader's it going to take to broaden that bridge by just one plank, I found myself wondering!'

ST SERAFIM AND THE BOMB

Anna now lived high up in a tower block on the summit of the 'yellow hills' of Saratov's Tatar name. It perched like a gull's nest in a cliff. Factories and housing blocks stretched over the hillside opposite. But way below tall poplars swayed in the breeze. Swifts screeched softly as they swooped past the window.

It was Sunday morning, and Anna had gone to church. 'So you've made your peace with Orthodoxy, then?' I asked as she changed into a modest skirt. Last time we met she was agonising between the Catholic Church and Orthodoxy. 'Well, there are things I still hate about it,' she replied in her categorical way. 'I wouldn't suggest someone in real trouble turned to our Church – it's incapable of helping anyone. They'd stand there, unable to understand a word, while the priest chanted in that weird monotone. The services are interminable. And I can't bear all that standing either. That stuff about having to wear something on my head, about not wearing trousers . . . Huh!

'But Catholicism – well . . . in the end I liked everything about it except what's at the heart of it. I was so fond of the nuns and Father Michael – the way they were with one another, the way they lived their lives. It was just the concept of Christ I couldn't take – this business about him being half man, half God . . .' She pulled a face. 'I can't explain it, though goodness knows I've read enough about it.'

Beside me on the window sill, Anna's hamster Anfissa was whirling round on the wheel in her cage. With Anfissa and her black cat, Lucy, Anna was tender and intimate. As a prominent journalist, her public manner was confident now. But without that professional armour, she still found intimacy hard.

How painful that break with Father Michael and the nuns must have been, I reflected. Her reason was almost the same as that

which precipitated the schism in Christianity in 1054. The Western
Church proposed a slight change to the Creed. They wanted it to
say that the Holy Spirit proceeded not just from the Father but
from the Son, too. The traditionalists of the Eastern Church
objected that the Latins were trying to make the Trinity too comprehensible, too rational: the relationship between Father, Son and
Holy Ghost *was* a mystery, and so it should remain. Ten centuries
later, Western Europeans like me were still itching to *understand*,
to bring reason into it, to keep changing things. At the start of
my travels, Anna and I both hoped naively that the fall of communism would change something in Russia. In retrospect, of course,
liberal democracy never stood a chance.

The night before the heatwave that gripped Saratov broke. Now,
even wearing all my summer clothes at once, I was still cold. I
paced up and down the flat, trying to keep warm. Once again
Anna had left her diary out on the table. This time I did not even
hesitate.

'This morning when I woke up I watched the light come up
and saw what it was that stopped us living in the light. But now
I feel ill and tired. Very tired. My nerves are shot. I can't just
comfort myself by saying, "You mustn't. Going through all that
again is meaningless." I'm tired and I long to go back to the church
which has got so many warm associations for me.' She must mean
the community of nuns in Saratov's Catholic church.

'I've got to go on, make good my choice, embrace the cross.
Though I find myself thinking: I'm too vulnerable psychologically,
there are so many things I can't bear – loud music, for example,
crowds, the company of people who make me feel uncomfortable
. . . Still I've got to do it, do what I can. First, I've got to stop
complaining, blaming God. For the fact that "we live in a country
like this" and all that. Be happy that you can bring at least a little
light into this darkness. How little, alas! So little that I can't even
seem to see it myself.

'Once, a long time ago, that silly little *S*** W**** (my italics)
wrote to me: "You're like a nun who lives in the world." I found
it funny then – I didn't like it. It didn't seem to fit me at all
. . . What's important is bearing the cross. In its totality. And that
I'm absolutely not capable of. My unworthiness starts right here
– with my whingeing, my inner struggle. I measure my whole life
by how good or bad I feel. My flat, my pay, blows of fate,

relationships with those around me. Yes, we feel defenceless when we're children. But we grow up. We have to decide how to relate to the world around us, to everything that happens to us. How to live, how to be. And that decision has to be radical, whole, focused. People like that can be positive, or negative. There was Serafim of Sarov and there was Lenin! But the principle's the same – wholeness, radicalism.

'Great joy saves people. Deep spiritual truth. It's that, not the outward kind of jollity, that attracts and saves people. Outwardly a person may be cheerful, but you can tell they're feeling bad inside. That kind of jollity is often noisy, exhausting, importunate, extrovert . . .

'A complex which grows worse with the years: I'm going to have to go on working – think how ridiculous I'll be, this babushka running around with her notebook. But what matters is how to work. If you do serious, principled work, rather than just earning your bread and butter, it doesn't matter one bit if you're a babushka . . .

'Very tired physically. Keep falling asleep. But I can still feel and see. There are some places, zones, that are alive and others that are burned-out, trampled, dead. Special feeling for the places that are alive – I'm drawn to them. But I'm tired. Horror, shame for the past, makes everything painful. It's hot and the brief showers of rain bring no respite.'

I closed the diary, stunned. There it was, the raw matter of Anna's daily struggle with despair, and the measure of her achievement. I once thought Anna might be a depressive. No, her despair was a rational response to the rottenness around her. Never once had she complained to me. But her days were spent chronicling the corruption of this city, the bottomless greed of its high officials at the expense of the powerless. If she was holding her own now, it was thanks to her faith. When I arrived and found her so buoyant, I thought perhaps she had found happiness. But no, she had just become more resilient. At what a cost.

Later, I found out more about Serafim of Sarov, whom she mentioned in her diary. An engaging character, he became a monk at the time of the French Revolution. After living on his own in a hut for twenty-five years, he came out into the world. He was credited with all sorts of miracles, including levitation and the gift of prophecy. But it was my guess that what appealed to Anna was the fact that Serafim was a mystic of a particular kind: he believed that anyone could reach the kind of mystical experience which was the ultimate reward of the contemplative's prayer.

The town of Sarov, where Serafim spent his life as a monk, has acquired another more sinister claim to fame. It lay further up the Volga from Saratov, by Arzamas-16, the secret military research base where the world's first hydrogen bomb was hatched. Andrei Sakharov worked there, among many other top Soviet scientists. So secret was their research then, and perhaps now too, that the scientists were not even allowed to talk to one another about it.

In 2003, Putin was among those who went there to celebrate the centenary of Serafim's canonisation. He now enjoyed a close relationship with the Church. Many Russians found this reassuring, though I am not sure why. The Church and the old KGB enjoyed the closest of relationships during the Soviet period, and that had not changed. The saint and Arzamas-16 were the icon and the axe, two faces of power. That remained the trouble with institutionalised belief, and not just in Russia.

THE CROOKED AND THE BEAUTIFUL

The communal taxi was jolting downhill from Saratov's industrial heights towards the old port. Misha and Tatiana had just flown in from their family holiday in Turkey, and I was going to stay with them.

Anna and I had been through a tricky couple of days, and I felt bad about leaving. First, there was the argument about Chechnya. Anna must have been reading about negotiations between the Spanish government and Eta over independence for the Basque region, as she suddenly burst out: 'Why are they negotiating with terrorists? This'll sound terrible to the liberals and democrats, but you've got to stand firm! They're always saying Yeltsin shouldn't have started the second Chechen war – but we *had* to fight it, or Russia would've fallen apart!'

'But Anna . . .'

'When Yeltsin pulled out in '96 it didn't *end* the war!' she steamed on.

'But it ended the fighting, which . . .'

'Let me tell you this story.' It was about a little girl from Saratov, daughter of a businessman, who was kidnapped and taken to Chechnya: 'They started sending her fingers home one by one. . . .'

'This is no way to discuss the rights and wrongs of a war.'

Anna was not to be stopped: 'It was wrong to withdraw in '96. Like a doctor who fights to save a patient, then gives up and says "You're cured!" when he knows the patient's getting worse!'

'Don't be absurd! You should be learning from the Spanish – that's what we did with the IRA over Northern Ireland, too. Things aren't brilliant there, but the war's over and the economy's growing.'

Suddenly Anna was listening. 'But you can't sit down with terrorists!' she concluded lamely.

*   *   *

The exchange left us both slightly shaken. It was a shock to hear that Anna wanted to disassociate herself so firmly from the 'liberals and democrats'. I hoped she had been saying this to me 'for the record', but it was a faint hope. Her friends told me she had become obsessively cautious as a journalist since Putin came to power. The particular trigger was the case that had been hanging over her since we last met. On the basis of a press release, she had written an article about weapons the police found in the garage of a Chechen living in Marx. The newspaper had destroyed the press release, and the police department which issued it had been reorganised and binned its records. So the man won his case. The paper was fined, and no one blamed Anna. But the incident had left her badly frightened: she had developed a mania for writing and rewriting, checking and rechecking every article, they said.

The following day, a public holiday, the familiar Saratov gloom descended on me. Longing to get out of Anna's dreary flat, I suggested we went to see the pilgrimage: some 300,000 pilgrims had started flooding into Saratov to see one of John the Baptist's fingers from some Serbian monastery which was doing the rounds of provincial cities. The notion of this ex-fortress of communism in the grip of religious fervour fascinated me. But Anna was categorical: it would be dangerous. 'Anyway, I *hate* crowds.' Too late, I realised my tactlessness: a couple of days ago a friend of hers had been run over and killed by a bus full of pilgrims.

'Well, let's think of somewhere else to go.'

'There *is* nowhere to go.' She shot me a withering look. So for the second day running we were stuck in Anna's flat. When I offered to help her with her English by recording something, she said brusquely when handing me the tape: 'Tell me about your family.'

I considered this as I looked out of the window, over the dancing heads of the poplars: Anna knew my husband was recovering from a serious illness, yet she had never even asked how he was.

'Sorry. I don't feel like it,' I said.

'What?'

'You're not really interested.'

'What?'

When I explained, she burst into tears. For the rest of the day she did little but weep, on and off. I felt terrible. My mistake was to take Anna's new resilience at face value. Drawn back momentarily into my own family crisis, I forgot how fragile Anna's equilibrium was. She was a formidably strong woman. But she suffered from the vulnerability of a person determined to remain true in a society where everything around her was crooked. I had no idea how to mend what I had broken.

I arrived at Misha and Tatiana's in time to watch France playing Portugal in the semi-finals of the World Cup. This was a big occasion for Misha, now chairman of the football club in Marx. In his mid-forties now, and brown from his holiday, his boyish good looks had hardened to a glint of steel. For Misha the French team played a beautiful game, but the Portuguese – pah! Each time a Portuguese player fell over, accusing a French player of foul play, Misha roared with indignation. Portugal's narrow victory left him inconsolable: it was the last straw, this most public triumph of the sly ones who snatched victory from the honest men by bending the rules!

Foul play was very much on his mind. The factory had twice as many storage silos as on my last visit; it was producing nearly three times as much virgin sunflower oil and they were farming ten thousand hectares of land too. Sales had spread beyond the Volga provinces, into the Urals. 'That's the problem,' Misha told me over breakfast next morning. 'Here, once you've grown large enough, you start attracting attention – and it's the wrong kind.'

Every year it was proving harder for the business to hold its own against the big manufacturers. *Solntse* was competing against farmers in the black earth region of southern Russia, where the same amount of land harvested twice the crop. 'The only way to stay ahead of the game is technology and know-how,' Misha explained. 'Farmers here are deeply conservative – when I came back from Germany last year, full of ideas, my people were horrified. My manager couldn't bear it – walked off the job.'

Viktor Goldantsev, the ex-boss of Murmansk's nuclear power station, would not have done that. But since my last visit Misha had lost the farm manager who shared his dream of modernising Russian agriculture. Viktor died in a car crash, swelling the hideous statistic of untimely deaths among Russian men. His photograph hung over Misha's desk.

The loss had left Misha no less determined: 'The Germans may think it's going to take twenty years for us to catch up, but I haven't got that long. Here, farmers still leave the earth fallow for a year. European farmers have given that up – good farming land's at too much of a premium. Last year we tried working it like that for the first time. But it's expensive – you've got to keep the soil well fertilised, as well as using pesticide.'

I asked him whether business had become easier since those chaotic early days. 'Oh – don't start me, we'll be here all day! It's hugely more difficult. The corruption's all in the state now, which means it's much more dangerous.' A neighbouring farmer had taken out a criminal case against him. The farmers of the region acted as middlemen for one another, selling on seeds and new technology. Last year Misha bought seed and sold it on. Everyone seemed pleased – except one farmer, who did not pay, complaining that the yield was less than he expected. 'He blames me! In fact he's just lazy!' Misha took him to court for non-payment, and won. Now the man was accusing him of fraud. In normal courts, there would be no case to answer, for Misha had sold the seed on in sealed packets. 'But this is Russia – the man's got close ties with the local police. Maybe he's just out to squeeze money out of me, but maybe someone's out to get me! There's no knowing!

'When Putin came to power everyone was longing for political stability. Now they've got it. But it's not the kind of stability business needs! What happened to Khodorkovsky could happen to any of us. Any day. Yes, of course there was a political dimension in his case. But it's true all the same – they can pick us off any day they want.' Mikhail Khodorkovsky, richest of the oligarchs, started using his money in the interests of democratising Russia. The tax police charged his oil company Yukos with owing billions of roubles in back tax. The company was broken up, and its assets redistributed among Putin's people. He was in prison in Siberia, in solitary confinement.

Had the new 13 per cent flat-rate tax Putin had introduced not made things easier, I wondered? 'In theory. But in practice the tax inspectors are bent and their powers unlimited. Take this business hanging over me – those inspectors could move into my office tomorrow and kill the business stone dead. If they're out to nail me, they'll find something to pin on me. I used to love doing business. But I've had enough. The trouble is if you get off the treadmill for a second it all comes to a grinding halt.'

I did not envy Misha. But what he was saying left me hopeful. While journalists like Anna had no power now, businessmen were surely different. At some stage, people like him, whom Russia needed to encourage if the economy was ever to escape its dependence on oil and gas, must become a force the state had to reckon with.

Before I left on the evening sleeper, Tatiana and I slipped off to walk in our favourite park, planted on the English model by an anglophile governor in the nineteenth century. The cold snap had passed and the sun was shining again. The paths threading through the dark oak trees were thronged with people. The swans on the glassy lake were imperturbable. A rash of smart new tower blocks now hemmed the park in along one side; there were rumours, Tatiana said, that the developer had bribed the authorities and the next lot of blocks were going to invade the park.

Business at the café was brisk. As we waited for our Siberian beer and sushi I asked after Misha's mother, whom I had not seen as she was living in the family's house in Marx. 'Well, she's better off there,' Tatiana sighed. 'Misha's working round the corner, and he drops round. She's got someone looking after her. And she can potter round the garden. But she's not happy. How could she be? All her life she's done nothing but work, and now there she is – blind, with nothing left to do.'

I looked over the table at Tatiana. Over the years, this pale northern beauty had grown into a snow queen, full-lipped and sensual. So what about her? She rarely talked about herself. Yet what I saw in her grey eyes struck me to the heart.

Over breakfast, I was looking through her family photographs. There was a faded snap of Misha on the day they met. He was just a boy, blond and wiry, with a cheeky grin. 'He doesn't like himself,' she whispered now, as if carrying on an earlier conversation. 'That's what drives him. He's got to outwit the lot of them. When he was young, it just made him a wonderful sportsman. But now if he's not working he's planning his next move. It's got so bad he can't relax. If we go out somewhere with friends he says he feels out of place. And if I look as if I'm enjoying myself he says, "There, you see, you don't need me."'

Recently, she admitted that she was sorry not to have developed the gift of healing which her grandmother wanted to pass down to her. But without being aware of it, she had done so. Of all those who befriended me in Marx, Tatiana, once the shyest, had become the hub of the wheel. Throughout that strange, upside-down time in Russia's history, she alone never lost her sense of balance. Perhaps it would have been easier for her if she had. Each of my other friends reacted to the fall of communism by going crazy in their own way. Each faced the task of reinventing themselves, as well as having to survive the suicide buried in their family. Tatiana just became more like herself with the years. Only now she carried the curse of memory, the unspeakable weight of the past.

GLIMPSES OF GRACE

About Anna, Tatiana was reassuring: 'Don't worry – next time you see her she'll have put herself back together again.' When we met up at the Moscow sleeper, it seemed Tatiana was right. While I read on my top bunk, Anna was chatting to the couple with whom we were sharing a compartment. They were gossiping about Ayatskov, the corrupt ex-governor of the province who still proved immune from prosecution.

'So what's he doing now?' asked the husband.

'Sitting in his palatial house, twiddling his thumbs,' replied Anna.

I listened with pleasure as she entertained our fellow passengers with gossip about Saratov personalities. Her professional persona was confident and relaxed.

When we reached Moscow Anna would be travelling on to the northern city of Novgorod. Her summer holidays were now spent exploring Russia's ancient heartland. In the sleepy charm of towns like Vologda she had found a Russia she could love. The walls of her shabby flat were lined with little coloured postcards of northern churches. They were the architectural embodiment of the spirituality she had embraced.

The train had stopped at a country station. On the platform an old woman was sweeping the path from side to side with wide strokes of her long broom, wielding it like a scythe.

Down below, the bulky couple were playing cards now. Yes, they too were using this shrivelled pack of cards. It was only the other day, when I was playing cards with Tatiana's daughter, Nadezhda, that I noticed it. The lowest card of the four suites was a six. There were no twos, no threes, fours or fives. These cards were just missing. When I asked the couple why they were playing with such a diminished pack, they looked at me blankly. Anna laughed: 'You're right – I first discovered how many cards the rest of the world plays with when I read *The Queen of Spades*!' In Pushkin's famous story these cards played a crucial role.

No one in the compartment knew what had happened to those missing cards. I guessed the Soviets deemed the very notion of the hierarchy to be counter-revolutionary. They probably wanted to chop out the whole royal family until someone pointed out that there would not be many card games left if they did. So they just cut the 'plebeian' cards, as if to announce that from now on they were all kings and queens . . . Now communism was no more, but these Russians were still making do with the same censored pack.

I took out the sheaf of poems which Anna had given me to read:

> I went out into a field
> by the quiet river one day
> and a sudden peace overcame me,
> the gift of a higher will,
>
> I stood there amazed at my fate
> as if it were not mine . . .
> That glimpse of grace
> of a soul not ready
>
> unaccustomed to understanding.
> If I could only remember how it had been –
> behind the village barns
> at sunset on that long summer evening.

A profound change had come over Anna's poetry, though the quality is lost in my translation. In Russian, the tranquillity she now managed to capture in her poems was the counterpoise to the painful struggle of her life.

> I look at a cloud, a branch
> A patch of asphalt and sand.
> What I took to be a shrimp
> Is in fact a folded maple leaf

And I walk along – glad of my mistake
ambushed by joy – towards
my favourite dacha – there's the fence
the green all patched with rust

the big lock on the gate
the cabbage forgotten on the table
the glistening threads
on the freshly dug earth.

Who is there I can tell about this –
the small, lost patch of asphalt,
the dimpled sand, slightly warmed by the
crimson horror of the drought?

The train passed a deep ravine etched into the steppe. In his novel
The Naked Year, Pilnyak described how bandit gangs hid in those
ravines when Russia's wheat bowl was being fought over by the
Red and White armies. Trains from the cities would crawl along
these tracks, crammed with starving people who had come out
here to forage for food. Was it surprising that the Russians had
such a fear of chaos? The 1990s were a ripple by comparison. But
the genetic memory it stirred up was traumatic.

All night I spent coming to terms
with my fate. I had almost managed.
But by daybreak the rain had breathed its way
through the planks, the plaster and the chalk.

And through the birch twig
through the spiders' web and the glass –
on the wall that smells of chalk –
a faint blueish patch of warm.

So does it matter really, what happens to me?
The damp stoop, the hook on the door
and the many-voiced silence
of the wind in the waving branch.

Yes, Anna had come to terms with her fate. But she found it hard to forgive those who failed to do so. Her cousin Sasha had killed himself recently, she was telling me: 'I went to the funeral, of course. But I couldn't cry – I was so angry. He was such a talented man, and so good at everything. How dare he do that to his family?'

FINDING THE GOLDEN WOMAN

Embarrassing though it was to discover that the source of Natasha's information about the singing cedars came from a best-selling fairy story, I wanted to know more. Luckily, so did Sasha and Ira. So what about all those settlements which the Anastasia books were said to have inspired? Later that summer, the three of us set off to visit one out at Konyaevo, some 150 miles east of Moscow.

Often by late September the golden days are over in Russia and winter set in. But we were lucky: it was a sunny morning and the air was crisp. The journey took most of the day. After turning south off the Vladimir road we found ourselves in an undulating landscape of lakes and birch forests blazing with yellow and gold. The day was still, without a breath of wind. Here and there a poplar trembled, like a hen shaking rain off its wings. We caught glimpses of the occasional village, tucked in the folds of the land, well away from the road.

As we drove, I considered what I had learned about the settlements since that first abortive visit to Vygovsky. The Anastasia books were nothing if not ambitious. They proposed that contemporary man was so swamped with trivial information that he had lost sight of the great issue as to where humanity was heading. Ever since the coming of Christianity Russians (and implicitly the rest of us) had been in the grip of a foreign ideology. Since then, all power had ultimately been controlled by the high priests, or their secular counterparts. The books, which had already been translated into dozens of languages, proposed that the key to liberation lay in the soil: everyone needed their own hectare of land, a place where they could live, grow their own food and reconnect with nature and God.

First, they proposed, you have to realise your dream in imagination. Then you will be ready to wind up your old life and buy your plot of land. After that other great changes will start happening. You will begin to recover the remarkable powers which man had lost. You will not just be changing your life: you will be joining the great cosmic battle against the forces of evil . . .

When we finally arrived at Konyaevo we found our way barred by armed guards. Baffled, we asked at the local shop. The plump shop assistant whispered that we'd come to a secret rocket installation. She'd heard there was another Konyaevo somewhere nearby – perhaps we'd got the wrong one? It was indeed the wrong Konyaevo. We drove on through the forest for a long time until we were waylaid by a sturdy tribe of old men and women in woolly hats, who put us on the right road in return for our loading the car with cranberries and jars of pickled mushrooms.

The red sun was spinning on the horizon by the time we turned down a dirt track leading through birch forests. The land, which some collective farm had claimed from the forest in Soviet times, stood waist-high in weeds. But a crop of idiosyncratic buildings was starting to rise up, each set on its hectare of land. The place seemed deserted. Then we spotted a man working on the frame of a wooden house. Sergei, a plump, curly-haired computer programmer from Moscow, made us a cup of tea on his camping stove. When the buildings were finished there would be some six or seven hundred people here, he said, half of them young. And was it really going to be possible to feed a family from one hectare of land as the books claimed, Sasha asked? The chubby programmer smiled, unruffled: we'll see, he said. Maybe it wouldn't have been in the past. But a lot of the settlers were technocrats like him; they may never have lived in the country, but thanks to the Internet, which would be powered here by solar panels, they had the benefit of the latest farming techniques.

Dark fell like a blackout curtain. We were a long way from the nearest town. Did Sergei know of anywhere we could stay the night, Sasha asked? 'Dunno – most people have gone back to the city by now.' Disappointingly, it was starting to look as if these were just city folk building second homes for themselves. As we drove on down the track into the old village the headlights picked out two women walking down the track. Sasha rolled down the window: 'Ladies, I wonder whether you could suggest where we could spend the night? We would pay of course . . .' 'You'll find no place here,' said a broad woman, clamping her jaws shut. But

Sasha teased her until she surrendered to his charm and invited us home.

Aunt Ksenia, buxom and bossy, lived in a traditional wooden house with her crimson-faced, monosyllabic husband, nine hens, five goats and three kittens. The clay stove was warm and the air sweet with the smell of animals and apples. Only seven people now lived in the village all year round, she said, and she was the youngest.

Over a meal of home-grown potatoes and tomatoes Aunt Natasha inveighed against the 'sectarians', who were ruining the countryside. They took all the firewood and bathed in the lake, naked. Most barbarous of all – they buried their dead on their plots of land! 'Disgusting,' she sniffed. We fell into bed early, weighed down by her indignation.

All night two kittens tore round the darkened room wailing and I lay awake thinking of the Siberian cedars whose singing led me here. Those cedars were the symbol at the heart of the Anastasia legend: Sergei was wearing a sliver of cedar round his neck and had planted a cedar by his house. Well, Vygovsky was right about one thing: the cedar business was clearly lucrative.

Next morning, a grey mist was still clinging to the ground when we left the village. In the middle of a wasteland rank with weeds three people were working on the roof of a skeletal house. A small, elderly woman with sun-bleached features explained that she and her son had come from Kazakhstan. With Russia facing demographic collapse, people from the old colonies were now being offered inducements to return. When Sasha questioned them about Anastasia and their dreams for the future mother and son looked perplexed. Simple people, they did not appear to be inspired by any great Russian Idea. They just needed a house and in Kazakhstan they had practised these pioneer skills all their lives.

We were about to head back to Moscow when the other young man, who had not said a word, spoke up: 'Hold on – there's someone I think you should meet – follow me.' He led us across the wasteland towards a wood of densely grown young birches. As we followed, the sun broke through the clouds and moved across the abandoned fields. By the time we reached the wood and were walking down a winding path the woodland floor was bright with red toadstools and yellow birch leaves. We came to a clearing with a small house built of whole trees. It had not a single window or door. Nearby, a heavy plastic sheet stretched between sticks was providing rudimentary shelter. A young man with a heart-shaped face and plaited headband round his long dark hair was shovelling it in an enormous hole. Damir was digging his pond, he said. We followed the sound of children's laughter down another path. In the next clearing, by a house of bright new wood, a young mother was tickling her child in a hammock, while a blond young man was laying roof-felt on the house. 'This is just the outhouse, but we'll overwinter in it,' the young man explained as he showed us his handiwork. 'I could've gone to university, but I didn't want to spend my whole life at the whim of some boss. My father works in the Prosecutor General's office, and my uncle's in the FSB – I could've done anything. But this is what I want! And I know plenty of people in Moscow who're dying to join us. They're just waiting to see how we get on.'

As he talked, a barefoot teenage girl had run down the path to join us. She had grey eyes, a slightly upturned nose and long fairish hair plastered flat. She stood in the sunshine very upright, quivering slightly, as though with the effort of holding herself in check. Her skin was burnished by the sun and she was glowing with excitement.

'Where did you sleep last winter?' Sasha was asking. 'Outside, of course, in the tents!' the girl broke in. 'It's fine, really!' Her words tumbled out like fish from a net. 'I knew very early on that I didn't want to live like other people. I'd go to the shops and I could never see anything I wanted to buy. Hems a little longer, hems a little shorter – just more things. And the longer you stay out here the less you need. You start to change.'

Damir's girl was a musician, like him. 'Would you like to hear us play?' she said, taking charge of us. 'Come back for our marriage next April,' called the blond young man as we followed her. 'Will there be a priest?' asked Sasha. 'Oh no – nothing like that,' he was emphatic. 'Everyone'll dress in glorious clothes. There'll be lots of games, and dancing.'

Damir's girl had run on ahead of us. She moved like a deer, leaping as she ran. While she and Damir took out their instruments – she a fiddle, he a guitar and mouth organ – they talked about how they had travelled across Russia, hitching lifts, earning their way with Damir's songs.

'Good morning planet, we greet you!' 'Thank you for the gift of life!' 'We are happy, happy, happy, today,' they sang. They were a musical couple, and their happiness was infectious, but my heart sank at the relentless cheerfulness. Ira, who clearly felt the same, said: 'That was lovely. But do you have songs for sad occasions too?' Damir's girl replied for both of them: 'But we've got nothing to be sad about!'

'Come on,' Damir's girl said, leading us across an abandoned field towards another wood. In a glade a swing had been hoisted between two tall trees. This was where they met up in the evenings to dance and sing round the bonfire. Ira asked about their plans: presumably they would start a family soon? 'Not for some time – there's an awful lot to be done before then,' replied the girl. 'The house has to be finished, then there's the planting. It's got to be perfect.'

'But you wouldn't mind if a little one came along before?'

'It won't,' the girl replied, a touch sharply.

I was swinging backwards and forwards, high in the trees, and I lost the rest of their conversation. But something about the way the two women were standing, heads close, taut, suggested that the conversation had taken an unexpected turn.

The couple showed us their secret spring: in a copse of birches the clear water rose languidly out of the earth and curled like a shell. At a lake fringed with birches we stripped off in the milky sunshine and dived in; the water was brown as tea, cold and pure. 'Now we've shown you all our favourite places,' Damir's girl said as we returned to the car.

'Aren't you afraid to be out here on your own?' asked Sasha as we said goodbye. 'What's there to be afraid of?' replied Damir's girl. 'Well, we've been hearing these horror stories about people who've bought land, then found some Chechen still owned the title deeds.' The couple looked at Sasha and smiled. 'Don't worry, it's all going to be all right,' Damir reassured him.

Yes, it would be, I reflected. Unlike their parents or grandparents these two were not afraid. If anything bad happened to them, they would head off and build a home deeper in the forest, like earlier generations of Russians who had rejected the incursion of state power into their lives.

As we drove back away, Damir's girl was standing waving in the autumn sunshine among the silver birches. I thought of all those European travellers who had returned home with stories about a golden woman hidden in the forests of Russia. For me, Damir's girl was golden enough.

I asked Ira what the two of them were talking about in the glade. 'She was trying – very delicately – to point out why she knew she wasn't going to get pregnant before they'd built their home – I was so obtuse, I just couldn't get it!'

'And?'

'She's a virgin.'

Only once they had built their home and taught themselves how to live off their land, and off the forests, would they live together as man and wife. That is what she wanted Ira to know. They were working their way back to a state of grace, rebuilding Eden for their children. They did not believe in Original Sin, though: organised religion was just another way of controlling people, preventing them from realising their freedom, she told Ira. Their children would be different.

Yes, what my golden girl and Damir were building was much more than a home. They really were reimagining Russia.

2008

In December 2007, President Putin ended a period of political uncertainty by announcing that he would step down after his second term of office. This must have triggered fierce squabbles over spoils at the top. For the information spilled out that Putin had amassed a personal fortune of $40 billion, making him the richest man in Europe.

His favoured successor was Dmitri Medvedev, First Deputy Prime Minister and chairman of Gazprom. In May Medvedev duly took up office, having been endorsed by the electorate. Putin assumed the post of Prime Minister.

No one knew how this novel combination was going to affect the political scene. The West and Russia's liberals were encouraged by the fact that Medvedev was a lawyer by training and did not come from a security background. They hoped that his appearance might herald a period of liberalisation and long-overdue institutional reform. But since Medvedev lacked any power base of his own, it was not clear how he could pursue any independent political programme, in the short term at least.

The campaign against corruption which Medvedev announced was a good example. It was the right objective: a third of the country's annual budget was being eaten up by corrupt officials, according to one official source. But how could such a campaign be effective without incriminating the very elite to which he belonged, and without rolling back the centralisation of the last eight years?

However, as long as the economy was booming, all things seemed possible. By June, the price of oil had doubled in a twelve-month period, reaching $147 a barrel in the following month. Russia's economy looked set to grow by more than 7 per cent. Now at last the country could afford to make the massive social investment that was required across the country's crumbling infrastructure, from pensions, education and health to the armed forces. The means were there for

Russia to transform itself from a corrupt, autocratic energy state into a confident, knowledge-based economy.

But in practice, there was little sign that the regime had the political will for much beyond self-enrichment. Despite the boom, cracks were already showing in the edifice. Quite apart from the corruption, inflation was slipping into double figures. In July, the stock market shuddered and fell by 5 per cent after Prime Minister Putin made critical remarks about the steel company Mechel: no one had forgotten that the state's dismemberment of Khodorkovsky's mammoth company Yukos, which produced 20 per cent of Russia's oil, started in this way.

Then, on 7 August, Georgia's President Saakashvili made a determined bid to regain control of the autonomous region of South Ossetia. After six days of heavy fighting, Georgian troops were repulsed. Russian tanks fanned out over Georgia and proceeded to destroy the country's newly modernised armoury.

Brief though it was, Russia's war with Georgia transformed the political scene. It was Russia's 9/11, proclaimed President Medvedev. The country had 'risen from its knees', the press exulted. The war buried any chance Medvedev might have had of pursuing a more liberal political agenda. It was announced that army funding would rise by 50 per cent over the next three years.

However, the regime's unpopularity was reflected on the international front. Russia had arguably only followed a precedent set by NATO in 1999 when it bombed Yugoslavia in defence of Kosovo's right to self-determination. But nevertheless, it found itself severely isolated by world opinion.

The West's ally had also played its propaganda well, and the sight of Russian tanks entering Georgia raised old Cold War ghosts. While Europe dithered, caught between distaste and self-interest, America's press exploded in Russophobia. All this served only to add a strong sense of grievance to the triumphalist mood back in Russia.

But world attention was soon diverted by the global financial crisis – one which had begun in the United States. Since the collapse of Soviet power, the banner of the free market had been fluttering over the world. Now suddenly it was in shreds. All over the world, markets were crashing. This was a crisis that was going to spare no one. For all the Cold War rhetoric, there was no ideological divide any more.

By the end of November, the price of oil had fallen from a high of $147 to below $50 a barrel. For Russia's oil-dependent economy, this was catastrophic. The poor faced hardship, since simply to meet its budgetary commitments the state had to dip into its reserve funds once the oil price fell below $70 a barrel. The rich were not spared either: Russia's once booming stock market dropped 70 per cent between May and November, the steepest decline of any worldwide.

HOW ABOUT A RIDDLE?

Russia's troops had not yet pulled back from Georgia when I boarded the sleeper from Moscow to Saratov. For the first time in all these years, I was apprehensive of the reception that awaited me in Saratov. How would my friends have responded to the war? Would they too have retreated behind a firewall of patriotic indignation? Although my three companions, young professionals from Saratov, looked pleasant enough, I retreated quickly behind the newspapers, wary of conversation.

I had reckoned without the lithe, dark-haired woman sitting opposite. 'Right, I'm Masha,' she said, shutting the door decisively and tucking her legs away under her. She was deputy director of a big Saratov factory which made soft cheese and margarine, she told us, and she was on her way home from a refresher course in Moscow. All three of them had been in the capital for similar reasons, it turned out. 'What are we going to talk about?' Masha went on. 'How about a riddle?' 'Oh, for heaven's sake,' groaned the large-boned young man next to me, who ran part of Saratov's pension fund. His suit was one size too large and his fair hair kept flopping over his clever face. 'Let's talk about Muscovites.' They proceeded to savage Muscovites as lazy, spoiled parasites, who raked in the money while a wretched, invisible black labour force of Central Asians somewhere on the outskirts did the real work.

I had just been reading about the Russian stock market, which had lost 50 per cent of its value in a matter of days. The day I flew into Moscow, Wall Street plunged to its lowest since 9/11. I asked my companions how much all this was going to affect them. All three laughed: 'Do you really imagine people like us have got stocks and shares?' Masha asked. 'Well, with the petrodollar boom . . .' I began. 'What boom?' floppy-haired Petr cut in. 'It's an illusion. Things are awful. Have been for ages. Inflation's far worse than they're letting on. It's those Muscovites. They're the problem. They're the only ones with money, and they've got so much they don't know where to put it.

'Property's gone crazy in Saratov. They're buying it up sight unseen – land, houses, you name it. They'll ring up. "It's on the Volga, is it? I'll take it." For the rest, middle class included, it's grim. Friends of mine have been selling off their DVDs and home computers just to pay the rent!' Masha and the young engineer agreed; the so-called 'boom' had lifted the oil elite and those who serviced it on to another planet, leaving the rest of Russia behind.

The ample woman in charge of our compartment brought round glasses of tea. I thought back to all the train journeys over the last sixteen years which had carried me across Russia's two continents and eleven time zones in search of friends and in pursuit of ideas. Sometimes in the '90s there was no tea, only hot water. Sometimes the collective anxiety was such that even the tribe of trusty railway stewards seemed suspect. Were they in cahoots with the gangs who were said to be robbing people in their sleep, bundling bodies off trains at dead of night?

Now at least we ate confidently from the food boxes provided. Back then no one trusted that food of unknown provenance was not part of some money-making scam that would leave them poisoned.

Masha, as if responding to these unspoken thoughts, nudged us back into conversation: 'If you could choose a favourite moment, between the end of Soviet power and now, when would it be? I'd choose '92–3. I don't care what anybody says – I loved it. It was a unique time. Just for a moment a person could think for themselves, be free.' I flashed her a grateful smile. These days it was fashionable to maintain that the idea of freedom was meaningless, a mere window-dressing for Western imperialism.

'Well, I was only seven,' began the quiet, doe-eyed engineer. Petr interrupted: 'I don't agree. All I saw was fear and insecurity. Don't get me wrong – I hate the way things are now. But you have to admit – it suits the Russian people. What do you expect? It's only a hundred and fifty years since we had serfdom. People would still rather be owned. Before anything changes they're going to have to *want* more freedom. As it is, the old days are back –

I'm sure you realise that there's a KGB person in every company again?'

'Well, there's certainly not one in our factory—'

'Take a closer look. The Party's back – it's just the name that's changed.' Petr was talking about Putin's party, Edinaya Rossiya. 'For two years they nagged me to join up. I refused. In the end they wore me down. OK, I said, I'll make a deal. I'll join, but on one condition – you've got to agree not to pressure any of my staff – they're not management, why the hell should they join? So far they've stuck to it. Turned out I was the only person in the entire ranks of management who'd been holding out! As for those vast, corrupt monopolies at the top, it'll take a couple of generations to break them up.'

This time there was a long silence. The train lumbered through a country station. An image from a news report of the recent war flashed through my mind. A truck full of raw conscripts with terrified faces was heading into Tskhinvali, the South Ossetian town which Georgian troops had attacked. Conscripts who came from backwoods places like this.

'How about a riddle, then?' asked Masha brightly. What was it with this woman and riddles. 'No! Let's talk about the war!' Petr whipped back. 'No. Absolutely not,' Masha cut in, too quickly.

Then I understood. That was what the riddles were about. Like me, she was worried that the war was going to divide us, rupture the harmony of our carriage. 'Fine! Let's talk about the war!' I surprised them by saying. 'You want to know what I think? They're all wantonly irresponsible – Georgians, Russians, Americans. I'd rather be governed by nine-year-olds.'

They looked at me in astonishment, all three of them, then started gabbling at once. Yes, the only people who benefited by the war were the leaders, and yes, this was only the beginning, it was going to get worse . . . The relief was palpable, and it touched us all. They hadn't expected my reaction, and I hadn't expected theirs.

'Can you believe it?' piped up the doe-eyed young engineer: 'A friend of my father's bought this suit the other day. When he got home he looked at the label. "Made in the US. 50 per cent linen 50 per cent cotton" it read. Then "Sorry our President's such an idiot".' We fell about laughing, with the solidarity of the powerless.

'Now will you let me pose my riddle?' Masha asked. This time we relented. 'Two women are standing at a market stall which sells pigeons. One says to the other, "I've got two children under school age."' Masha was away. I hated riddles. 'Their combined ages are the number of pigeons on that stall. How old are they? And by the way, my oldest's called Borya.'

For my own part, I had never intended to spend so many years puzzling over a different, insoluble riddle, the one Churchill famously posed. 'I cannot forecast to you the action of Russia,' he told the British after declaring war on Germany, when it was not clear which side Russia would join. 'It is a riddle, wrapped in a mystery, inside an enigma; but perhaps there is a key. That key is Russian national interest.' It still was the key. But the answer to the riddle came out very different, depending how you defined that national interest.

The three of them argued over the riddle with an engaging degree of enthusiasm while the train rumbled on over the darkening steppe. Out came the paper and pen. At one point Masha, suddenly unsure whether it really was solvable, rang her boss. 'Haven't you got anything better to do with your Friday evening?' her boss grumbled. We took to our berths without having found the answer.

Meanwhile, I had been reading the papers. There was an article about the Tunguska meteor, whose mysterious site I had passed on the trip into the taiga to visit the Old Believers. All this time, no one had been able to work out how such an enormous object – some 50–100 metres across – could have hit the earth without leaving a crater. Was it a UFO, dark matter, a nuclear explosion? Now, a hundred years after the event, two Russian scientists had come up with a mathematical model which proved how the asteroid, or comet perhaps, had disintegrated into tiny fragments on its way into the earth's atmosphere, exploding and bouncing away from the earth's surface while barely having touched it. One mystery solved.

Others were going to remain unsolved. I had no reason to doubt the chilling warnings of my enchanting Professor Kaznacheev about the dangers of mind-control weapons, designed to manipulate people's mental functions at a distance. Indeed, they were substantiated when the Duma banned the use of such weapons on Russian territory in June 2001. Since then, discussion about them had dried up in Russia. In the USA, there was no proof that the government had ever developed such weapons. They stuck to their line that no such technology existed, or that all such information was subject to the law on National Security. Congressman Dennis Kucinich had introduced a bill in the House of Representatives in 2001 that would have obliged the President to start negotiations on the international ban for which Russia and the EU had been pressing. But it got nowhere.

In the middle of night, when the men were asleep, Masha leaned down to me from the berth above with a bit of paper covered in equations. She had finally worked out the answer to her riddle. Lucky her. I was still a long way off finding an answer to mine: how long were the Russian people going to endorse the idea that Putin's 'sovereign democracy' was in their national interest?

THE WORM TURNS

It was a sunny Sunday, and Tatiana was driving us out to Marx in her smart jeep to visit Misha's mother. Her daughter Nadya, who was now twelve, was whispering to her friend in the back of the car. We were sitting in a traffic jam. These days there were traffic jams all day long in Saratov's city centre; 4x4s and gleaming jeeps like ours sat nose to nose as far as the eye could see. There was plenty of time to register the new dress shops, the Irish pub, the shopping malls, restaurants and the rash of stylish little cafés. Time enough to register that with a few, dazzling exceptions, these frontages had been attached to buildings that looked more derelict than ever.

Saratov was being run by an honest man now, they said. Poor fellow, it was no qualification for running this city. The previous incumbent was sitting in prison, facing fourteen criminal charges, including bribe-taking, non-distribution of taxpayers' money and exceeding his authority. As for his predecessor, the master crook who had held the job for years before that, people referred to him almost nostalgically now, as of someone who 'knew how to get things done'. He had survived all attempts to finger him.

I was in a jaundiced mood. I had come here to see my friends. But with the exception of Tatiana, they seemed to be avoiding me. I had calculated my visit so that Anna and I could spend time together over the weekend. But she had not invited me to stay, and had come up with a flimsy excuse for not joining us in Marx.

The day I arrived, Misha had also left for Germany, prompted by an 'unexpected invitation'. Tatiana, of course, had done her best to make up for this by being more loving and attentive than ever. She had lost weight and looked like a tragic queen, stabbed through by an icicle. I dared not ask her about herself.

The roads had improved. Clearly, this had been necessary to

expedite the escape of the jeep-owners from the sight of the limb-
less war vets, lurching drunks, piles of rubbish, bedraggled high-rise
blocks, overloaded trams and hollow-eyed grannies begging
beneath hoardings advertising holidays in Australia costing only
$4,000. Where the jeeps were heading became clear once we
reached open country.

Rows of pale, svelte high-rise towers reared up against the
Sokolov hills, tall and striking as bulimic models. Around their
foot stretched gated estates of gabled houses with vivid russet and
blue roofs. These were the homes of the 15 per cent who belonged
to Russia's new economy. As in a traditional steppe town the cows
peeled off from the herd of an evening and made their own way
to their front gate, so those 4x4s peeled off the road to adorn the
forecourt of each imposing mansion. Sixteen years ago, when I
first came down to Saratov, I little dreamed that Russia's new
beginning would look like this.

Of all my friends, Misha was the one whose dreams had most
spectacularly come to fruition during the years I had known him.
Before he left on the train we had spent the afternoon together,
but it was not long enough. I had come down here intending to
celebrate his success. Misha had become a manufacturer entirely
by his own efforts, rather than by appropriating a factory, or the
wages of people from some factory, as was common in the 1990s.
He had started farming at the right time, too, when across Russia
people had turned their backs on the collective farms, when millions
of acres were lying abandoned.

This time Misha was more affectionate with me, more genuinely
present, than I had ever known him. He was looking good too,
younger, having lost a lot of weight. But things on the farm had
not been going well, he admitted. 'The problem is that the new
technology I've ploughed my profits into hasn't yielded the results
I expected. In fact, it's been performing badly even by comparison with traditional methods! I've lost a lot of money.'

Misha, ever the gambler, had been relying on modern European
farming techniques, drilling rather than ploughing, as well as using
the latest in fertilisers and pesticides, to make the Volga steppe
competitive with farms in Russia's fertile black-earth country. Last
year, those black-earth fields yielded 3.3 tons of wheat a hectare,
and would yield more when properly managed. He was so far
only managing 3 tons a hectare. 'I may not be doing it right yet,'

he brooded. 'I'm a novice at farming – when I started I made every mistake in the book! Or it may be that the local farmers have got a point – they've always said my techniques won't work here. It's tricky farming country. Time will tell. But this year I'm hedging my bets, farming half my land in the traditional way.'

Misha was being hard on himself, as usual. Three tons a hectare was not at all bad. Overall, the average yield per hectare in this vast, northern land was only 1.85 tons. He had disappointed only his own ambitious expectations.

Last time I had been here, he was fighting a court case. Someone had accused him of selling them on bad seed. He was very worried then. How had that gone, I asked? 'Well, I've more or less won – the man just didn't have a case. But the case is dragging on. I'm innocent, but that's no protection – he's got powerful contacts. It's all very tiresome. I've got to keep sucking up to these judges, giving them presents, to make sure the case doesn't come undone again.'

Misha's real legal headaches lay elsewhere now. Since the price of land had risen, everyone was after it. Of the 1,011 hectares he farmed, some 300 were not his. It was land that belonged to Russian Germans who died or had left for Germany in the early 1990s. It was lying fallow, so Misha started farming it. But people were now coming up with pieces of paper that proved their right to bits of it, or so they claimed. The judges were inclined to give in to these little claims, on the grounds that Misha already had quite enough land. 'What's so frustrating is that I know perfectly well that most of these claims are just a try-on – they've got no basis in fact.' This legacy of the chaotic '90s was wearing him down, he complained.

These were all trivial problems, I reflected as the car bowled across the steppe to Marx. On either side of the road, vast fields stretched away. Right now, the perspectives for a farmer were extraordinary. Thanks to high global grain prices, the big investors had looked at the map and realised that 8 per cent of the world's cultivable land lay in Russia. They had started investing billions. Land prices here were soaring, but it was still ten times as cheap as land in France. Misha was in the right place at the right time.

Before the Revolution, the Volga had been Russia's great wheat bowl, and there was no reason why it should not be again. Russia was going to become the world's largest wheat exporter, and Misha was bound to be part of that success.

Outside Marx we stopped by a lorry piled high with green mottled watermelons. As a lad clambered over the green globes to reach a golden one for us I noticed that Tatiana was frowning. 'What's the matter?' 'Nothing. It's just that I loathe Marx – Lyuba's the only reason I'm still prepared to come down here,' she replied. So fast did she whisk through the town centre that I noticed only a blur of new shops.

Their house was on the outskirts, in the district where the Soviet bosses used to live. This was the original Thieftown, as opposed to the New Thieftown which had sprung up since the fall of communism. Back then, the grandees used to live here, but now the houses were going cheap. The sight of them made me nostalgic for the old days, when the thieving was so modest. They might have been built by blind men, with their small, awkwardly placed windows and badly laid brick walls festooned with electric cables. They cowered behind tall fences, as though ashamed of their appearance.

Over the gates of one house someone had hoisted lines of doggerel, written in crude, loopy letters. The gist of it was this: 'All year I waited for my pension. The postman got so embarrassed he'd be lying, blushing./Hunger's no joke. But as you'll find, prison's a lot worse./You may be living it up now, Baguette you bastard!/But you'll get your come-uppance!/Give us our pensions! We fought for our country!'

'Baguette' was the head of the regional administration. When I first started coming to Marx he was a rough lad who ran a bakery, hence the nickname.

The sound of church music floated out to us as we approached Tatiana and Misha's house. Tatiana winced: 'She plays it day and night. It drives me nuts.' Lyuba, eighty this year, was sitting on the side of her bed, white kerchief round her head, flowered smock, growth stunted by malnutrition, blind eyes closed, folding and refolding her huge, knotted hands in her lap. 'Ah, Brooksevna! Brooksevna's back!' She called me by my father's name, hugging me fiercely, lavishing a torrent of earthy Ukrainian endearments on me. 'How is your husband? Is your daughter married yet? Any grandchildren? In my prayers I remember you all, ask God to give them, the girls, his grace. That your one and Polina should bring us grandchildren.' She had forgotten nothing.

Back then she was weeping every day for her lost home, the

rose trees she kept watered through the hot summers, the raspberries and potatoes, the apple trees and the brindled cow. When
she arrived four years ago the doctor said she'd not survive long
('they never do, when they're moved'). She finally came to terms
with the move only this summer. 'This is where I want to see out
my days,' she told me, patting my hand decisively. 'The children
weren't good to me, they didn't want me. But here my heart's at
peace. Tanyochka, my little sunshine, is more daughter to me than
my own. She never makes me feel I'm a trouble, though I do no
work. I pray for her though, for you all, every day. I can peel
seeds too – here, take these.' She fished a bag of sunflower seeds
out of her cupboard. 'I roasted them myself too'.

In the evening, Tatiana's brother, his wife and their little boy
arrived with a sack full of crayfish for our supper. I remembered
Tatiana's sister-in-law as a shy, retiring woman. This time, something about her intrigued me. She occupied the room differently.
She had attitude. Yes, she explained as we scrubbed crayfish
together, a lot had happened since we last met. She had become
one of the moving spirits in a stubborn, grassroots revolt in Marx.
It was about their daughter's lycée, the only good school in the
district. Eight months ago, Baguette had announced that it was
closing. The explanation he gave for the decision was utterly uncon-
vincing. Everyone assumed some developer had paid him fairy-tale
sums for the site.

Baguette can never have expected resistance. But out here, what
hope people had was vested in their children's future. That meant
education. The worm turned. The parents got together and took
the matter to court. Twice, they won their case. Twice, the judges
were bought off and Baguette won. After that, the parents and
children simply refused to leave the school. Although the teachers
had been reassigned to other schools, they also stayed on, though
the gas had been switched off and there was no way of feeding
the children. When word got out that lorries were coming to
strip the school of furniture overnight, the mothers organised a
rota and started spending nights there.

Such was Baguette's power that not a single deputy from Marx
(including the school's founder, who had gone into local politics)
backed the children. Anna had written up the story for her paper.
But the paper's editor rewrote it, to support Baguette's version.
The best Anna could do was remove her name from the article.

This was just a little revolt against those palaces on the hill. It was hardly going to go down in history alongside the great rebellions launched on the Volga by Pugachev and Stenka Razin, which had shaken the Russian empire. But then, as now, grassroots revolts remained the only way ordinary people could make themselves heard by autocratic rulers.

Putin's government had seen off all legitimate outlets for opposition. But early in 2005, they were badly rattled when thousands of pensioners took to the streets in cities across Russia, protesting at an attempt to 'rationalise' their pitiful pensions. Terrified by this massing of the powerless, the government caved in. Here in Marx, with its cult of obedience, this eight-month-long battle by mothers and children must also have sent shock waves through Baguette and his crew. 'They'll win in the end – we're running out of options,' said Tatiana's sister-in-law, before adding with a gleam in her eye. 'Still, we'll never be the same. Any of us.' That included Baguette's own daughter, who was at the school, and had come out against her father.

THE PRICE OF DREAMS

Lyuba was already there, at the head of the table, when we sat down to eat the heaps of pink crayfish. She sat quietly, nibbling at a potato, a diminutive old woman who appeared to be drifting downstream, focused on some drama the rest of us could not see.

Then all of a sudden, in answer to a question of mine, she started talking. She talked about growing potatoes from seed, about preserving tomatoes with the green stem on, but what she said was not the point. Even the children fell silent, watching her pull on the words like oars, as she rowed back against the current towards us.

In the old days, they made dishes, boots, buckets and clothes, Lyuba was saying. Yes, even the cloth. You'd take the hemp, only the female plants mind, soak them for a month, collect the strong strands and weave them. That was what she and her mother did of an evening.

That dialect of hers, as rough and dark as freshly ploughed earth, conjured up a whole way of life, a peasantry which Russia's rulers had decided to kill off, in the interests of modernisation. There was a time when I had hoped to bring the past of this town, Marx, to life, through the memory of old people. But with a few dazzling exceptions, most of them were too fearful. The past was not a place they dared return to.

In Cherkassk province, eastern Ukraine, before the war there wasn't much they didn't grow or make, Lyuba was saying. That included music. Her oldest brother played the fiddle at local weddings. She played the balalaika, like her father. And she sang. She was famous locally. The family would all play together in the evenings. On high days and holidays the villagers would come round to listen, as we were doing now.

Something was happening to Lyuba as she talked. There were

pink spots in her cheeks and she spoke with such vigour that she had to keep pushing her white kerchief back over her hair. The years were falling off her. Then all of a sudden she was singing, in a clear, sweet voice. She sang about a husband who beats his wife. 'Right, I've had it', says the wife, gets into a little boat and floats down the River Dunai. Home comes the husband. The children are hungry, the dishes are dirty. Bitterly then does he regret what he's done. But it's too late, by that time the River Dunai has carried her far, far away.

Lyuba sang on, singing herself back from the edge of death, back down the years, back under the skin of that vanished peasant life. The tunes were merry, but the words were about violent husbands who got their come-uppance. Songs written by women, wreaking musical vengeance. Only when Tatiana implored her 'Sing something cheerful', did she pause, stuck to find happiness in the grown-up world, before starting off again on the children's songs.

While Lyuba was singing, the wood-lined *banya* next door was sighing and creaking as it heated up. When everyone else had gone to bed, Tatiana and I retired into it. Afterwards, light-headed, smelling of honey and wet birch leaves, we floated out to the kitchen and sat in dressing gowns, drinking tea.

'What did you really think about what Misha said about the war?' Tatiana asked me. 'It's exactly what I expected,' I replied, truthfully. Misha had become genuinely emotional on the subject. 'You know how critical I can be of this country,' he burst out. 'But on this one I'm right behind Medvedev and Putin. There's a lot this country can learn from the West about how to run itself. I know that. But surely we've got the right to defend our own borders from attack! What's Russia done to the West to deserve being provoked in that way? You tell me that.

'As you know, my family's from Ukraine. So all this is very close to my heart. Half Ukraine's population is Russian, or almost. Our language, our culture, it's practically the same. Whatever that puppet Yushchenko says, there's no way we'd stand for Ukraine being taken into NATO. It's rubbish! What's more, if push comes to shove, the West's got a lot more to lose from such a conflict than we do. Europe depends on Russian oil and gas! We may not be in great shape domestically. But we've got what it takes. We don't need the West! It's going to take us a generation or two to sort ourselves out, but we're smart people – we're on our way now!'

Misha had indeed been remarkably consistent in his views. In those early days in Marx, when the rest of the group were still stunned by the trampling of their hopes for democracy and freedom in Russia, Misha's vision had been distinct. A regular guy, a talented sportsman, he did not just long to be rich. Even then, he was dreaming of the day when Russia would be strong again.

It was another of his dreams that had been realised. On entering Gori, in Georgia, the youngest Russian conscript would have known that the one building they could not fire on was the hut where Stalin was born. Back home in Russia, the Georgian had just topped polls as the country's all-time favourite hero. As Russia's tank commanders rumbled into the port of Poti, their heads were full of memories of childhood summers on the Black Sea. The Caucasus was Russia's Ireland. Putting things to rights there was a task which had occupied her army since the days of Tolstoy and Lermontov.

It was clear from the expression on Tatiana's face that she did not share her husband's views on the war. 'Let's talk about something more cheerful,' she proposed. I turned to Lyuba's dazzling performance. 'You know, I'd never heard her sing before,' Tatiana said, before adding enigmatically, 'If Misha'd been here, she'd never have been like that.' 'What do you mean?' 'She felt safe, loved.'

Misha had just rung up from Germany. He was amazed by Tatiana's account of our evening. He said his mother had sworn she would never sing again, after the last of her brothers died thirty-three years ago – the one who returned from the war, terribly wounded. Until tonight, she had never done so.

I mentioned a strange story Lyuba had told us of how the village healer had brought her mother back from the dead after her accident. 'My mother, *matushka moya*, was only twenty-seven when the lightning got her,' Lyuba told us. 'Right down her spine it went. When they brought her in she was a corpse, lifeless. *Babushka*, her mother that is, started laying her out, but the *znazhar* said, "Hold it! Don't be in such a hurry to bury your daughter!" He dug this great hole, buried her up to her neck in the earth for three days and three nights. When they dug her out she was not just alive. She'd recovered the use of her limbs. She could even work, though she remained in great pain.'

I knew that she had killed herself years later, when she could bear the pain no longer. But it was only now that Tatiana told me Misha was the one who found her hanging there. 'He was three. I think that's one of the reasons he's so troubled now,' Tatiana muttered. 'I don't know about that,' I said. 'He seemed on rather good form to me.' 'You're right, he was lovely with you, the way he always used to be. But when he's drunk he's different. Crude, awful.'

He had started drinking a couple of years ago, she said. Was that because things were going wrong on the farm, I asked Tatiana. 'No, it was because he became too confident. He thought he could do it all. He thought he'd got it licked. But now he's started drinking, he can't control it. He's spending more and more of his time down here, with Marx's local bosses. And that's what they do when they get together. Drink. They bring him home legless.

'He's particularly bad with his mother, for some reason. He's her favourite child. Before, he always used to be so good with her. He'd talk to her, spend time with her. Not any more. When he's drunk it's her he takes it out on. And she, well, she just sits there and takes it.

'I've come to admire Lyuba enormously,' Tatiana went on. 'She's not just strong, she's intelligent. I watch the way she can take a tiny bit of information and use it as the basis for making a much broader judgement. When Misha comes in drunk, she always manages to work out what lies behind it, for instance. And she's never far from the mark.'

Four years ago, when Misha brought his mother here from Ukraine, the two women were dreading the prospect of living together. Now they had become close allies, mutually supportive in the face of their shared problem. Tatiana's loving care was what had given Misha's mother her new lease of life.

As for Misha, who had always been so gentle, such a meticulous manager, the drink was affecting his work, Tatiana said. 'When things go wrong he loses his temper, blames it all on his subordinates. He spends time on the farm and the factory starts slipping. He concentrates on the factory, and the farm suffers. But he won't delegate,' Tatiana sighed. 'He's a maximalist, as you know. He thought he could change everything at once. But what he took on was too much for one person.'

We sat in silence, listening to the creaking of the cooling *banya*.

A cat appeared in the open doorway, stalked round the kitchen and retired outside to feast on crayfish shells under the full moon. How sad, I thought. Misha had realised his dream. But he had paid too high a price.

His youthful appearance was deceptive too, Tatiana confided. In fact, he had just spent three weeks in hospital, after being taken ill on holiday in Turkey. Years of unremitting work were taking their toll. The doctors were clear: he'd got to change the way he lived, or else . . .

As we shut the cat out and headed for bed Tatiana told me that Misha was just about to stand for election in Marx, as a deputy for one of the small opposition parties. If he got in, he would be working with that rogue Baguette. Tatiana sighed: 'Sometimes, I look at him and think, yes, Marx has won.'

PILNYAK'S ISLAND

Early next morning, we climbed into the car and headed back for Saratov, half-awake, driving too fast. Tatiana and I had overslept. Nadya and her friend were going to be late for school. This time, we drove back on the old road, through the town of Engels. A week ago, it was from here that two Tupolev-160s, each carrying twelve nuclear warheads, had taken off bound for Venezuela, bearing the message to the United States that two could play at fomenting trouble on each other's borders.

Tatiana had been trying to help me reach Natasha and Igor, my own efforts having failed. The war with Georgia had left me worried about them and their underground newspaper in Sevastopol. Suddenly, the derelict naval port was in the geopolitical spotlight. Since its military triumph, Russia was viewing the map differently, as a foreign policy pundit had been telling me in Moscow.

America's days of unchallenged global supremacy were over, he said. A new, multi-polar world would emerge sooner or later, one in which Russia was destined to play a major role. But before that could happen, Uncle Sam was going to have to admit that it had failed in its bid to impose its vision of liberal democracy on the world. Until that happened, the world was going to be a dangerous place. Opportunistic conflicts were bound to break out in places like the Caucasus, borderlands between the spheres of influence. Whether this was a prediction or a threat I did not know.

By any reckoning, Crimea was high up among those potential flashpoints. Russia's rusting navy still lay in the inlets of Sevastopol. Although Khrushchev had rashly bequeathed the peninsula to his native Ukraine, 60 per cent of Crimea's population was still Russian. Russia's sense of historical entitlement had been stirred up now. The weaker the economy at home, the more Russia's leaders would be tempted to find a rousing cause to distract attention from their failures domestically. How long was it going to be before Russia's military moved to reclaim land where so much Russian blood had been spilled? Perhaps the first move had already been made. For one of Russia's tame opposition parties had started championing its marooned compatriots in Crimea. They were arguing that Crimea's Russians should have passports, that they should have the right to work and be educated in Russia.

I would like to have had more confidence that a new incumbent in the White House would steer clear of stirring up trouble there. But the worse the US domestic economy became, the more attractive it might seem to keep pressing on with the crazy policy of expanding NATO right up to Russia's borders, to include Ukraine and Georgia.

Natasha and Igor had lived their private lives rashly. But I knew my friends well enough to be confident that they would do whatever they could to help Crimea's Russians resist becoming political pawns. At least there was no history of ethnic tension to exploit between Ukrainians and Russians, as there had been in South Ossetia. The only group in Crimea with a declared interest in separatism were the increasingly politically organised Crimean Tatars, men such as Igor's friend Evdan. For them, the memory of Stalin's wholesale deportation in 1944 would never fade. In any conflict, they would always side with Ukraine.

Tatiana had tried ringing Natasha's sister in Novosibirsk. When she asked for news of Natasha, her sister slammed the phone down. 'I'm not surprised,' Tatiana sighed. 'In Marx I remember watching Natasha throw away a pile of unopened letters. "I don't know how to manage long-distance friendships," she said when I asked her why. "They're just an imitation of friendship."' Knowing how wounded Tatiana had been by the way Natasha broke off contact when she left Saratov, I said quickly: 'I don't know what it is about Natasha. But there's something inevitable about the way she's ended up in the eye of the political storm yet again, don't you think?'

When the car rumbled over the old bridge across the Volga, I was looking out for Pilnyak's Island. Pilnyak (né Wogau) was the popular 'bourgeois' writer from Marx whom Stalin hounded to death for having hinted that the Great Leader ordered the elimination of his rival, Frunze. There the island was stretched out below, its two long white sandy beaches looking like a pair of tights laid out to dry. A long time ago, Pilnyak tells us, a barge had sunk there. Over the years sand had built up around it, until finally it surfaced in that island.

It was an image that mattered to Pilnyak. He returns to it again and again, even in the atrocious Socialist Realist novel Stalin forced out of him in a final act of creative humiliation. What did it mean to him, I wondered? Was he protesting against the Soviet faith that you can refashion history, and human nature? Was he objecting that while the river flowed on, the sunken barge remained? It was a more ambiguous image than that, though. For the island kept changing shape.

This autumn, Putin had been launching an ambitious bid to do just that, to impose a new shape on Russian history. He had given his enthusiastic endorsement to a new standard history textbook for secondary schools. Western commentators construed it as an attempt to repeal the revelations of the glasnost years and return to the pre-Gorbachev version of Soviet history. So I tracked the book down in a Saratov bookshop when I arrived and spent a long time huddled on a stool, leafing through it.

It certainly contained a fulsome litany of Soviet achievements, imperial, economic and technological. But it was not just a return to the old Soviet view. It was altogether more ambitious, a considered attempt to make the notion of 'sovereign democracy' mean something.

Teachers were being offered ways of presenting Russia as having a special destiny, one which could not, should not, be measured by any Western yardstick. Yes, Russia's Eurasianists had finally come in from the cold. Nineteenth-century Orthodox autocracy and Stalin's imperial vision were finally reconciled in a single narrative whose underlying theme was Russian exceptionalism.

In the Soviet period there had indeed been bouts of repression and execution, the revisionist argument went. But the rationale for them needed to be understood. There had been famines too, there was no denying it. But the numbers who died had been vastly exaggerated (1–2 million perhaps, not the 7–10 million the detractors claimed). Stalin, 'the most successful leader of the USSR', had been acting entirely rationally. How else could an industrial state have been forged from a peasant society in such a short time? How else could the fascist enemy have been conquered? Yes, Stalin did deport whole ethnic groups, 'in order to keep the monolithic character of the system'. But Russia emerged victorious. Russia's greatness had been realised.

As we left behind the aching, bloodstained Volga countryside and dropped Nadya and her friend at school I was wondering what these bright twelve-year-olds were going to make of this rebranding of their country.

Tatiana dropped me off at the handsome Radishchev Museum. Framed by great plane trees, it stood on its own in the heart of the city. It had been closed for years, this fine, neoclassical building, one of the first purpose-built provincial museums in Russia. 'For repairs', they said. People wearily assumed it had been grabbed by some powerful organisation. But when I arrived this time, I heard it had been reopened.

I spent the morning treading the magnificent wrought-iron staircase, marvelling at the renovation, checking in with my favourite paintings. I had started coming here sixteen years ago, when Benya's boat brought me to this old closed city. Inflation was taking off and the privileged workforce of those armaments factories were in a rage at their sudden impoverishment. This was where I would take refuge when I could no longer bear the hostility my foreign accent provoked.

Now hard times were setting in again. Long before world markets started crashing, there were already fears of an impending catastrophe if Russia's government did not use oil revenues to improve people's lives. All over the world, the myth of the free market had gone to the heads of elites, but nowhere more than here. The price of oil was tumbling. Judging by the newspaper reports, xenophobia was on the rise: attacks on anyone non-Slav in appearance had been on the increase for some time. If the regime continued to stoke up anti-Western feeling a time might come when my accent again provoked hostility.

I was hunting for my favourite painting, by the remarkable Kuzma Petrov-Vodkin. Born in the Saratov countryside, son of a cobbler, he bicycled all the way from Leningrad to Paris, and from there to Italy to study the art of Western Europe's Middle Ages and Renaissance. Where was it? There it was, hanging high up in a corner. Two girls were getting dressed after bathing in the Volga. Their outstretched arms filled the canvas. The painting was a feast of lemon yellow, fuchsia, scarlet and Giotto-blue. Petrov-Vodkin had brought together the legacy of medieval Russian iconography with that of Europe's Middle Ages and Renaissance. The composition was modern, yet ancient, an everyday image suffused with intimations of transcendence.

One of the girls looked like Tatiana when we first met, a clear-browed beauty with pale skin, pale hair and wide grey eyes. Then, she was still a shy provincial girl, under the influence of the sophisticated Natasha. Now, she had taken her place in the army of Russia's strong women, as the point of first and last resort for the old and the young, the single and the frail, the idealists and the honest. All of these stood far more frighteningly exposed in Russia than in the West. For them, family and friendship were the only safety nets.

When things fell apart, it would be Tatiana who absorbed the anger and fear, kept her judgements to herself and supported those around her, as Lyuba had done, as women down the centuries had done in this unyielding northern landscape.

Matushka moya, mother of them all. The clarity with which Tatiana understood all that went on around her was the burden she had to carry. After our *banya*, when we were sitting in the kitchen she had talked, in her balanced way, about the Georgia war and the difficulties of living in this post-ideological age. 'I don't believe in anything they tell us in the mass media. I know it's all propaganda.

'Twenty years ago it was different. We did all believe in communism – we accepted it, like the weather. You don't demonstrate against the rain. But I remember as a child this feeling of shame, listening to those leaden speeches they used to make in the name of the Party. I knew it was false – children can tell these things. Not that I was especially sensitive. I've talked about this with other people of my generation – they all had the same feeling, a sort of inner chill.'

However much they pushed Putin's new history textbook in the schools, I reflected, they were not going to be able to shape the minds of Tatiana's children in the old Soviet way. Some of the gains of the last twenty years could not be undone. Russians would remain free to talk, to travel the world and use the Internet. A return to monolithic control over information was a technological impossibility.

FESTIVAL OF DEAD LEAVES

'Of course I despise my Fatherland from head to foot, but I mind when a foreigner shares my feelings.'

Alexander Pushkin

I woke up during the night, fretting about Anna. We were back at Tatiana's flat in Saratov. But Anna had not asked me to stay. She had not come over. She had not even rung. I was accustomed to Anna's strangeness. I had learned not take it personally. This was different, though. She had never avoided me before. That hurt.

When I first arrived on this trip, she had been there to greet me at Saratov station. Her lean, tanned face lit up by a lopsided smile, she dodged my embrace as usual. She returned with us to Tatiana's flat, and stayed for a meal. It was long enough for me to register the change in her.

Anna had somehow grown into her skin, become womanly, attractive. There was a new animation about her. She had let her hair grow for the first time, and wore a striking plaid jacket and trousers. Strong colours suited her. I wondered fleetingly whether she was in love. She slipped away after the meal and I was longing to see more of her.

There had been times back in England when I was trying to write about Anna that I was so maddened by her elusiveness I almost fancied she didn't exist, that she was merely the part of myself that I left behind in Russia when, with regret, with relief, I returned to the daylight world of the West. Now, when she was looking so vibrant, when she was only half a mile away, she had dropped out of sight.

Being with Anna had never been easy. Silences had been the

other, the constant companion of our friendship. But since she had written me that wonderful letter after we met I had never doubted the connection between us; the fact, as she put it, that I was a-little-bit-her. Was that no longer true?

I remembered those early days, when we were both looking for answers to the same question: what does it mean to be Russian, now that communism has gone? We shared the same hopes for Russia, too. Her enthusiasm for the ideals of liberal democracy was untarnished. And I, her friend from the West, was the living representative of her hopes. Even then there were good reasons why she needed to retreat into silence, I reflected. Hers was a country with volatile politics and a venerable tradition of punishing people for their opinions. Before we ever met she had lost her job and her flat simply for having come out in support of Marx's Russian German community.

Then there had been the time when a Moscow journalist picked up on her account of a hysterical attempt by Marx's leaders to provoke rebellion against the region becoming a Russian German homeland. So crushed was the community by the mocking article he wrote in a popular paper that when I arrived in Marx shortly afterwards, no one would talk to me. Anna had been the agent of their humiliation, albeit unwittingly. Muscovites were dangerous enough, foreigners far more so.

The reasons for Anna's silences had changed over the years. Though I was often left struggling to understand what lay behind them, I never doubted that she was challenging me to try to understand. After Putin came to power, after Russia's relationship with the West became strained, there had been a tacit agreement between us that I would not expose her to unnecessary difficulties by asking her directly about politics.

Increasingly she had turned her energies inwards and started exploring her spiritual world. But even then she wanted me to bear witness to her life. Or so I thought. Had I been kidding myself? The thought was unbearable.

Perhaps the problem was connected with the Orthodox Church? I had watched her wavering between the two branches of Christianity, Western and Eastern. I saw how she struggled to resist the comfortable lure of Catholicism. She battled to breach the outer defences of Russia's Church, the obscure language of its liturgy, the way it made no effort to help the uninitiated. That was a journey where I could follow her only so far. But she had clearly broken through long ago, found her way to something that nourished her. She had discovered a Russia she could love. I was even a little envious.

The problem, if there was one, was that the relationship between Church and State in Russia has always been so close. In its idealised form it amounted to a quasi-mystical 'symphonia' between them. 'Orthodoxy, Autocracy and Nationhood,' ran the old tsarist rallying cry. When Putin embraced the notion of sovereign democracy, the regime was setting itself up as the legitimate inheritor of that autocratic tradition.

I noticed with alarm how other formerly liberal friends, now pious believers, had started investing Putin with the reverence traditionally accorded to the tsars. Had the burst of popular patriotism prompted by the war with Georgia affected Anna in the same way? Had she felt challenged to go the full stretch, to embrace the notion that if she loved her country, she must support the values and actions of its rulers?

The thought was so alarming that I was now wide awake. Outside in the street, a cat fight had started. I switched on the light. So that was it, was it? Anna had thrown in her lot with sovereign democracy. She could not cope with our friendship any more. All this time, I had never really been more than a function of her idea of the West. Or was it just that the distance between Russia and the West had grown too great? Either way, the connection between us had snapped.

The rubbish vans came and went, roaring hungrily, collecting refuse along the street. Dawn broke, and I got up early, waiting for the moment when Nadya would be at school and I could discuss my fears with Tatiana. She would tell me the truth. She knew Anna well.

Tatiana was unequivocal. 'No, that's all nonsense. Anna's just being Anna,' she told me firmly. I felt a rush of relief. The night devils slunk away. What on earth had got into me? Then she added, in her emollient way: 'You're her conscience – and she can't bear it.' That seemed highly improbable. Anna had more than enough conscience of her own. Tatiana was just trying to make me feel better.

After that, I insisted that Anna and I spend an evening together. Perhaps I should not have tried. For the occasion comically recapitulated our first, painful evening in Marx sixteen years earlier. There was I, longing to talk, to catch up on her, find out how she was. And there she was, deploying her words like well-placed guns, behind whose cover she kept contriving her retreat back into that hinterland of silences.

Topic after topic, she simply vetoed. 'Don't let's talk about my work – I'm fed up with it. I'd love to leave, but there's nowhere else to go. They're not interested in serious, objective journalism any more. It's all become – well, very political.'

Anna dealt with the subject of the war with Georgia with equal dispatch, chopping it up like an awkward joint of meat. 'How did people react to the war?' she growled. 'They didn't. Oh yeah? So they're killing each other in the Caucasus again? My boots need mending.' Then she added bleakly: 'Still, you get to the point where there's nothing you can do *but* back your government. Living in a weak country's no picnic. We tried that. It's preferable to live in a strong one. Now let's talk about something more cheerful.'

So we focused on the good news, her summer holiday exploring the glorious churches of the far north, the Moscow periodical *Arion*, which was publishing more of her poems.

Lucy, her beloved cat, who had survived falling seven storeys from the window of her flat since my last visit, did her best to keep me entertained while Anna made a fuss about the fact that the hot water hadn't been turned on as promised. She rang to tell the building manager off. Then she ran a very deep cold bath into which she dangled a small electric element, which might or might not warm the water up enough to give her a bath around midnight.

Meanwhile, I could hardly fail to notice that she had no furniture or carpets. Money had proved another taboo subject. Anna had been proud of her earnings. Now she was visibly struggling. Inflation was running a good deal higher than growth, and prices had shot up. The price of bread alone had risen by 22 per cent since the beginning of the year. According to one survey, Russia's middle class was shrinking, down from 25 per cent of the population last year to 18 per cent this year. Half Anna's salary went in rent, her friends reckoned. Meanwhile, her parents, now old and infirm, needed her help to survive on their basic pension of $74 a month.

Anna had moved home since I was last here. She had just

redecorated her old flat when the owners decided to sell it. This one was wretchedly dark and shabby and all but empty, except for a pile of periodicals thrown in a corner and a bookcase which the owners had left behind. Tatiana said she had refused all offers of furniture, in order to be prepared for further, involuntary moves. Anna slept on the floor now. Only her icon corner looked cared for. There, on a small chest covered with a freshly laundered cloth, lay her Bible and a few small paper icons.

Stilted though our evening was, I came away reassured that Anna had not lost her head and become a rabid nationalist. Nor was she trying to distance herself from me. She was just under greater pressure than I had ever seen her, struggling with the unexpected descent back into poverty, with having no home, hating her work, hedged around with constraints it would have been dangerous or demeaning to talk about.

Anna's recent articles revealed more about her than she was prepared to admit to me directly. The brash tabloid for which she worked had always been a mine of interesting stories. It was tame now. Page after page of celebrity gossip was leavened here and there by patriotic articles. Russia's popular press had morphed into its Western counterpart.

A Moscow friend was clear about her judgement of this development: 'What we've got today is much more damaging than Soviet censorship was. It keeps people mindlessly occupied so they don't have the time or inclination to think for themselves.' All this was true. Anna's articles were different, though. There had been times after Putin came to power when her articles were bland, constrained by her anxiety to keep out of trouble. Not any more. Now they were bold.

They offered a compelling glimpse of the dark malfunctioning of power in Saratov. Take the ongoing topic of the murder of the province's harsh but honest Chief Prosecutor six months earlier. For a long time, the police got nowhere with their search for the culprit. Then the murder was pinned on the boss of one of the city's most powerful factories, Hammer and Sickle. (I remembered it, of course. In the 1990s, the manager's hair turned white overnight when the boss was beheaded for refusing to surrender his factory to a criminal gang.)

Anna did not bother to hide her scepticism at this turn of events. With one hand the prosecutor's office was handing out awards to those responsible for the arrest, she noted coolly. With the other they were refusing the defendant his choice of lawyer. Back at his factory the disbelieving workforce were asking what possible motive their boss had for murder. Their view was that his arrest was the beginning of another hostile takeover attempt.

To add to the mystery, shortly before the murder an extremely personable swindler had been offering to 'replace' the doomed prosecutor with a more amenable candidate, for a cool $1.5 million. The tape recording of the conversation played in court was collected by an ageing police stooge with dark glasses and a puffy face who gave evidence in a tremulous voice. He died quite suddenly, mid-trial. Self-assured, amused, Anna picked at the holes in the evidence presented by this Gogolian cast of characters.

Reading these articles left me feeling chastened. How unimaginative I had been! No wonder Anna did not want to talk to me about her job. As her paper's legal correspondent, each time she wrote an article she was picking her way through the minefield of a corrupted polity. The law served a state whose leaders had no higher vision than self-enrichment and the perpetuation of their rule. It was a terrifying job. But she, who had always seemed so fearful, was not just chronicling these cases. She was daring to make her own judgements clear.

Sometimes she even appeared to be enjoying herself. She had become a virtuoso at negotiating such moral complexities. And she could pull it off because all the lawyers, prosecutors and politicians knew her to be incorruptible. I felt ashamed to have doubted her.

When Tatiana took me to Saratov station to catch the sleeper back to Moscow, Anna joined us, wearing a smart pink jacket ('second-hand', she told me proudly). Ten years ago, you had to push through a swarm of hawkers, beggars and displaced people with bundles to get to the platform. Now the place was spotless. This morning, the Indian summer spell had finally broken. The golden light which had touched Saratov with grace during the days of my visit had given way to drizzle. 'You're taking the sunshine with you,' said Tatiana with a rueful smile. Her face was whiter than ever today, and her eyes were dark holes. Anna on the other hand looked perversely vital, even amused as she shifted from foot to foot and hunched her shoulders against the rain.

Further down the platform a school brass band was seeing

somebody off, rum-pa-pa, rum-pa-pa. We stood there, pretending everything was normal, talking about future plans. There was a piece by Anna I was going to publish in the magazine I edited. I would meet up with Tatiana's older daughter when I was in Moscow . . . The words were not the point, they were just a promise that whatever lay ahead, our friendship would hold fast.

We had shared a great grief in the years of our friendship. In the strangled silence between us lay our aborted hopes for a new Russia, one which would at last come to prize its own people, rather than hoisting itself up on their bones. All of us had bowed to the conventional wisdom that our hope for Russia at the end of communism was naive. But was it? Surely what was wrong was just that it was not stubborn enough. Hope is sacred, the fine point of the fulcrum of change.

What my friends were really feeling I hardly dared think, dare not even now. I was feeling cowardly, longing to be gone, to leave behind the plague of emotions bearing down on me. Guilt was the worst of them. I had never imagined leaving them to face such a difficult situation. Before we next met, relations between Russia and the West looked likely to get worse. Russia's economy depended on selling oil and gas to Europe. The world recession, triggered in the West, was going to hit long-suffering Russians. And the harder it hit them, the more Moscow's war party were likely to beat the nationalist drum and seek out confrontation with the West as a distraction. 'We can't afford to look ahead, any of us. It's too awful,' Tatiana was saying over breakfast. 'All we can do is live in a continual present, manage each day as it comes.'

This was the political backdrop against which my book was going to come out. My intimate account of the last sixteen years of their lives was going to appear in English, in the West. How would that play out for them, living here? There were times, much earlier on, when I believed that it might offer them protection. Not any more. Ghosts from Russia's Soviet past were giving me a hard time.

So how was it going to play out? The question was so delicate that I had not dared raise it with them. My friends had stayed clear of it, too. Now, as Anna evaded my embrace in her usual way, as I hugged Tatiana, the risks to which I was exposing them hit me like a truck.

I hurried on to the train and settled into my compartment

without looking back, without waving. That Russian phrase about 'leaving in the English way', meaning without saying goodbye, came back to me. It had always seemed so funny, so un-English, and there I was doing it. Their unspoken question followed me in: could they trust me? These were the people who had taught me so much about friendship. Here in Russia, where everyday life was a battle against poverty, bureaucracy or corruption, friendship was the true currency, the resource that made all possible. How would I turn out to have repaid that friendship with this book? Would it have repercussions on their lives? The questions were painful, and there were no answers.

My hope was that the positive lessons which my brave, independent-minded friends had drawn from the 1990s would not turn out to have been in vain. Whatever happens to my friends and to Russia, those lessons will always be there, in the compost heap of history which Anna Akhmatova evokes in her *Poem without a Hero*:

> As the future ripens in the past
> So the past rots in the future –
> A fearful festival of dead leaves

INDEX